The Astral
Journey

By the Same Author

THE NEW WORLD OF DREAMS

THE BOOK OF PSYCHIC KNOWLEDGE

PREMONITIONS: A LEAP INTO THE FUTURE

THOUGHTS OF THE IMITATION OF CHRIST

HOW TO DOUBLE YOUR VOCABULARY (SECOND EDITION)

IN DEFENSE OF GHOSTS

The Astral Journey

HERBERT B. GREENHOUSE

Doubleday & Company, Inc.
Garden City, New York
1975

133
G

Library of Congress Cataloging in Publication Data
Greenhouse, Herbert B
The astral journey.
Bibliography: p. 341
Includes index.
1. Astral projection. I. Title.
BF1389.A7G73   1975   133.9
ISBN 0-385-06750-X
Library of Congress Catalog Card Number 74–17610

Contents

The author is grateful to all whose experiences are in this book, to D. Scott Rogo for valuable comments on the Robert Crookall chapter, to Jo Filardo for the generous loan of his library, and to Kathy Gavan for her research assistance. Thanks are due also to Dr. Karlis Osis, Marian Nester, and other helpful staff members of the American Society for Psychical Research; Dr. Robert Morris and Blue Harary of the Psychical Research Foundation; Dr. John Palmer of the University of Virginia; Dr. Russell Targ of the Stanford Research Institute; and Mrs. Judith Skutch of the Foundation for Parasensory Investigation. Much source material was provided by the British Society for Psychical Research, the American Society for Psychical Research, the Psychical Research Foundation, the Parapsychology Foundation, the British Museum in London, and the National Library of Scotland in Edinburgh.

To the Double,

which is indestructible

Overview

Chapter 1

A "Trip"
to the Ceiling

It was three o'clock in the morning. I woke up with a strange sensation—I was rocking gently back and forth. I felt myself lifted and moved to the side of the bed, then lowered to the floor. I started to rise to the ceiling. I was weightless, without substance. What was it? What was happening?

I was not in my body, yet I was still very much alive. My physical self lay inert on the bed below, while "I" hovered near the ceiling. Was it a dream? No, I was fully conscious, enjoying this feeling of lightness and freedom. I did not wish to go back. But with this thought I began to fall very rapidly and was once more in my physical body.

But "what" had gone out? What had escaped from the physical organism that I had always identified with myself and became "me" for a few brief moments near the ceiling?

It happened in the summer of 1972, on a very hot August night. I had been living in a sublet apartment in Greenwich Village, New York City. It was an unusual apartment, with a stairway leading to a small balcony and a ceiling twenty feet high. I had been visiting a friend and had come home about 1 A.M., quite tired and in need of a good night's rest. Two hours later I was out of my body.

I was not frightened. I was pleased at finally having what I knew was an OOBE—an out-of-body experience. Although I do not regard myself as a psychic, I have had other extrasensory experiences —seeing objects and hearing voices beyond the range of my eyes and ears, sometimes catching the unspoken thought in someone else's mind. I have seen and written about ghosts. I have had visions of the future. But going out of my body? I couldn't picture it.

I wanted to have an OOBE. I wanted to write about it, as I have written about other psychic events I believe in. But I felt that I should know about it firsthand. I had had many vivid dreams when I may have left my body, but I could not be sure. In one dream a young lady came into my bedroom and took my hand. Together we soared at great speed above the clouds. Flying dreams have been classed by psychics as out-of-body dreams. This also could have been a wish-fulfilling dream. Freud and his confreres competed in my mind with mystics and parapsychologists.

Once I woke up in the middle of the night and felt that I was split into two persons. The lower part of my body was rigid, paralytic, a condition that often accompanies OOBEs. But there were two upper halves, as with Siamese twins, leaning in opposite directions. I tried desperately to coax one of my two selves out of my physical body. It refused to leave. I learned later that anxiety, excessive emotion, could stop an incipient OOBE.

Before I go further, let me state for the skeptical reader that I am of sound mind and body and also that I approach the supernormal with an attitude of wait-and-see. I firmly believe that it is necessary to separate psychic wheat from chaff, and before I put one word on paper, I determined to make a careful, exhaustive investigation of OOBEs. Prior to my own experience, I read many books and papers on the subject, detailing thousands of cases throughout history. I examined the reports of parapsychologists who study the phenomenon in the laboratory. I spoke with and tape-recorded the stories of psychics and non-psychics who claimed they were astral projectors.

I still felt, however, that until I too could be alive outside my physical body, it was all coming to me secondhand.

The Search for Evidence

The objective evidence for OOBEs was highly impressive. At first I picked up fragmentary information in my reading, and I had to read further, dig more deeply. I heard rumors of out-of-body experiences that had to be tracked down, stories to be proved or disproved. Many of the accounts turned out to be exaggerated, overblown. Many checked out to my satisfaction. I found that there were similar patterns that kept reappearing in these accounts —the same process by which the projector left his body, the same state of mind and body, often the same reason for leaving.

What were my sources? History gave me many examples of OOBEs. In the first century A.D., the writer Plutarch told about a soldier in Asia Minor who, while unconscious, roamed for three days in another dimension. Five hundred years earlier Plato wrote that "we are imprisoned in our bodies like an oyster in a shell." OOBEs were known in ancient Israel, Egypt, Persia, and India and were mentioned by St. Paul in the Bible.

Primitive tribes have always taken out-of-body experiences for granted. African witch doctors, Siberian shamans, American Indians have practiced rituals that helped them to escape from their bodies. Even today Australian aborigines put themselves into a trance and make astral journeys when their tribes need information. Legends from prehistoric times tell of the wise men who left their bodies and communicated with the gods.

The Church has recorded many out-of-body experiences. Saints such as Anthony of Padua and Alphonsus Liguori were seen elsewhere while their physical bodies remained in church or monastery. Emperors, kings, philosophers, writers, and scientists have reported being out of their bodies. The scientist-mystic Emanuel Swedenborg visited many dimensions and wrote detailed accounts of what he saw. Thomas De Quincey left his body while smoking opium. It was rumored that Napoleon, just before his death, traveled astrally from St. Helena to tell his mother in Rome that he was dying.

The First Investigators of OOBE

Are these stories true? Since many of them are remote in time, we cannot be altogether sure. But there is a scientific approach to

OOBEs as well as to other psychic phenomena that began in 1882 with the formation of the British Society for Psychical Research (SPR). The Society's investigators made a thorough study of each case, weighing the evidence carefully, judging the reliability of the person who reported the experience, interviewing witnesses. Many of these researchers, university-trained, were skeptics and yet intellectually curious and open-minded.

What they discovered about OOBEs was more or less a by-product of the search for evidence of extrasensory perception and the survival of the soul. The SPR studied cases of apparitions, particularly those seen at the time of death, and the phenomena at seances, where the dead either materialized or in some way manifested through the bodies of mediums. Of great interest also were the cases of multiple personality—two or more distinct personalities alternating in the body of the same person. It was suspected that some of the personalities might be "possessing" entities, dislodging at least temporarily the true "I" of the patient.

Richard Hodgson, William James, Sir Oliver Lodge, and others from the Society investigated cases in which apparitions of the living as well as the dead appeared to friends and relatives. Many of these cases were written up in the monumental *Phantasms of the Living,* published in 1886. The investigators also studied mediums, such as the famous Leonora Piper, whose bodies were taken over by invisible entities while they, the mediums, went somewhere else. This kind of "possession" was benign, however, arranged by mutual consent, in contrast to the devil-possession recorded in the annals of the Church and recently dramatized in the movies. When the possessing entity, or "control," had finished his business with those in the seance room, he retired from the medium's body and allowed her to return.

Hodgson also investigated and wrote an account of perhaps the strangest case of possession on record, the "Watseka Wonder." In 1865 a girl named Mary Roff died in the village of Watseka, Illinois, at the age of nineteen. Thirteen years later another Watseka girl, Lurancy Vennum, who had been an infant when Mary died, had what Hodgson calls "a sort of fit" and was unconscious for five hours. The next day she went into a trance and said she was in touch with heaven and the dead. Lurancy seemed to change into other personalities, first an old woman and then a young man. She claimed she was controlled by evil spirits.

A doctor suggested to Lurancy that she allow a more reasonable control to take over her body, rather than the devil-spirits who caused her to have fits. Lurancy said that the dead Mary Roff wished to enter and control her body. The next morning she woke up saying she was Mary Roff, and her speech, personality, and memories were apparently those of the dead girl. She insisted that the Roffs were her parents and went to live with them.

In the three months that followed Lurancy stayed with the Roffs and seemed to know everything that had happened to Mary, recognizing and calling by pet names friends and neighbors of the Roffs who had known Mary before she died. Once Mrs. Roff showed her a velvet hat that had been worn by Mary, and Lurancy exclaimed, "Oh, there is my headdress I wore when my hair was short!"

On May 21, 1878, Lurancy told the Roffs that she would have to leave them. Then she went into a trance and woke up once more as Lurancy Vennum, now cured of her illness. She went back to her real parents and was normal from that time on, but occasionally she would be aware of Mary Roff's presence for short periods.

Although in this book we are dealing mostly with the concept of leaving the body during one's lifetime, the Vennum-Roff case suggests that consciousness may live on after death as the spirit or soul. A question that remains unanswered, however, is where Lurancy's consciousness went during the time that Mary's spirit was occupying her physical body.

Most projectors, contemporary or past, have gone out of their bodies involuntarily, as I went out of mine, but some of them have learned to project consciously. The late Eileen Garrett, an outstanding psychic of this century, did one such voluntary projection as an experiment, with a secretary taking notes and a psychiatrist present as observer. Mrs. Garrett sat in an apartment in New York City and willed herself to the office of a doctor in Reykjavik, Iceland. The doctor sensed her presence and asked the invisible Mrs. Garrett to look at the objects on a table. At the same time she described the objects as she sat in a chair in New York.

Then the doctor took a book off the shelf and silently read a paragraph about Einstein's theory of relativity, which Mrs. Garrett recited verbatim in New York. While he was reading the book, the astral Garrett noticed that the doctor's head was bandaged, but back in New York the psychiatrist said, "This cannot possibly be true. I had a letter from the doctor a few days ago and he was quite well then."

The next day a telegram arrived from the doctor stating that he had had a head injury just before the experiment. A day later he sent a letter verifying everything that Mrs. Garrett had described on her out-of-body trip, including the objects on the table and the paragraph about Einstein.

A Tour of OOB Laboratories

In recent years the astral experience has joined telepathy (reading other minds), clairvoyance (seeing objects out of visual range), precognition (psychically knowing the future), and psychokinesis (mind over matter) in the laboratory. Today, in a California university, a parapsychologist attaches electrodes to the head of a young woman who claims she can go out of her body when she wills it, and as she lies in bed in another room, he watches her brain-wave tracings. When she tells him over the intercom that she is leaving her body, he notices unusual patterns on the EEG machine (electroencephalograph).

In New York City I have talked with parapsychologists and technicians from the American Society for Psychical Research (ASPR) who have designed an OOB experiment in which psychics project their "I" from different parts of the country to a room in the Society's building. Later they describe by mail or phone what they saw in the room during their visits.

In Durham, North Carolina, the Psychical Research Foundation (PRF) conducts tests in which a psychic projects to a room occupied by human beings and animals who may sense his presence, and by machines that can record any change in the physical environment of the room. Two physicists at the Stanford Research Institute (SRI) in Menlo Park, California, are doing an experiment in which a subject lying in an electrically shielded room describes a location unknown to him where members of the staff have gone by car.

In England a graduate geologist, Robert Crookall, examines thousands of out-of-body cases and charts the features common to all. By this method of content analysis, he has established a theoretical basis for understanding astral projection.

Tape-recorded Stories of Projection

But the most exciting and fruitful part of my search for the reality of OOBEs was talking with people who had projected, some of them practicing psychics, most with only occasional paranormal experiences. What they told me will be detailed later in the book along with results of my reading and laboratory researches. Their stories add up to some of the most spectacular cases on record—the double who appeared in a state of pregnancy, the women who witnessed their own operations, the man who solved a murder by going back in time to the scene of the crime, the young lady who previewed a dinner engagement by astrally smelling what was in the oven, and many more.

Housewives, students, businessmen, the old, the young, the middle-aged, children—all have told me and my tape-recorder of their out-of-body journeys. I have met my projectors everywhere—at parties, dinners, lectures, even on a lonely road in Massachusetts, where I picked up a young hitchhiker who had many times left his physical body. Most of them were eager to describe their experiences, but a few were reluctant, in some cases for deeply personal reasons, in others because they were afraid of ridicule.

One of the most startling of these experiences happened to Paul Lachlan Peck, a college administrator. In February 1972 Peck was driving across an intersection in New York City when a large car went through the red light and hit his small Toyota broadside. Just before the crash he escaped from his body and hovered over the Toyota, watching himself slumped unconscious at the wheel. Peck, who is a psychic healer, could see into the interior of his own head and he noticed that a blood clot was forming. He gave himself a quick healing and then went back into his physical body.

He lost consciousness again and was rushed to a nearby hospital. After an examination that lasted forty minutes, Peck was released with no apparent injuries, his blood clot dissolved. It developed later that he had hurt his neck and knee, but it was a miracle that he was neither killed nor hospitalized with serious injuries.

When I probed deeply enough, I found that there was usually a reason, a motivation for projectors to leave their bodies, even in involuntary cases when the process is more or less unconscious. Peck, for example, left his physical body to avoid the pain that would have followed the accident. There are many OOBEs in wartime, when soldiers literally jump out of their skins to escape the horror of gunfire and exploding bombs.

People leave their bodies to visit other people, sometimes to help or be helped by them. Mothers "go out" to see sons, fathers "travel" to visit their daughters. One woman, worried because her little grandson always stood too near when his mother was ironing, flew astrally five miles one night, appeared in her daughter's bedroom, and pointed to an electric iron in her hand, a thought form she had created, warning the daughter to be careful.

The Body That Leaves

But what is it that goes out? That can live apart from its own physical body? One of the important questions of this book is not only whether there is out-of-body projection, but what the substance is that encloses the departing consciousness. Because this substance or vehicle has been seen by both the projector and witnesses, it is called the "second body," or "double," as distinct from the physical body. It is also known as the "duplicate body" because it frequently appears as an exact replica of the physical body but is thought to be composed of finer, less dense material.

These terms have come to us from various cultures, along with such esoteric expressions as "astral body," "etheric body," "subtle body," "soul body," and many more. For the purpose of this book all terms are more or less interchangeable, but "OOB," "second body," and "the double" will be used most often. We will also speak of "astral travel" and "astral projection," although these terms have special meanings in occult circles.

Sometimes, mostly during sleep but frequently when the astral traveler is awake, the second body moves out of its physical shell, glides around the room, floats to the ceiling, or perhaps just takes a walk down the road. The second body may also travel great distances, often to foreign countries. Sometimes it finds itself in unfamiliar, even unreal surroundings, where shadowy figures move through mist and fog. Other times the setting is heavenlike, with brilliant light and vivid colors. Many astral travelers have gone forward and backward in time.

The Plan of the Book

In addition to the results of laboratory experiments, we are going to explore several kinds of evidence for the reality of the human double: the awareness of the projector that he has left his physical body; the information that he brings back from his travels; the testimony of witnesses who have sensed, seen, heard, or even touched their astral visitor; cases in which the second body has been able to move objects; and instances of written or spoken conversation between the projector and his host or hostess.

We will observe the process of leaving the body as experienced and reported by projectors. Watch for the following sequence that is often part of the process: the physical body falls into a trancelike, frequently cataleptic state just before or after projection; there is a momentary blackout just before the bodies separate; the second body rises to a horizontal position above the physical body, then uprights itself; the astral projector looks back and sees his physical body lying on the bed or relaxing in a chair where he left it; the projector sees a cordlike connection between the two bodies; the projector returns to his physical body the same way he left it, with the steps reversed. The second body may also rotate out of the physical body in a spiral motion and return the same way. The second body generally feels very light, usually weightless, and sometimes gives off a glow that may illuminate a dark room.

The above phenomena do not occur in every case, but they are common to a large percentage of OOBEs. My "trip" to the ceiling followed a familiar pattern: the rocking or vibrating motion in the beginning, the feeling of weightlessness, the sensation of falling, then swiftly rising (although in most cases the projector is conscious only of an upward motion), the swift descent over the same route on my return to the physical body. During my partial projections, when the upper half of my double was trying to get out, my physical body was cataleptic.

We will also ask other questions: in addition to motivation for astral travel, what are the physical and mental conditions that generate it? Why do some people see their doubles while they are still in their physical bodies? Why do a few persons project while they are in motion—walking, riding, flying, sometimes just talking? What are the cases of double and triple projection, when two or more persons out of their bodies at the same time "travel" together and communicate extraphysically?

And what of the physical body? What is it doing while its astral counterpart has gone off on its own?

The OOB files now contain thousands of cases, cases that are alike in their essential patterns but different in details, just as people themselves are basically alike but differ in personality structure. There are cultural beliefs, too, that cause variations in out-of-body patterns. In Norway, for example, there are many cases of the "arrival" phenomenon—a host who is waiting for his guest sees the double of the guest first come into view, then disappear, followed soon after by the guest himself in his physical body.

Thus we have a general idea of what an OOBE is, and we have posed questions to be answered about the nature and purpose of the out-of-body experience. The evidence I am going to present was gathered bit by bit over a period of years until all pieces of the puzzle seemed to fit—except one. I knew all about the human double but I didn't know the reality of it—until August 1972, when I too was for a few moments alive in two bodies.

Let us go back and retrace the steps of my search, so that I may fill in the details. I would like to take you first on a flight to ancient times and primitive societies, then cruise slowly back to the present, observing the astral travelers of the past, among them many great men, as they float, fly, and glide by. Then, after examining the criteria of a valid OOBE and the motivations and physical/psychological conditions that make it possible, you'll join me and my tape recorder as we go by car and plane to Maine, Massachusetts, Pennsylvania, Ohio, Virginia, North Carolina, and other states as far west as California. We'll leave the country, too, and visit Canada and Great Britain.

They're all waiting—the students, scholars, subjects and experimenters in out-of-body laboratories, along with my astral projectors in homes and offices. All are eager, I am sure, to tell their stories to you as they told them to me.

I hope this will prove to be the most exciting "trip" you have ever known.

Chapter 2

A Journey
to the Past

We discover what the ancient world thought about out-of-body experiences by consulting the writers, philosophers, religionists, and rulers of many countries: Plutarch, the Greek biographer who wrote books about Alexander the Great and other famous men of earlier centuries; Herodotus, the Greek historian who went from country to country interviewing officials and recording many stories of psychic phenomena; the biographers of the Indian Gautama Buddha, who was said to leave his body many times; the Romans Pliny the Younger and Suetonius; and many more.

The Bible describes what may have been the most famous second-body materialization of all time—the resurrection of Christ. St. Paul informs us in his Epistles to the Corinthians that "if there is a natural [physical] body, there is also a spiritual body." Then, speaking of himself in the third person, he continues: "I know a man in Christ . . . (whether in the body, I know not; or whether out of the body, I know not; God knoweth) . . . how that he was caught up into Paradise, and heard unspeakable words, which it is not lawful for a man to utter."*

* I Corinthians 15:44; II Corinthians 12:2–4.

St. Augustine tells the interesting story of a man lying in bed one night who saw the double of a philosopher-friend standing in the room. His astral visitor began to discourse on Plato and the man was puzzled—his friend had always refused to explain Plato when in his physical body. When the two men met the next day, the man asked his friend why he had broken his silence.

"I did not do it," said the philosopher, "but I dreamed that I did."

The Double in the King's Bedroom

We hear of four rather striking out-of-body experiences in the classical period, each the forerunner of different kinds of OOBEs occurring in the 2,000 years that followed. The Israeli leaders of the present day who are trying to cope with hostile Arab neighbors would do well to read the story of Ben-hadad, the King of Syria, who was tearing his hair out because every time his army launched a "surprise" attack, they found the Israelites waiting. Ben-hadad finally called the members of his council together and demanded to know who the traitor was. Who among them was tipping off the Israelites?

One of the council members had his own theory, which he had expressed privately, and it was to him that the other council members turned. The King looked at him and said: "Will you not show me which of us is for the King of Israel?" The man, who was known to be something of a psychic, replied, "None, my Lord, O King. But Elisha, the prophet that is in Israel, telleth the King of Israel the words that thou speakest in thy bedchamber."

Ben-hadad nearly went into shock. Who was this Elisha, this mortal with the attributes of a god? The council member replied, admiration in his voice, that this Elisha was many things—a medium, a seer, a healer. He had once restored to life a boy felled by sunstroke. He had cured the leper Naaman of his disease. He had recovered for the son of a prophet the lost head of an ax that he saw clairvoyantly in the river. This superpsychic was consulted many times by the kings of Judah and Israel. Elisha could put himself into a trance by listening to the music of a minstrel and while in this condition would travel in his second body.

Ben-hadad snorted and vowed that his army would smite down Elisha. He sent his troops to encircle the city of Dothan, where the prophet lived. Elisha's servant trembled with terror, but his master comforted him: "Fear not; for they that are with us are more than they that be with them." Elisha created a ring of horses and chariots of fire around his house and asked God to strike the Syrians blind. He then led the sightless soldiers to the King of Israel and prayed for restoration of their vision. And now they saw that they were the prisoners of Israel.†

Using the second body to visit offices and bedchambers and learn state secrets may be a psychic weapon of the future, if not the means of immobilizing an entire army. The crash program of the modern-day Russians in developing psychics could pay off in OOB espionage.

Doubles Who Visited the Dead

Elisha was clairvoyant in his second body; that is, he could go among the living and get information not available to him through sense channels. Doubles in ancient and modern times have also gone to the land of the dead and on rare occasions have stayed there. The ancient Greeks, in fact, seemed concerned that too-long absence from the physical body might result in premature burial.

The sixth-century B.C. philosopher Hermotimus of Clazomenae, like all Greek philosophers, was curious about the state of death and used his OOB talent to investigate it. He often fell into a trance and wandered away from his body, which became cataleptic and deathlike. On one such occasion his wife, annoyed at these astral departures or perhaps anxious to get rid of him, quickly had him declared dead and cremated. According to César de Vesme in *A History of Experimental Spiritualism*, mediums later reported that Hermotimus was quite upset when he came back and found that his physical body had disappeared.

Two other OOB tales from ancient times involved brushes with death, but the endings were happier. In his *On The Delay of Divine Justice*, Plutarch tells of one Aridaeus of Asia Minor, who in A.D. 79 was knocked unconscious and immediately taken out of his body. With his perceptions immeasurably sharpened, as in many modern OOBEs, he could see on all sides at once. Aridaeus met and spoke with the dead, one of them an uncle who greeted him warmly. The dead man reassured the astral traveler that he—Ari-

† II Kings 6:11, 12 et seq.

daeus—was not dead because the rest of his soul was firmly anchored to his body.

"The rest of his soul," explained the dead uncle, was a cord connecting the two bodies. So long as the cord was still attached to his physical body, Aridaeus would remain alive. Aridaeus could also see the difference between his double and the doubles of the dead. His own second body had "a faint and shadowy outline" while "the dead shone all around and were transparent." While he was studying this phenomenon, he was suddenly "sucked through a tube by a violent in-breath" and awoke once again in his physical body. The "tube" is similar to the "tunnel" that many projectors experience on leaving and returning to their physical bodies.

The story of Curma is a dramatic one and was first reported in the fifth century A.D. by Augustine, Bishop of Hippo, in Numidia, North Africa. Curma, a senator, was seriously ill and in a coma for several days. As he left his body, he heard his name called from somewhere and thought that he was being summoned to death and judgment. But, as in the case of Aridaeus, the dead he met assured him that he was still alive. There was another Curma, they told him, a goldsmith who had just died and was on his way to the other world. Curma the senator noticed that the spirit world contained not only the dead but those like himself who were alive and merely on out-of-body excursions.

When Curma the senator woke up in his physical body, he said, "Send someone to the house of Curma the goldsmith and see what he is doing." A messenger was dispatched and returned with the news that Curma the goldsmith had recently died.

A Classical View of the Second Body

The double had a different name in each of the ancient countries. The Hebrews called it the *ruach*. In Egypt it was known as the *ka*, an exact replica of the physical body but less dense. The Greeks knew it as the *eidolon*, the Romans as the *larva*, while in Tibet it is still referred to as the *bardo* body. In Germany it was the *Jüdel* or *Doppelgänger* and in Norway the *fylgja*. The ancient Britons gave it various names: *fetch*, *waft*, *task*, and *fye*.

In China the *thankhi* left the body during sleep and was seen by others. The ancient Chinese meditated to achieve out-of-body travel, the second body being formed in the solar plexus by the action of the spirit. The double leaving the body through the head and other OOB processes familiar to students of astral projection were depicted on seventeenth-century wooden tablets.

The ancient Hindus spoke of the second-body principle as the *Pranamayakosha*. The Buddhists called the double the *rupa*. Tantric Buddhist scripts of Tibet and parts of Mongolia, cited by D. Scott Rogo in the *International Journal of Parapsychology*, describe astral projection and state that the Buddha did not approve of his followers trying to leave their bodies.

Most ancient cultures postulated other bodies along with the duplicate body. The Buddhist *linga sharira* was part of the double that still retained something of the physical substance. The Egyptian *ka* was also part of a composite astral body that was closely attached to the physical body and stayed near it at death. Ancient Egyptians called the soul that separated from this astral shell the *ba* or *bai*. In addition, there was the *khou*, or intellectual body, that returned to its source, the sun, and the *ab*, or soul of the heart.

The Parsees of India spoke of man as being composed of five elements: at death the physical body returned to the earth, the life to the wind, and the form to the sun, while the soul and spirit were immortal. In *The Possibility of Miracles* Anna Maria Roos writes of the pre-Germanic theory of man as composed of six elements ranging from the physical body to the spirit. Among these elements the *litr* was a very fine substance that built the physical body known to the senses. At death the spirit and intelligence ascended to the judgment seat, while the *litr* went to the world below.

Chinese philosophers believed in the sevenfold nature of man. The Hebrew Kabbala had an even more complicated body system. *Nephesch* was the body, *ruach* the soul, and *neschamah* the spirit, but each had three subdivisions, making nine in all.

In this book we are staying close to the simple second body and will speak later of the theoretical composite body, but the philosophical systems of the ancients contained many bodies in addition to the physical, each of a rarer substance and culminating in the bodiless spirit that goes on forever. The Theosophists, whose system is based on that of the ancient Hindus, speak of an "etheric body," a "subtle body," a "desire body," and many more, each with its designated place in a spiritual order.

The Double After Death

"Approaching the borderland of death, I stepped over the threshold and was conducted through the elements. Although it was midnight, the light was brilliant. I stepped into the presence of the gods."

The speaker was the Roman philosopher Apuleius, who had just come back from an astral journey as part of the ceremony of initiation into the Mysteries of Isis, the Egyptian goddess. According to Roos, the first objective of the initiation was to release the double through self-hypnosis and ritual and finally come to learn what Paradise was like: "The highest aim to be achieved was the union of the spirit with the Highest God, the One."

Ancient cultures all seemed to have the same notion of how the second body leaves at death and what happens to it later. The Phrygians and other peoples believed in something similar to the Christ resurrection: the astral body remained as a shell for three days after physical death, then disintegrated, while the soul body went on to permanent residence in the next dimension. That the Hebrews shared this belief is reflected in the words of the prophet Hosea: "Come, and let us return unto Jehovah; for he hath torn, and he will heal us . . . After two days will he revive us: on the third day he will raise us up, and we shall live before him."‡

In *The Other World* M. K. Spencer quotes the Zoroastrian Scriptures, written 550–330 B.C., as saying that it takes three days for "the spirit of a departed person to find its home in Paradise. The Parsees [of India] offer intensive prayers during these three days."

The *Bardo Thodol,* written by Tibetans in the eighth century A.D., and in modern times translated as *The Tibetan Book of the Dead,* tells the reader that the departed second body wanders about a Hadeslike Bardo region for three days before the separation of physical and astral bodies is complete. A lama has traditionally assisted the dying in finding their way during the process of separation. In *Magic and Mystery in Tibet,* Alexandra David-Neel, for many years a resident of Tibet, describes how the lama helps the dying man to make the transition. She first learned of the practice when she was returning from a trip one day and heard a

‡ Hosea 6:1–2.

strange, animal-like cry. She saw two monks seated under a tree and crying "Hik!" in a shrill voice.

Her guide told her that the lama utters this cry in order to free the spirit of a man as he dies, causing it "to leave the body through a hole that this magic syllable opens in the summit of the skull." After "hik" the world "phat" is shouted and this assures a proper separation of body and spirit. A Tibetan must "learn the art of dying well," and mystic initiates generally know how to keep their minds clear while their personalities are disintegrating. But an ordinary Tibetan who has not mastered the "science of death" needs help in the separation process.

The dying man must hold his consciousness as his soul departs. The lama instructs him to concentrate on the "special consciousness" of each sense as it leaves—the eyes, nose, tongue, ears, and so on. After the second body has made its successful departure through the skull, the dead man presumably has a series of visions. As he travels through the Bardo region, he sees a very bright light. There are "radiant beautiful beings" and "hideous forms." He has many choices of paths to take, and if he can follow the lama's instructions, he will choose the right road "that will lead him to be reborn among the gods, or in some other pleasant condition."

The Tibetans, of course, travel astrally before death as well as after. David-Neel writes that some of the projectors visit places on earth while others go to "paradises, purgatories, and the Bardo." Astral travelers who visit the Bardo and meet the dead before returning to their physical bodies are called *delogs*, "those who have returned from the Beyond."

The evidence of astral travel from the classical period in history is difficult to corroborate because we hear of it through writers whose sources we can no longer check out. Still, many of the phenomena of modern OOBEs, which we will examine later, keep recurring in the old stories. Astral projection happened during sleep and dreams, in a state of mild or cataleptic trance, during illness and especially coma, and when there was an accident. Projectors reported seeing the connecting cord, leaving their bodies through the head, going through a "tunnel," and having sharper perceptions in their second bodies. They visited both the living and the dead and often brought back information they could not have obtained through physical channels.

Chapter 3

"To Open the Gate of Distance"

Ngema Nzago, chief of the African tribe of Yabikou, enjoyed great prestige among his people because he was a fetish man. He could heal the sick, conjure up money for the poor, and make life pleasant for the tribesmen in many other ways through his psychic powers. He was preparing now to join the magicians from other tribes in the M'fang country who met from time to time to discuss the secrets of their craft. Their meeting place was the plateau of Yemvi, a journey of four days away.

"I shall be there tomorrow," said Ngema to Father Trilles, the missionary. Father Trilles looked puzzled. How could Ngema cover a distance of four days' travel in less than one? There was no other means of travel than by foot.

Ngema smiled.

"Oh, I shall go there but I will also be here at the same time. But I see that you do not believe me. Well, come this evening to my hut. I shall leave from there."

Still skeptical, Father Trilles presented himself at the door of Ngema's hut that evening and found the chief rubbing a reddish liquid on his body and muttering a chant. He did not completely disbelieve the chieftain, having seen many examples of Ngema's clairvoyance. Still, his Western mind needed proof, evidence that Ngema had actually made the journey in his second body.

"On the way to Yemvi," said the priest, "at the foot of the hill, you will go through the village of Nahong, where my catechist, Esaba, lives. As you pass his door, please tell him that he should come at once and bring me the cartridges of the gun I loaned him."

"It will be done. Esaba will get your message this evening and will set out tomorrow."

Ngema then stretched out on the mat and was very still. After several minutes of silence, Father Trilles was startled to see a snake fall from the roof and wrap itself around the chieftain's rigid body as he slept on the mat. The priest, avoiding the snake, stuck a pin into Ngema's side, but there was no response. A slight foam appeared on the sleeping man's lips, but his body did not move. Father Trilles retired to a corner of the room and sat down, prepared to spend the night.

The serpent mysteriously disappeared.

All night Ngema lay in a cataleptic trance while Father Trilles watched him. The next morning he stirred, then awoke and smiled at the missionary.

"I have given your message, and I have been to the meeting of the magicians."

Three days later Esaba the catechist arrived at the mission house of the Yabikou and asked for Father Trilles. He handed some cartridges to the missionary. Father Trilles was impressed. Did Esaba actually see Chief Ngema, who was all that time lying on the mat in his hut?

"No, Father, but during the night I heard him call from outside my hut. He told me that you wanted these at once."

Astral Powers of the Medicine Men

Father Trilles returned from Africa in 1906 and told a French lecture audience about Ngema's astral journey. The story appeared later in De Vesme's *A History of Experimental Spiritualism*. De Vesme also wrote about other African witch doctors who projected astrally to get needed information for their tribes or for missionaries and explorers. David Leslie, a South African hunter, was worried because his elephant hunters had not arrived as scheduled. He consulted a native witch doctor who promised "to open the gate of distance" and travel through it.

The witch doctor asked for the names of the hunters, then lit eight fires, one for each hunter, and cast roots into them. He inhaled the fumes of a medicine and went into a trance for ten minutes. When he awoke, he raked out the ashes of each fire in turn and described the eight hunters. The first hunter had died of fever. The second had killed four elephants. The third had been killed by an elephant. The other five had survived but they would not return for three months and would take a different road from that originally planned.

The information proved accurate in every case. It is remarkable that at the time of the out-of-body trance, the hunters had already been scattered over an area of several hundred miles. The witch doctor had somehow telescoped time and space during his astral journey.

North American Indian tribes often used the powers of the medicine man to get clairvoyant information. Father Lafiteau, a Jesuit missionary of the eighteenth century, tells of a projection by an old sorceress of the Huron tribe. Seven Huron warriors, off on an expedition, did not return on schedule and the sorceress was asked to go out and find them. She retired to her hut and went through a complicated ritual that ended in a state of delirium. When she came out of it, she told exactly what had happened to the warriors —the road they had taken, the villages they had passed through, and where they were at present. On the third day the lost warriors filed back into the village and verified all that the sorceress had said.

A Trip to the Great Spirit

It was not just the medicine men or sorceresses who had OOBEs. Sometimes a member of the tribe would find himself out of his body with no preliminary warning or preparation. In one case the projector's fellow tribesmen thought he had died and were about to bury him when he came out of his trance, very much alive and eager to tell about his astral adventure.

White Thunder was a chief of the tribe of Spotted Tail. One

evening while his squaw was making supper, he lay down for a nap but woke up and saw two of his tribesmen in the room, dressed in white robes. They signaled him to follow them. He called out to his wife that he would be gone for awhile, but she paid no attention. This puzzled him and he looked back and saw that his physical body was still asleep on the mat.

Then he must be dead! The men in white robes reassured him— they were merely taking him on a journey but would bring him back, and he would continue to live for many years. He and his guides seemed to float away and White Thunder found himself above "a great shining river" that reached far into the sky. His guides told him that the river wound through the land of the Great Spirit, where all good Indians went when they died.

White Thunder saw familiar wigwams along the shore of this river and was overjoyed when many of his old friends, now dead, came out to greet him. But when he reached the largest wigwam, where a Great Spirit lived, he was told that he must return to his body and deliver the message that all men were brothers and should be kind to one another.

When White Thunder came back to his own wigwam, he found his sleeping body tightly bound with cords, his wife sitting beside the mat and crying, his children tearfully calling his name. He looked with indifference upon his physical body and turned to go back to the land of the dead. But his guides barred the way and told him solemnly that he must re-enter his body. The next moment he lost consciousness, then awoke in his body, panic-stricken as he struggled to throw off the cords. With a cry of joy, his wife cut the cords and said that they thought he had died and had prepared his body for burial.

The story of White Thunder appeared in Major C. Newell's *Indian Stories*. White Thunder told Major Newell that he had been out of his body for "three sleeps."

Projection Through Fasting and Drugs

Stories like those of Ngema, the African witch doctor, the old sorceress, and White Thunder have come to us from primitive societies everywhere—from Australian aborigines, from North and South American Indians, from Zululand, Siberia, New Zealand, Tahiti, and elsewhere. The pattern is similar throughout. Shamans from many of these tribes seem to project at will. They go through a preliminary ritual, their bodies become rigid or passive, and after a short or long sleep, they wake up with information of what is happening at a distance. Other members of a tribe project accidentally while sleeping, napping, lying ill in bed, or being in some other condition that also generates OOBEs in urban societies.

Primitive peoples know the principle of altering the state of the physical body in order to release the second self. In *The Sacred Mushroom* Andrija Puharich writes about the shamans of Eastern Siberia, who subject their physical bodies to an ordeal that leads to out-of-body flight. First the shaman goes through a period of "fasting, meditation, and exposure to hardship," then takes part in a ceremony by "beating on a special drum . . . improvising chants and hymns to the spirits that are to be called to assist in the separation of the soul from the body." He then goes into a feverish dance that leads to near exhaustion and consumes alcohol or a hallucinogenic drug extracted from the *Amanita muscaria*. After a period of even more vigorous dancing, he "suddenly collapses and passes into a deep trance state," and his astral travels begin.

Hallucinogens and Shamanism, edited by Michael J. Harner, describes how the shamans of South American Indian tribes take a hallucinatory drink made from the *ayahuasca,* or *yagé,* vine to release the second body. The projectors feel a "spinning in the head, then a sensation of being lifted into the air" as they begin their journey. The Jivaro Indians of eastern Ecuador believe that part of the soul leaves the body "with the subject having the sensation of flying, returning when the effects of the drug [*yagé*] wear off."

After imbibing *yagé,* Jivaro shamans can clairvoyantly see persons far away and describe what they are doing. Sometimes the shaman solves crimes by piercing the time barrier while out of his body, witnessing the re-enactment of a killing or a theft. The shamans and their tribesmen travel astrally not only to familiar places in the tropical forest but sometimes to the unfamiliar cities of white men hundreds of miles away, which they can accurately describe.

The members of a tribe in the Ucayali River region of Peru frequently go off on astral trips as a group. Sitting in a circle and drinking *yagé,* a proposal is made to visit a certain location together. Once someone suggested, "Let's see cities!" and off the group went to a distant urban center none of them had ever visited in the flesh. Later they met white men who lived in this city and asked about the *aparatos*, strange objects that "run so swiftly along the street." They were describing automobiles, which they had never seen with their physical eyes.

The Body That Survives Death

Native tribes throughout the world have their own theories of the second body that often include additional bodies, as in ancient and Theosophical beliefs. The Zulus of South Africa speak of the physical body as *inyama* and the duplicate non-physical body as *isithunzi*, which at death stays on as the vehicle of the spirit, or *umoya*.

Many primitive societies believe that the second body can be observed leaving the physical body at death. In *The Phenomena of Astral Projection*, Sylvan Muldoon and Hereward Carrington quote the words of a missionary to Tahiti from *The Metaphysical Magazine* of October 1896:

> At death the soul was believed to be drawn out of the body, whence it was borne away, to be slowly and gradually united to the god from whom it had emanated . . . The Tahitians have concluded that a substance, taking human form, issued from the head of the corpse, because among the privileged few who have the blessed gift of clairvoyance, some affirm that, shortly after a human body ceases to breathe, a vapour arises from the head, hovering a little way above it, but attached by a vapoury cord. The substance, it is said, gradually increases in bulk and assumes the form of the inert body. When this has become quite cold, the connecting cord disappears and the disentangled soul-form floats away as if borne by invisible carriers.

The Culture Shapes the OOBE

The culture determines the pattern of an out-of-body experience. In eastern Peru, after the shaman takes *yagé*, he imagines that his soul is leaving his body in the form of a bird, to go off and kill an enemy in the distant forest. In some tribes the connecting cord appears as a snake, in others as a tree or vine. Some Asian tribesmen view the cord as a ribbon, thread, or rainbow. Africans see it as a rope, and the natives of Borneo as a ladder.

The ladder suggests the myth of ascent to the sky that appears in both biblical and primitive lore. An example in the Bible is the story of Jacob's ladder. In *Shamanism*, Mircea Eliade tells of prehistoric shamans who left their bodies and communicated with the gods. The shamans of some modern tribes fly to heaven on horse staves of wood or iron that are used in the rituals.

Primitives have not only seen the connecting cord during out-of-body flights and watched it disappear at death, but have also caused it to appear symbolically in their ritual ceremonies. Ronald Rose has devoted a complete chapter in *Living Magic* to the importance of the cord as a symbol in the rituals of Australian aborigines. During an initiation ceremony a man lies on his back and goes into a trance. His body shivers and his mouth begins to open, a cordlike object writhing out of it like a snake. It stretches to the length of a man's ear, then leaves and crawls about on the ground, finally withdrawing into the initiate's body.

Do the onlookers see something that is not there? Is self-hypnosis generated by the cultural fascination with snakes? Did Father Trilles only imagine he saw a serpent come down from the ceiling when Ngema was in his trance? Possibly, although it becomes more difficult to explain away what happens as more witnesses report seeing it. Rose comments that "the phenomenon of the magic cord as recounted by aborigines resembles the phenomenon of ectoplasm reported by spiritualists and others."

It is apparent that OOBEs and the cord attachment have been known for thousands of years. It is an experience common to all of mankind, and what was once accepted universally as an ascent to the gods and then discarded as superstition is now being more seriously considered as symbolic of the process of astral projection.

The main difference between OOBEs in primitive and sophisticated societies, in addition to cultural variables, is that primitive people *know* that they happen, while in so-called civilized countries we keep questioning, doubting, weighing, and we are never quite sure that this phenomenon really occurs—even when the evidence is overwhelming.

This difference is pointed up in the area of dream theory. Freudian-oriented cultures make a strict separation between the real and the dream world, with the latter an imaginary stage on which the dreamer's conflicts are dramatized. In many primitive societies, however, past and present, the daily life and the dream life are merged into one reality. When the sleeper takes a trip in his dream, he is actually out of his body. Anthropologist Edward Tylor writes:

> Certain of the Greenlanders . . . consider that the soul quits the body in the night and goes out hunting, dancing, and visiting . . . Among the Indians of North America, we hear of the dreamer's soul leaving his body and wandering in quest of things attractive to it . . . The New Zealanders considered the dreaming soul to quit the body and return, even traveling to the region of the dead to hold converse with its friends . . . Onward from the savage state, the idea of the spirit's departure in sleep may be traced into the speculative philosophy of higher nations as in the Vedanta system, and the Kabbala.

Today more and more people are beginning to realize that the primitives may have been on to something—that a sleeper's double may project many times from his physical body during dreams as well as when he is awake. The rest of this book will examine that curious notion from many angles.

A Look at
the Evidence

Chapter 4

"I Know I Am Out of My Body"

So much for the reality of astral projection in classical and primitive societies. But since we live in the age of science, we must take a closer, more analytical look at the out-of-body experience in our own time and culture. We must ask ourselves whether there is indeed enough hard evidence to regard it as a fact, or at least as much a fact as telepathy and clairvoyance, which have been demonstrated experimentally.

How can we be sure when someone tells us he has gone out of his body? It may be that in some way he has projected his thoughts to another part of the room, even to another house or town, or that he only *thinks* he has left his physical body and traveled in another, non-physical vehicle. The mind can play tricks at times. Illness, hysteria, fatigue may produce such illusions, and we know that mental institutions are filled with persons who claim the ability to travel astrally not only on this earth but to other planets.

There are several ways to test the statement of an astral projector, just as there are tests of other paranormal phenomena. Does he or she appear to be a stable, truthful individual, one who does not mistake fantasy for reality? The author has interviewed many men and women projectors who would not be mistaken for other than normal by their friends and families. Among them are a stock-broker, a swimming-pool salesman, the proprietor of a bookshop, an opera singer, and a nurse. Granted that neurotic or psychotic persons may have illusions of astral travel, it then becomes the task of the investigator to make a judgment based on his evaluation of the person plus the objective evidence in the case.

Once the credibility of the projector is established, other questions should be asked: Did he have a vivid, realistic sensation of being in another body? Did he go through a process of leaving his physical body similar to that reported by other projectors? Did he see his physical body lying on the bed or sitting in a chair where he left it? Did he see a connecting cord between the two bodies? Has he brought back evidence of what he observed in the place he claims to have visited? Has his second body been seen, heard, felt, or sensed by witnesses? Did his second body cause any changes in the physical environment, such as making objects move?

The I-Consciousness of the Projector

In this chapter we will deal with the awareness of being in another body, the "I-Consciousness." Good psychics know the difference between the sensation of astrally traveling to another place and seeing that place in their mind's eye. Vincent Turvey, a leading psychic of the early twentieth century, had both telepathic-clairvoyant and out-of-body experiences. Here is how he distinguished between them: "In plain long-distance clairvoyance I appear to see through a tunnel which is cut through all intervening physical objects, such as town, forests, and mountains." In out-of-body projection Turvey was fully conscious of being in his double, he could see his physical shell where he had left it, and he had a vivid sense of moving through space to his destination.

A middle-aged woman named Caroline Larsen decided to retire early one night and listen in bed to the music of her husband's chamber group playing Beethoven in the living room downstairs. As she lay in bed still awake, Mrs. Larsen was in a mildly emotional mood brought on partly by the music, but suddenly her quiet enjoyment changed to a feeling of "deep apprehension and oppression." She felt her body becoming numb limb by limb until she was in a total cataleptic state. There was a momentary black-out, then she was standing on the floor beside her bed and sur-prised to see a stranger lying where she had been a moment before.

No, it wasn't a stranger. It was her own pleasant, middle-aged face and body, "the arms and hands . . . limp and lifeless beside the body." She looked around the room and found everything as natural as it was before. She could still hear the music, the second violinist a bit off pitch, the cellist playing a trifle too loudly. The only unnatural circumstance was that she was in another body, not her own as she had known it.

She decided to try out this new vehicle. It worked as well as the old, even better. She walked springily to the door, passed through it and into the hall. She tried to turn on the bathroom light but her hand went right through it. Actually, she needed no light for the room was lit up by "a strongish white light" that emanated from her body and face. When she looked in the mirror, she had a very pleasant surprise. She saw not a middle-aged woman but a very beautiful young girl of eighteen, the girl she remembered herself to be. Her face and body were rather transparent. Her eyes were much more luminous than her physical eyes and "shone with such lustre that the mirror reflected their penetrating beams." She wore not her nightdress but "the loveliest white shining garment imag-inable."

The music, which never left her consciousness, now changed from Beethoven to Mendelssohn. She decided with some amuse-ment to go downstairs and let the musicians see her in her new-found beauty. She bounced gaily into the hall, delighted with the lightness of her astral body for she now "moved with the freedom of thought." As she walked down the stairs, the music grew louder, just as it would if she had been listening with her physical ears.

But now a strange thing happened. Standing on the stairs was a woman spirit who barred her way.

"Where are you going?" demanded the woman. "Go back to your body!"

Regretfully, Mrs. Larsen turned and went back upstairs, through the hall, and into her bedroom. She looked at her physical body, as still as in death, with a feeling of disappointment, but she knew she would have to re-enter it. The next moment she, her I-Con-sciousness, was back in her body and woke up in it.

Mrs. Larsen had many more astral experiences after the first one and wrote a book about them, *My Travels in the Spirit World,* published in 1927. Had she been dreaming? She assures us that she had her projection while still awake, listening to the music. During her OOBE, she continued to listen to the playing of the group, which followed a sequence later verified by her husband.

There were many features of her experience that recur time and again in other accounts of OOBEs, whether they come from ancient history, from distant countries and cultures, or from our own cities and towns: the momentary blackout or tunnel effect on leaving and returning, the numbness of the physical body, the more acute senses of the double, the ability of the double to pass through objects, the feeling of weightlessness of the second body, the light emanating from the second body.

"It Was Different from a Dream"

Ernesto Bozzano, a highly respected investigator of the paranormal, tells about his friend Giuseppe Costa, who was studying for an examination on a very hot night in June. Feeling tired, Costa threw himself on the bed without putting out the lamp on the night table. Accidentally knocking over the lamp as he turned in his sleep, he woke up to the smell of heavy smoke that was filling the room.

Suddenly he found himself in the middle of the room, yet his physical body still lay on the bed, still asleep. He now saw the room with much keener sight than with his physical eyes, "as though a physical radiation penetrated the molecules of the objects." He could see into the interior of his own body with "its clusters of veins and nerves vibrating like a swarm of luminous living atoms."

He felt "free, light, and ethereal." When he tried to open the window of the smoke-filled room, however, he was unable to do so. He could see through the wall into the next room where his mother lay sleeping. Her body gave off "a luminosity, a radiant phosphorescence." He watched her hurriedly get out of bed, run out of her room into the hall, and rush into his room and over to his bed, where she shook his physical body. At that moment he woke up with "parched throat, throbbing temples, and difficult breathing."

Costa said that until this night he had never heard of OOBEs and he insisted that he was not dreaming, that the quality of his experience was totally different from that of a dream. He writes, as so many other projectors have written: "Never had I so vivid a sensation of existing in reality, as in the moment when I felt myself separated from the body." Bozzano adds that Costa was "a highly cultured and really scientific man, so that he was able to describe his own impressions minutely and with rare analytical penetration."

In many respects, Costa's OOBE parallelled that of Mrs. Larsen. It was the first projection for both, and Costa did not even know what an OOBE was. Both projected while lying in bed feeling very tired. Both felt much lighter and freer in their second body. The senses of both were unusually keen, especially the ability of Costa to see not only through the wall but also into the interior of his own physical body. Mrs. Larsen also saw her physical body, and this is what usually makes projectors realize that their consciousness has transferred to another vehicle. Both physical bodies lay passively in bed, Mrs. Larsen's in a state of numbness and rigidity, the familiar cataleptic state.

A final factor and certainly a very important one was the careful, analytical approach of both to their experience. Mrs. Larsen wrote about her OOBE thoughtfully and in detail, and she gives a feeling of reality to what happened. It should be added that her husband was a professor on the faculty of Middlebury College in Vermont, and it took courage and conviction for her to publish a book about her experiences. Costa, a scientist, was endorsed by a scholar, Ernesto Bozzano.

"I Was Laid Horizontally in Space"

Another projector who gives the impression of integrity and believability was the Reverend Dr. O. A. Ostby. (OOBEs have been quite common among the clergy, and a later chapter will discuss the miracle of bilocation as recorded by the Catholic Church.) In 1904 Dr. Ostby awoke from sleep one night "in full clear consciousness" and, as in the other two cases, found himself standing by his bed looking at his physical body. He thought he had died and was "perfectly happy" about it, but worried about the shock to his wife and baby boy who were lying in bed beside him.

Then he felt himself lifted from the floor, "laid horizontally in space, and pushed slowly, inch by inch, into the physical again." The sensation of leaving the body horizontally, then moving into an upright position and returning in reverse order, is common in OOBEs. Dr. Ostby woke up outside his body, but it is possible that his double first moved upward in the horizontal position as he lay sleeping and unconscious of what was happening. Many projections start this way in sleep before the projector is aware of being in another body.

Ostby's story was quoted by Sylvan Muldoon in *The Case For Astral Projection*. Both Dr. Ostby and Caroline Larsen had several OOBEs after their first one and eventually learned to project at will. In most cases, those who learn the technique of voluntary projection had their first experience spontaneously and did not understand at the time what was happening to them.

Robert Crookall has described a case of awareness during the horizontal movement of the second body. A Scottish woman was lying awake in bed one night when she felt energy starting to build up in her solar plexus. Then her double rose above her physical body and parallel to it. Still in the horizontal position, she swung around so that she—her I-Consciousness—was diagonally across the bed, then reversed direction and floated out of the house.

"Like a Snake Skinning Itself"

Some projectors have their first OOBE during the daytime, while relaxing on a chair or couch. In *The Phenomena of Astral Projection*, Muldoon and Carrington describe the daytime projections of Fräulein Sophie Swoboda in Germany. Fräulein Swoboda had a headache one day and lay down on her bedroom sofa to rest. Waking up from a deep sleep, she saw her mother quietly leave the room. Feeling very light-bodied, her headache gone, Sophie followed her mother into the living room and watched her sit down and begin to knit, while her father read aloud from a book. Puzzled because they paid no attention to her, Sophie went back to her bedroom and saw her physical body sleeping on the sofa, "pale and corpselike." At that moment she was "hurled back" into her body.

Later she repeated word for word the text of the book her father had been reading and gave a verbatim account of her parents' conversation. It is possible in cases of this kind for the senses to be unusually acute (hyperthesia), so that speech is heard that would normally be out of hearing range. There were, however, two rooms between Fräulein Swoboda and her parents, and all the doors were closed.

Another time Sophie was sitting in the living room of a friend's home, listening to her friend's daughter playing the piano. As she closed her eyes, she felt herself crossing the room and standing beside the piano. The pianist's mother, sitting on the sofa, stared in amazement at Sophie's double walking to the piano, then looked at Sophie's physical body sitting next to her. The momentary restfulness induced by closing her eyes plus the effect of the music may have brought on Sophie's OOBE.

Muldoon and Carrington also tell about a Colorado man who was plowing soil one day. He worked all morning, then after feeding and watering his horses, lay down beneath his wagon to rest for an hour or two, his old battered hat under his head. Relaxed but not asleep, he felt his feet growing numb. The numbness traveled up his legs, and his I-Consciousness traveled with it—up his body and through his head "like a snake skinning itself."

The next moment he was floating in the air and could see the wagon and his physical body resting beneath it. His vision was far more acute than it had ever been. His double then floated to the ground and walked toward the wagon. As he came near it, he felt himself turned around and thrown back into his physical body with a sharp cracking sound "like that made by a steel trap when sprung."

The man, Bert Slater, had several more OOBEs after his first, once while he was again settling down after lunch for a nap under a tree, and once following an accident, when he was knocked unconscious while climbing a cliff. In each case he was vividly aware of his I-Consciousness in another body and could see his physical body back on the ground. As time went on, Slater learned to project at will.

Projection During the Drowsy-Dreaming State

Sleeping, dreaming, lying in bed awake, resting on a couch or on the ground—all are situations in which an out-of-body experience may happen. At these times the person moves away from normal awareness of his environment into what is called an "altered state" of consciousness, a state that is favorable to psychic experiences.

Another altered state is that of just falling asleep or just waking up, a prelude to many OOBEs.

In *Casebook of Astral Projection* Crookall tells about a dozing-off case in which a woman felt her toes tingling, a sensation that moved upward through her body. When it reached the top of her head, she felt "a violent pull upward," then found herself floating around the room. She looked back and saw her body "lying open-eyed on the bed." Then she passed through the closed door of her bedroom.

In another drowsy state projection reported by Crookall, a woman was dozing in an armchair when she began to float near the ceiling. Unable to move her physical body or open the eyes, she was certain that she had had a stroke or had died. Since then she has had many projections while drowsy that start with "a kind of whirring in the head." She insists that "projection is quite different from ordinary dreaming."

A View of the Silver Cord

Seeing the connecting cord is another way in which projectors realize that their "I" is now in the second body. Since the cord usually extends from the forehead or solar plexus of the physical body to the back of the astral head, it is not often seen unless the projector happens to look back. The cord has been compared by modern projectors to a thread, a string, a tape, a ribbon, a garden hose, a chain, even an umbilical cord. A woman who became frightened while out of her body felt that she was guided back through "a kind of pipeline."

Other projectors are conscious of a light that pulsates from the cord. The "silver cord" is mentioned in the Bible. One man, after rising horizontally above his body and stopping a foot from the ceiling, looked down and saw a "silver light" between the duplicate and physical bodies. Another projector saw the cord as a "stream of light" coming from behind. Reine, a French model who had hundreds of projections in 1913, compared her cord to "a ray of sunlight filtering into a room."

In *Psychic News* of August 12, 1961, a man wrote that he once woke up and found himself in his second body sitting on the roof of his house. "I noticed that a cord, which appeared to be about one inch in diameter, was attached to the back of my head and, stretching down the roof, disappeared over the edge." Wondering where it led, he climbed down from the roof to the top of the bedroom window and saw that the cord went inside, giving off a steady, whitish light. It ended in the forehead of his physical body lying on the bed.

In the accounts of most projectors, the cord appears to be about two or three inches thick when less than ten feet away from the physical body. As the second body moves further away, the cord thins out, but it remains connected even though the double may journey hundreds of miles.

The I-Consciousness seems to vibrate across the cord between the physical and astral bodies, resident in one or the other, sometimes for a brief period in both. The life principle may be more inherently a part of the second body than of the physical body, and when the two coincide, it animates both. When the astral body leaves, however, it appears to carry this vital principle with it, sending mental and spiritual nourishment across the cord to the passive, sometimes corpselike physical body that awaits its return.

The cases in this chapter, unlike the stories from classical times and primitive cultures, were examples of fairly simple projections, in which the projector, fully conscious, did not stray far from his physical body and either walked or floated in his bedroom or elsewhere in the house. As we forge the next link in the chain of evidence for OOBEs—bringing back clairvoyant information—we will travel with our projectors to more distant locations and more exciting astral adventures.

Chapter 5

The Second
Body Is Clairvoyant

The key point in the Larsen, Costa, and Ostby cases as well as others mentioned in the last chapter is the very real consciousness of the projector that he or she was in another body. The next question to ask is—can he prove it to our satisfaction? One way is to bring back evidence that can be verified of what he has seen or heard on his astral trip. And so much the better, if there are witnesses who saw or sensed his presence or even in some way communicated with him.

The British Society for Psychical Research has on file the case of a man who during a dream found himself in front of another house a few miles from where he lived. There were several men present, four of whom he recognized as his tenants, and a woman with a basket on her arm. One of his tenants was being attacked by some of the men, and our projector pitched into the battle and hit two of the men, but his arms seemed to go right through their bodies without hurting them.

When the sleeper woke up he felt stiff and sore, and his wife told him that during the night he had been throwing his arms around as if trying to hit someone. He described his dream and gave the names of the tenants he had seen. The next day he received a letter from his agent, stating that the tenant attacked in the dream had been found dying of a skull fracture in front of the house that had also been in the dream. There was no clue to his assailants.

The dreamer informed the authorities, who apprehended the three tenants he had recognized in the dream and the woman with the basket on her arm. All four stated that between eleven and twelve o'clock on the night in question, they were walking down the road when they were stopped by three strangers, two of whom attacked the other tenant.

Was this an OOBE? Perhaps. The dreamer brought back clairvoyant evidence of having been on the scene, with all the details of what happened verified and the characters in the dream identified later. The sense of reality that the dreamer felt and his emotional response are characteristic of the dreams in which OOBEs take place. But since he had no certain consciousness of being out of his body and no one saw him, two important elements are missing —awareness of being in a second body and the testimony of witnesses. Yet the fact that very many if not most OOBEs happen during sleep and dreams makes us suspect that he may have actually been out of his body.

Muldoon calls this a case of "psychical somnambulism," in which the subject merely dreamed of what was taking place at a distance. The fact that the man thrashed around during the dream and woke up stiff and sore suggests to Muldoon that he was having a clairvoyant dream rather than an OOBE. Later, however, we will consider cases of a physical body remaining active while the I-Consciousness is in the second body, although this is rare and usually happens when the two bodies are near each other.

"Down a Long, Dim Tunnel"

Still, for the moment we are looking for examples of second-body awareness plus clairvoyance. In *The Mystery of the Human Double*, Ralph Shirley quotes a letter from a woman correspondent: "Whenever I desire to know how and where a friend is whom I have not heard of for some time, I go and find them . . . I can do it sitting quietly in my chair in the day or before going to sleep when in bed at night, perfect quiet being the only condition necessary . . . l close my eyes and have a feeling of going over backwards . . . I find myself going down a long, dim tunnel which is warm and as if it were moss-lined. At the far end is a tiny speck of light which grows as I approach into a large square and I am 'there.' In nearly every case I can describe the room my friends are in, the clothes they are wearing, the people they are talking to."

Although Shirley does not give corroborating testimony, the details of the experience sound authentic. "Going over backwards" during an OOBE is a frequent occurrence. The feeling of being in a tunnel or experiencing a blackout is almost universal. The correspondent does state that on one occasion she was seen by a friend who spoke to her, but she doesn't make the extravagant claim that this happens all the time.

In some of the I-Consciousness cases of the preceding chapter, there are also what appear to be clairvoyant details. Caroline Larsen, when out of her body, could follow the sequence of the music played by her husband's string quartet. Yet she could have been hearing the music in her physical body, since she was in the same house. Costa clairvoyantly saw his mother get out of bed and run to his room. The case is weakened somewhat by the fact that this is just what she would do if she woke up smelling smoke and was worried about her son.

Although Sophie Swoboda was able to repeat for her parents every word of their conversation, her sense of hearing may have been considerably sharpened as she dozed. She claimed, however, that there were three closed doors between her room and the one her parents were in.

An out-of-body experience involving the I-Consciousness plus clairvoyance in the same house was reported by the late medium Gladys Osborne Leonard, and it gains credence because of Mrs. Leonard's reputation through the years as a reliable and talented psychic. The first time that Mrs. Leonard "went out," she was resting in bed in the middle of the day. Still fully conscious, she had a feeling of being lifted off the bed, then she looked down and saw her physical body below her while her double was rising in a horizontal position above it.

Mrs. Leonard heard her husband open a door and talk in a low voice to someone in the hall. Immediately she found herself standing by her husband's side and realized that she must have passed through the closed bedroom door. The man in the hall was from the gas company. At this point a maid from an upstairs apartment came down the stairs, and Mrs. Leonard saw her husband hand a coin to the girl.

Mrs. Leonard then went back to her bedroom and lay in a horizontal position just above her physical body. At first she was fearful that she would be unable to get back into it, but she mentally calmed herself, then gradually sank lower and lower until she had merged with her body.

Mr. Leonard verified all that his wife had seen and heard. Aside from the consciousness/clairvoyance elements of Mrs. Leonard's OOBE, there are other significant aspects. She looked down and saw her physical body. Her double was in the familiar horizontal position as it left her body and assumed the same position on its return. Her fear that she would not be able to return is common among those having an OOBE for the first time. If she had not calmed herself, she might have slammed back into her body and given it a shock. As it was, she went back in slowly and with no ill effects.

Long-Distance Astral Travel

There are cases in which clairvoyance-plus-consciousness takes place at a greater distance from the physical body and not in the same house where hyperthesia (sharpened senses) may be operating. An example is Dr. Ostby, who woke up outside his body during his first OOBE and thought he had died. Later, when he learned a technique of projecting at will, he decided to contact a certain man he had never seen who was living in Chicago, far from his own home. When he left his body, however, he felt intuitively that the man was now living in California, but Dr. Ostby didn't know where.

Almost instantaneously Dr. Ostby found himself in a strange town in California and in front of a bungalow. He went inside and saw the man, learning that he was a dope addict. Later Dr. Ostby secured photographs of the man and the bungalow he was living in, both exactly as he had seen them in his astral body. All other items checked out, including that fact that the man was taking dope.

Another long-distance traveler was an Australian woman, who not only was fully conscious during her trip but also brought back an interesting piece of evidence. She left her home, flew over a harbor with many boats in it, passed through a cloud layer, and reached an area she did not know where her husband had been reared. Here she saw a boyhood friend of his, a man named Mitchell who had grown a black beard. Several months later the woman and her husband, who had been skeptical of her story, took a trip to the town where he had grown up and stopped on a road near some houses. As if by a signal, Mitchell walked out of one of the houses, sporting a black beard.

What are the modes of travel during an OOBE? How does a long-distance projector cover large areas in a short time, as the African chieftain Ngema Nzago and Dr. Ostby did? Sylvan Muldoon, perhaps the best-known of all projectors, often just walked around his bedroom or took a stroll down the block as he would do in his physical body. Sometimes the projector glides rather than walks or moves in an up-and-down wavelike motion. When traveling great distances, he may rise high above the ground and move at lightning speed while the landscape flashes by him. The speed of travel may be so fast that he may not be conscious much of the time of covering vast stretches of territory. Many projectors, however, just think of where they are going, as Dr. Ostby did, and immediately find themselves there.

Conversation with a Double

Along with consciousness and clairvoyance, witnesses add a strong third element to the reality of astral projection. Sometimes the testimony of the witness is the *only* evidence we have. It is especially strong in the automatic writing and direct voice type of case when the double may have no consciousness of being present, yet carry on an intelligent conversation and show marked personality characteristics. (See Chapter 17.)

A man may be napping or dreaming with no awareness of leaving his body and yet be seen by friends somewhere else. In cases of what is called "deferred percipience," he may try to project to a friend, then go to sleep thinking he has failed, only to learn later that he was seen by the person he wished to visit. A Harvard professor tried this experiment one night but nothing happened and he fell asleep in his chair. The next day his friend told the professor that he had seen him staring through a crack in the door.

The professor may have merely sent a thought-form to the home of his friend. But when a projector in full consciousness not only brings back evidence of details he has observed but is also seen by a witness, we have impressive evidence of an OOBE. Ralph Shirley, at one time editor of one of the leading magazines devoted to the paranormal, the *Occult Review,* may have come across such a case.

Shirley told about a woman who enrolled her two sons in an English private school and thought they would be assigned to two bedrooms at the end of a hall. That night, while resting at home, she projected to the school and noticed that one of the rooms was empty. Her oldest son was in the other. She asked him where they had put the other boy, Brian, and the lad replied that he was in a room at the opposite end of the hall. A few days later she received a letter from her older son stating that he had seen her come into his room and ask where Brian was and that he had given her the very answer she had heard astrally.

The woman told Shirley that she was able to go to anyone she chose by closing her eyes and concentrating on that person. Sometimes, when she was not sure of the direction, she stood in the middle of the room and turned around slowly, her arms outstretched. At some point her hands would seem to stop and she knew that this was the direction in which she must travel.

Cases such as this are rare in which a projector is not only seen but actually carries on a conversation with the witness. An OOBE of this kind is described by Robert Dale Owen, United States minister to Naples in the last century, who wrote one of the definitive books on psychic experiences, *Footfalls on the Boundary of Another World.* A woman woke up one night and found herself standing by her sleeping physical body. Thinking she had died and pleased that death had been painless, she passed through the bedroom wall and went to see a friend, with whom she spoke. Then she woke up at home in her physical body once more, surprised that she was still alive.

Two days later her friend came for a visit. The projector, saying nothing about her astral trip, mentioned that she was going to buy a new bonnet and have it trimmed in violet. Her friend replied that she knew the projector liked violet because, she said, "When you came to see me Wednesday night, you were robed in violet."

The projector feigned surprise.

"I appeared to you on Wednesday night?"

"Yes, about three A.M. We had quite a conversation."

Doubles Who Visit the Dying

There are innumerable accounts of OOBEs at a time of crisis, particularly when someone is dying. Most of the time it is the person on his deathbed who projects to the other (see Chapter 31), but sometimes the healthy one's conscious or subconscious knowledge of a grave illness causes him to project.

In one of the most dramatic cases of this kind, reported by Robert Crookall in *More Astral Projections,* a woman in South Africa, worried about her sister who was dying of tuberculosis, traveled astrally to the patient's bedroom and noticed unusual details: her sister's bed was in the middle of the room and she was lying on her right side with her left arm over the edge of the bed.

The projector knelt down and took her sister's hand. The latter opened her eyes, smiled, and said, "Oh, Bet, I'm glad you've come! I've been so frightened! I'm dying!" The astral projector comforted her: "There is nothing to be afraid of." Then she woke up back in her body with the conviction that her sister had died. Two days later news came that death had occurred at that very time. The projector also learned that her sister's bed had been put in the middle of the room, just as she had seen it. When the young woman was found dead in the morning, her body was on its right side, her left arm over the side of the bed.

This story is very striking in its consciousness-plus-clairvoyance aspects. Since the projector's sister was found dead, however, there could be no actual proof that the conversation had taken place.

A similar case reported by writer J. A. Hill gives strong evidence that the projector was seen. A Mrs. Napier, lying in bed one morning and worrying about her father who was ill, had a feeling that his condition had worsened. She left her body and journeyed through space to her father's home, going inside the house and walking up the stairs to his bedroom. He was sitting up in bed. He turned his head, saw her and called out her name, "Mabel!" She was then drawn back through space and into her physical body.

Mrs. Napier immediately wrote to her mother, telling about her projection. Their letters crossed, the one from her mother stating that her father was much worse and that on the night Mrs. Napier projected, he saw her standing in the doorway and called out to her.

Mrs. Napier described how she projected: she would feel a "prickling" sensation as though an electric current were passing through her body, followed by a state of catalepsy, after which she would have a "very pleasant flight" through space. In many of her projections she brought back information that was later verified, such as the state of her father's health and his seeing and speaking to her.

The Astral House Hunter

There are also practical reasons for projecting and the results can often be amusing as well as giving solid evidence for OOBEs. In one case of consciousness-plus-clairvoyance-plus-witnesses, a woman living in Ireland was looking for a house to buy and found it while out of her body. It suited all her requirements—it was the right size, the furniture and decor were just right, and the colors of the walls pleased her. There was only one problem—she didn't know where it was.

She went back astrally many times to look at the house and liked it more each time. The following year she and her husband decided to move to London. Answering a newspaper ad in the real estate section, she was amazed when she walked into the home of her dreams. When the owner saw her, she screamed, "You're the ghost!" The house had a reputation for being haunted and finally was sold at much less than its value—to its own ghost.

Some of the cases in this chapter were investigated by the British Society for Psychical Research. Some were evaluated by writers and researchers from personal conversations and letters. All have features that are common to the out-of-body experience. The strongest are those in which the I-Consciousness aspect is supported by details accurately noted by the projector at the same time that he is seen by one or more witnesses. In rare and astonishing instances the witness reports that he has spoken with his astral friend.

Chapter 6

Astral Mind-over-Matter

Witnesses have not only seen and spoken with astral projectors; they have reported that their supernormal guests knock on doors and walls, ring bells, lift and carry objects, blow out candles, and in many other ways affect the physical environment. Even when the projector himself has not been seen, he has made his presence known this way.

There are two kinds of astral mind-over-matter. In one, physical objects prove no barrier to the second body, which can pass right through them. The other kind, which is the subject of this chapter, occurs when the double can create sounds, handle and move material objects, and make physical contact with people. Most of the time the I-Consciousness knows that its astral hands are performing as they would in the physical body. Sometimes, however, the double causes such things to happen even when it is not near the object or person.

Generally, projectors who have the one kind of mind-over-matter ability are not capable of the other. Those who can pass through barriers cannot manipulate objects, and vice versa. The difference seems to depend on how much of the physical substance is retained by the second body when it starts its journey. Scholars of OOBEs such as Robert Crookall believe that the double is a composite, made up in varying proportions of a semiphysical body and a soul body. The more there is of the semiphysical component, the more the double behaves as it would in the physical body and the less able it is to pass through matter. But when this component, which Crookall calls "the vehicle of vitality," is dropped off and returned to the physical organism, the soul body is then free to move through physical barriers but can no longer influence matter.

In *The Study and Practice of Astral Projection* Crookall mentions a Mrs. Joy who once had to open the door with her astral hand and on another occasion lifted up a window. Another woman found that at different times her body seemed to have different weights that affected her ability to pass through barriers. She said that when her second body was "thicker," the slightest object would be a physical impediment. Yram, the Frenchman who wrote about his astral experiences in *Practical Astral Projection,* projected one day in a double that was more physical than usual. The walls blocked his passage and he had to open a window astrally before he could leave the house. At other times his soul body was in the ascendant, and he went through all physical barriers and traveled long distances at great speed.

Eileen Garrett said that when the separation of her bodies happened accidentally, she was usually unable to pass through matter, but when she projected experimentally, she went through all barriers. Some psychics I have spoken with who can project at will seem to do so in what may be called the "soul body." This is not a strict rule, however, and many involuntary projectors report passing through physical objects.

The double-through-barriers experience is quite common, but the double-moving-objects is a rare occurrence. When it happens, however, it may be the strongest link in the chain of evidence for an OOBE: the I-Consciousness of the astral traveler is aware that the double has impinged upon the physical world, and the case is buttressed by the testimony of witnesses.

A Mr. Rose once decided while lying in bed to project his second body to the home of a woman friend and her daughter. He visualized himself walking to the house, going up the front steps, and ringing the doorbell. Meanwhile the woman, who was in bed at the time, saw him enter in a luminous mist, while her daughter, in another bedroom, woke up and heard his footsteps. At the same moment the maid went to answer the doorbell.

There are many cases of astral knocks on doors. A woman resting in her garden one afternoon decided to visit her friend Stella without physically moving from her chair. She was conscious of traveling through the air and then standing on Stella's doorstep. She knocked on the door with her astral hand, but no one answered. She tried once more, this time hitting the door with all the force she could muster, then heard someone moving inside. Stella's sister opened the door but saw no one and went back to tell Stella, who was in a chair reading a book. A day later the projector received a letter from Stella, saying that she had heard a faint knock on the door about 3:30 P.M. (the time of the projection) followed by a very loud knock. Her sister had opened the door, but no one was there.

One of the strangest of all astral mind-over-matter happenings was reported by Sylvan Muldoon in *The Projection of the Astral Body*. He dreamed one night that he was standing near a metronome in the living room, which was next to his bedroom. He woke up and after a pause of one second heard the clicking of the pendulum that sets the tempo of a piece of music. It clicked six times, then stopped. As Muldoon points out, metronomes do not start by themselves—someone or something must have activated the pendulum. Weeks later it happened again: a dream, the awakening, and now an interval of two seconds before the pendulum started to click back and forth. This time the metronome ran for about twenty minutes.

The conventional explanation would be that in his sleep Muldoon heard the metronome going and accommodated his dream to the action. But the device did not start clicking until he had awakened, and he had to go into the next room and turn it off. The most likely explanation, if one accepts the OOB hypothesis, is that Muldoon, who projected quite often while asleep or awake, actually set the metronome in motion and then returned to his physical body just before he heard it. An unexplained mystery, however, is why there was a pause before the clicking began.

It is also possible that while lying in bed Muldoon unconsciously exerted some kind of psychokinetic energy upon the instrument. This kind of energy is believed to cause the well-advertised poltergeist phenomena. In houses plagued by poltergeists there are mysterious noises caused by no known human agency, and objects float or fly around a room or are hurled with great force. Parapsychologists theorize that in these cases an unusual amount of energy may be generated by the hostile feelings of teenagers living in the house. It is also possible that the agile astral body of the disturbed person is working overtime to discharge his feelings.

In another incident described more fully in Chapter 13, Muldoon was aware of being in his double when an object was moved. Going upstairs astrally to wake up his mother, in some way he caused her mattress to lift up and throw her and his little brother out of bed. This is a case of the double not knowing its own strength, since the mattress moved without his laying an astral hand on it.

Vincent Turvey said that on one of his astral excursions he lifted a bed with two persons on it. In his physical body he was so weak that ordinarily he could not even lift a small child. There are numerous other examples of a double that seemed to have more strength or at least could generate considerably more energy in the astral than in the physical body.

A remarkable case of a double carrying an object from one room to another was reported in the *Journal* of the British Society for Psychical Research. In September 1955 Lucian Landau lay ill in his home in Kent, England. His girl friend Eileen, who later became his wife, stayed in the spare bedroom across the hall and came in astrally each night to check his pulse and respiration. As a test, he asked her one evening if her double could pick up his diary, which was on a desk in her room, and bring it to him.

The doors of both rooms were left open that night. At dawn Lucian woke up and saw Eileen's double standing near the window and wearing a nightdress. Although her face was pale, her figure was opaque and lifelike. She began to glide backward and Lucian followed her into her room, where she vanished. He saw her physical body asleep in bed.

When he returned to his room, he noticed a toy rubber dog on the floor that had been sitting on the dresser in Eileen's room. The next morning he asked her why she hadn't brought the diary, and she replied that she couldn't lift it and decided that the dog might be easier to carry. She remembered leaving the bed in her double, going to the desk, trying to pick up the diary, then taking the dog into Lucian's room. She said the dog did not seem heavy or difficult to hold.

There was certainly good evidence that a projection had taken place. Eileen was conscious of leaving her body, Lucian saw her double, and the toy dog was moved from one room to the other. The question arises why Eileen couldn't carry the diary, since doubles seem to have greater rather than less strength than their physical counterparts. The dog weighed 107 grams and the diary only 37, yet she found the dog relatively light. She stated later, however, that as a child she had been told never to handle other people's letters or diaries. Psychologically, the diary was extremely heavy for her.

There have been witnesses to changes in the physical environment caused by the double. In New Guinea the second body of a man was seen and heard by two persons, his footsteps depressing the matting on the floor as though he were walking across it. The British Society for Psychical Research also investigated a case (later written up in *Phantasms of the Living*) in which the double snuffed out a candle.

Pierre-Émile Cornillier, a French artist, wrote in *The Survival of the Soul* about a series of OOB experiments he conducted in 1912 with his young model, Reine. Cornillier hypnotized Reine and asked her to project her double to homes of persons he knew. Once he told her to visit his friend O and relate what she saw. Sitting in Cornillier's studio with her eyes closed, Reine said that O was at his desk, writing. Cornillier told her to "manifest her presence." She said she touched O and thought he was reacting. Then she "concentrated with all her force" to make O's eyeglasses fall off his nose. The next moment she burst out laughing.

REINE: "It's done! It fell!"
CORNILLIER: "You are sure, Reine, absolutely sure, that you made the eyeglasses fall?"
REINE: "Oh yes, I know I did! He picked them up, and fixed them on his nose again."

Cornillier later checked with his friend O, who spent much of his time traveling, and found that he had been home on the afternoon of the projection. Unfortunately, Cornillier says nothing about O's eyeglasses. Did they fall off his nose, as Reine claimed? In many other projections, however, she brought back information that was later verified.

In other OOBEs we have the testimony of witnesses that they have been touched, stroked, fondled, kissed, even pushed, punched, and pinched by doubles. Husbands away from home have come back in their second bodies and embraced their wives. Wives separated from their husbands have flown over land and sea to find their spouses and kiss them. In one case reported by the British Society for Psychical Research, a man willed his double to the side of his fiancée as she walked up the stairs in her home, and she felt the pressure of his arm around her waist.

Some projectors are not so gentle. Robert Monroe, who did conscious projections for more than fourteen years, tells in *Journeys Out of the Body* how he flew to the home of a lady friend and roguishly pinched her as she slept. When they met later she showed him the brown and blue marks left by his astral hand.

In *The Mystery of the Human Double*, Ralph Shirley describes an even more painful contact between a double and her witness. Ann Amherst dreamed one night that she went into the bedroom where her friend Mary de Lys was sleeping and stuck a pin into the forefinger of Mary's right hand. Mary grimaced as though in pain and said, "Oh, this pin! How it hurts! Why did you do it?"

The next morning Ann went downstairs and saw Mary in the library holding her finger and with the same facial expression as in the dream. Mary's first words were "Oh, this pin! How it hurts! Why did you do it?" It was the forefinger of Mary's right hand, as in the dream. Both bedroom doors had been locked all night.

This incident could possibly be explained as a case of reciprocal dreams rather than as a trip out of the body. Ann dreamed that she had stabbed Mary. Mary dreamed that she was stabbed and her mind caused her finger to feel the pain, which was still there in the morning. However, the attempt to explain away one theory of a paranormal happening by another also difficult to understand brings in more problems. Why, for example, did Mary repeat the very words in the morning that Ann had dreamed of the night before? Was precognition operating? Perhaps Ann did visit Mary in her second body and stab her with the pin.

Shirley gives us no clue as to what motivated this astral attack. What was the relationship of the women to each other? Did Ann harbor some underlying resentment that might have generated the act of her double? It is important to uncover, whenever possible, the circumstances in which an astral projection occurs and the reasons why the double may behave in a certain way, whether as friend or antagonist.

Most physical encounters between astral travelers and their hosts or hostesses are affectionate rather than hostile. In one of Robert Crookall's cases a woman visited her aunt and touched her on the shoulder. The aunt turned around with a puzzled look. Crookall also tells a very striking story of a woman who fell asleep one night thinking of her cousin who had just been killed and whose funeral she was unable to attend. A friend had gone in her place.

The woman woke up in the familiar horizontal position a foot above her physical body, then floated out of the room, down the stairs, and through the door. With no consciousness of traveling, she found herself standing upright in the dining room of her cousin's home eighty-six miles away. She noted the position of the night lamp on the table, the place in the room where her cousin's body lay, and the color of the casket. Then she went into her friend's bedroom and pulled the sleeping woman's arm. Her friend opened her eyes and saw her, and an instant later she was in the horizontal position above her physical body, then back in it.

When her friend returned a day later, she told the projector that she had felt the pull on her arm, then awoke and saw the double, which faded away. Thus all the elements were present to prove that an OOBE did happen: the woman's I-Consciousness of being in her double, the clairvoyant details of the objects in her cousin's room that were later verified, and the testimony of her friend, who both saw her and felt the pressure of her astral hand.

The astute reader will object that this woman, who was able to pull her friend's arm, also passed through the door of her own home. Every case of astral projection is not one of either/or when it comes to mind-over-matter. The second body is not a fixed entity and may vary in its composition from moment to moment. Some projectors have been able to pass through physical objects and also manipulate them, sometimes on the same trip. The over-all evidence seems to suggest, however, that the double borrows varying amounts from the physical body, and what happens during a projection is influenced by how much of the physical component is present.

Can the double touch his own physical body? Muldoon claims that it cannot be done, but there are instances to the contrary. Monroe says that he could not only feel his astral body when it was out but could touch his physical body. Celia Green in *Out-of-the-Body Experiences* tells of a woman projector who touched her own body to find out if it was cold and discovered that it was "warm to the touch." Another of Green's cases shook her own shoulder gently. Her physical body stirred and she awoke "with a strong start, sitting upright in bed."

The Double Writes on a Blackboard

Do projectors ever write with their astral hands? In cases of automatic writing when a living communicator is identified, the latter may be actually present if invisible, writing with the arm and hand of the medium (see Chapter 17). Sometimes the double is seen as a lifelike figure writing with his own hand. In a celebrated case of the last century, the first mate of a ship, Robert Bruce, saw a stranger in the captain's cabin, writing on a slateboard. The stranger disappeared but the slate bore the words "Steer to the Northwest."

The incredulous captain at first refused to believe Bruce's story, thinking it a hoax. He pointed out that the ship had been at sea for several weeks, and it would have been impossible for another man to come aboard. He then asked the first mate and the rest of the crew for samples of their handwriting, but none of them matched the writing on the slate. The captain, utterly mystified, decided to change the ship's course from due west to northwest.

The next day they sighted another ship icebound in the North Atlantic and were in time to save the passengers and crew. The first mate recognized one of the passengers as the man he had seen in the captain's cabin. The captain asked the man to write the words "Steer to the Northwest" on the other side of the slate. When he turned the slate over, the handwriting was the same. Then the captain of the icebound vessel recalled that this man had taken a nap about the time his double was seen. When he woke up, he announced with certainty that they would all be saved.

The story appeared in Robert Dale Owen's *Footfalls on the Boundary of Another World*. Although it came to Owen secondhand from a marine officer who had heard it from the first mate, the officer swore that Bruce was a man of the utmost integrity and should be believed. It is one of the strangest OOB cases on record. How can an astral hand grasp a piece of chalk and write a message

on a slateboard? Once we start, however, with the assumption that
there is an astral body, we should not be surprised that it is capable
of many supernormal feats.

This is one case in which the I-Consciousness did not accompany
the second body, but the writing on the slate plus the appearance
of the double and later identification by Bruce are good evidence of
an OOBE. It is an example, also, of out-of-body experiences during
sleep, most of them not remembered by the dreamer.

Psychic Rods and Ectoplasmic Extensions

Crookall and other theorists believe that many of the physical effects caused by the astral body may result from "projected ectoplasm." Ectoplasm is the substance that comes from the body of a
medium during seances and is allegedly used by spirits to materialize their forms. Ectoplasm may be the substance of the second
body, at least in its semiphysical phase. The mind-over-matter phenomena during seances—raps, table tilting, the playing of instruments detached from any human agency—may actually be generated by the second body.

Philosopher C. D. Broad believes that an "invisible and intangible" body could put out "arms," "pseudopods," "psychic rods," or
"ectoplasmic extensions" and cause the mysterious movement of objects. Crookall calls these the "extruded portions" of some doubles,
the semiphysical component that shares the double with the soul
body.

In *A Casebook for Survival*, A. T. Baird tells what happened
when Thomas Mann, the famous German novelist, attended a seance given by medium Willy Schneider. Although the skeptical
Mann held Willy's knees between his own while someone else held
the medium's wrists, a typewriter in the room began to type by itself. No one was near the machine as it merrily clicked away. Perhaps it was the extruded portion of the medium's second body that
was doing the typing, his "ectoplasmic extensions," or perhaps the
second body itself had left Willy's body during his trance state
and manipulated the keys. Mann reported that as the machine
drew to the end of each line, he could hear the bell ring, the carriage being drawn back, and a new line beginning.

The medium D. D. Home could cause an accordion to play although it was some distance from where he was sitting. During one

of Home's seances, a disembodied hand was seen hovering over a gas jet. The gas went out and at the same time eight jets in other parts of the house also went off.

Mind-over-matter phenomena in the seance room, whether it is caused by ectoplasmic extentions or another kind of paranormal power, may differ in kind from mind-over-matter events that occur during astral travel. Or the two kinds of phenomena may be related. The answers may be simple or they may be complex, as is the case with the psychic world in general.

Yet the evidence for astral mind-over-matter cannot be brushed aside for want of a definitive explanation. When a young woman feels the pressure of a friendly though unseen arm around her waist, when another woman feels the prick of a pin in her finger although she is alone in her room, when bells ring and repeated knocks are heard although no one is physically there, when mattresses seem to lift up by themselves, when a toy dog is mysteriously moved from one room to the next while the person responsible is asleep in bed, and when astral projectors are aware of making all these things happen and others see what they are doing—then the evidence for OOBEs becomes more solid than ever.

Chapter 7

What Does the Double Look Like?

What does the second body look like? What is it made of? How do others see it? How does the projector see himself?

The double has appeared to both astral travelers and witnesses as everything from an insubstantial presence to a body that is the duplicate in all respects of the physical organism. In a letter to Robert Crookall, a woman described her double as "an exact replica of my physical body." She experienced herself as solid, she breathed and was normal in all other ways, except that she could see her physical body on the bed below. At the other extreme, some projectors never see their doubles or even believe that they have one. They are aware only that their consciousness is out of their physical body and moving to another point in space.

Celia Green, director of the Institute of Psychophysical Research at Oxford University, issued a press and radio appeal to persons who had had OOBEs, then did an analysis of their experiences. She used the term "ecsomatic" for all OOBEs in which the I-Consciousness was not in the physical body and divided these into "parasomatic" when the projector was aware of being in another body or at least "a spatial entity" and "asomatic" when he had no awareness of a second body, only that his I-self was separated from the physical self.

The most tenuous of parasomatic projectors had a feeling not of a second body but of an extension into space of his I-Consciousness. One of Green's subjects had "no substance or form of any kind" but thought that there was "an area of control" vaguely oval in shape, about 2½ feet in breadth and about a foot in depth. Another projector felt "like a single eye that is lit up and about 2½ inches in diameter." Psychic Paul Neary experiences himself as a "mist" during his astral travels while psychic Alex Tanous thinks of himself as "a blob of light." Others have seen their doubles as "gauzy," "gossamer," "smokelike," and so on.

In a large number of cases, the double can be recognized as the personality who has projected, appearing in all gradations from a translucent figure to a solid physical body. At times only the head is seen, with either no body or shoulders or just a shadowy outline. In *Mysterious Worlds* Dennis Bardens writes of a young college student whose father's head appeared in his room, the face "shrouded in darkness." His father was making a conscious projection.

Sometimes the double first appears in rather intangible form, then coalesces into the second body, with distinct features. The man who projected himself to his lady friend's house and astrally rang her doorbell was first seen by her as a luminous mist, before he condensed into a duplicate of his physical body. The double is often ovoid in form or is seen within an egg-shaped envelope. Paul Lachlan Peck, who healed himself of a blood clot when out of his body after an accident, described his double as an egg-shaped glow, in hues of purple, blue, and white.

One of Celia Green's correspondents wrote: "I rose out of my body like a white cloud the same shape as my body but without weight." Second bodies vary in density, depending upon the conditions in which they project, or, to put it in Dr. Crookall's terms, how much of the vehicle of vitality is retained in the double. Most projectors feel no weight in their astral selves nor are they aware of heartbeat, breathing, or other functions of their physical bodies.

Another of Green's cases had an OOBE while in a dentist's chair and sensed himself in both bodies, a case of dual consciousness, but with his self-awareness more strongly in his double. He could feel "solidity and weight" in the physical body in the chair but a lack of solidity and weight in "himself."

The second body may be altered to fit the desires of the projector, who often sees his double as much younger than his physical body, especially if he can observe it in a mirror. Caroline Larsen was middle-aged when she looked in the bathroom mirror and saw herself as an eighteen-year-old girl. Many projectors discover, too, that they are taller or larger than in their physical bodies. A traveling salesman staying overnight in Omaha, Nebraska, felt himself as a "fleecy ball" while coming out of his physical body. When the ball took the shape of a man, his second body was three feet taller. Reine, the French artist's model, also had a larger second body, probably because she was rather sickly in her physical body.

In a large percentage of cases, the second body gives off a glow that illuminates even a totally dark room. Many projectors, including Caroline Larsen, have awakened in the middle of the night in their doubles and could see so clearly by their own light that they did not have to turn on the room lights. A projector quoted by H. F. Prevost Battersby (*Man Outside Himself*) from P. Gibier's *Analyses de Choses* could see through the wall into the backs of pictures in his neighbor's apartment: "I found that I could perceive quite plainly what appeared to be a ray of light emitted from my epigastrium [abdomen] which illuminated the objects in the room."

Witnesses also report seeing projectors in bright light. When writer Dennis Bardens had a projection, he appeared to his wife in bright colors. During Reine's astral excursions, she had a good look at the second bodies of other living persons. Cornillier, the artist who hypnotized her, wrote: "She sees them as different and distinctive, in density, color, and attitude, as each individual is. The color red seems to indicate, for Reine, a heavy material substance, to be inferior; while the superior and more ethereal double is bluish or whitish."

What Is the Double Made of?

What is the ultimate substance of the double? Is it physical, semiphysical, or superphysical?

The semiphysical component, or vehicle of vitality, may be made of ectoplasm, or what Crookall calls "the ultra-gaseous or electromagnetic part of the total physical body." In its purer form there is evidence, to be developed as this book progresses, that the second body may be composed of white light. There is also evidence that the double is basically electrical in nature.

Robert Monroe once felt his double traveling along telephone company lines. Mrs. Napier, who paid an astral visit to her dying father, first felt "a sort of prickling sensation" through her body "like an electric current." A. J. Davis, a psychic of the last century, thought that the astral body was related to the physical through "vital electricity." Medium D. D. Home, while projecting, could see his own nervous system as "thousands of electric scintillations, which here and there, as in the created nerve, took the form of currents."

(A later chapter will elaborate on Harold Burr's theory that electrodynamic fields hold together all living organisms, and its implications for the second body.)

Many psychics claim that they can see the second body as a colored aura around the physical body. Mrs. Garrett called this aura the "surround" and saw each person "as if he were set within a nebulous egg-shaped covering of his own." Dr. Walter Kilner, an Englishman, and Hector Durville, a Frenchman, were able to see the aura through the use of chemical screens. When Durville hypnotized his subjects, the aura would sometimes disappear from the passive physical body and reappear near a calcium sulphide screen some distance away. Durville also saw a cord that extended from the navel of the physical body to the double.

What are the boundaries that separate the physical body from the semiphysical vehicle of vitality and both of them from the nonphysical soul body—the boundaries between a solid physical organism, an ectoplasmic substance, an ovoid form, a mass of electrical energy, and pure light? Since there is a constant shifting, blending, melting of astral forms one into the others, it is difficult to make sharp divisions. Some experimenters and many psychics, however, believe that these boundaries can be seen in the aura.

Colonel Albert de Rochas, another French experimenter of the early twentieth century, postulated several layers around the physical body, the first about an inch and a quarter thick, the last about seven or ten feet away. In *Breakthrough to Creativity*, psychiatrist Shafica Karagulla mentions a psychic called Diane who sees three psychic bodies in the aura. The closest, about an inch or two away, is the "energy body," a replica of the physical body appearing as "a sparkling web of light beams." A foot or a foot and a half farther out is the "emotional field," ovoid in form, with colors and energy patterns that reveal emotional states. Two feet or more beyond the physical body is the "mental body."

Other psychics have seen as many as seven bodies in the aura. What each sees, of course, depends on his sensory perception and subjective evaluation. That there is an aura, however, has been demonstrated scientifically by high-speed photography and other experimental procedures in Russia and the United States. While the connection between the aura and the double is not clear, the reality of the double and its nature as a composite have been established by evidence from many sources.

The Clothes That Doubles Wear

What do astral travelers wear when they go visiting? Witnesses have seen them in a variety of outfits—conventional suits and dresses, sports clothes, uniforms, pajamas and nightgowns—mostly apparel that is familiar to their host or hostess and gives the projector a natural look. The woman who visited her friend "robed in violet" was wearing a color her friend recognized as her favorite. Another young lady was surprised by a visit from her boss's double, wearing the same checked tie he usually wore in the office.

The dress of the double is often appropriate to his problem of the moment. In *The Facts of Psychic Science and Philosophy*, A. Campbell Holms tells the story of a man in England who desperately needed the advice of a woman friend. The friend, however, was sleeping in an Egyptian hotel at the time. How does one dress astrally for a consultation in the middle of the night? The woman heard someone calling her and saw the man's double walk into the room. She said later: "He appeared most eager to speak to me . . . So clear was his figure, that I noted every detail of his dress, even to three onyx shirt studs which he always wore."

In another Holms case, a young lady in London was sitting at her kitchen table when the double of her brother, on sea duty off the coast of Australia, walked in and sat down. He was wearing his sailor's uniform, a monkey jacket, and a cap that were all dripping with water. Speaking in a natural voice, he said, "For God's sake, don't say I am here," then disappeared. The girl realized from his clothes and his manner that he was in some kind of trouble. When she saw him in the flesh later, he explained that he had been ashore without leave and when he returned to the ship after midnight, he fell into the water and nearly drowned.

The projector may wish to be dressed as she was in the past rather than in the present. Caroline Larsen, who saw herself in the mirror as a young girl, was not wearing the nightclothes she had retired in but "the loveliest white shining garment imaginable—a sleeveless one-piece dress, cut low at the neck and reaching almost to the ankles." Mrs. Larsen may have worn such a dress when she was a young girl of eighteen—or it may have been an idealized garment.

The clothes may be associated with something that happened in the past, something the projector wishes to call to the attention of her host or hostess. A London woman staying in a country house lay down one evening with the hope of projecting to her husband at Wimbledon. Instead, she appeared at her London flat, occupied at the time by a friend, who was reading a book. The double said, "Give me that book," then opened a door and passed through it. She was wearing an evening frock and an embroidered Indian shawl she had not worn physically for two years.

Since there are no more facts available in this case, one can only guess why the woman appeared not to her husband but her friend, why she went home instead of to Wimbledon, why she demanded that her friend give her the book, and why she was wearing the likeness of an Indian shawl that was gathering dust in a closet. The shawl may have represented something in her past that came to mind at the time of her projection, if only in her subliminal mind, and the book may have been associated with the same incident. Many cases of OOBEs give only sketchy outlines, but more probing could bring to light the motivations of the projector.

During the sleeping hours the astral traveler usually chooses a more circumspect outfit than the nightclothes he may have been wearing, but often such formalities are ignored. When Lucian Landau was ill, Eileen came to him in her astral nightgown, seeing no reason to dress up merely to check his pulse and respiration. In most cases of husband-to-wife projection (and vice versa) at night, the projector usually shows up in the clothes he wore to bed. Most projectors, however, will appear to their friends and relatives in street clothes and sometimes evening clothes.

The garment worn in the astral may be a faithful copy of the physical garment, or it may be an improved version of it. On one of Frederick Sculthorp's astral journeys, described in *Excursions to the Spirit World,* he was wearing his "everyday clothes, reproduced in every detail, even to a small stain that was on them." In Crookall's *More Astral Projections,* however, there is the case of a woman who fell down while she was carrying a hod of coal and found herself standing beside her prostrate body. Although she was wearing the same clothes, her astral garments were spotless while her material clothes were wet and sooty.

Instead of conventional clothing, projectors often find themselves in a flowing robe such as Caroline Larsen's "white shining garment." These have been described as "a long, trailing garment of white chiffon," "a gauzy white robe," "a pool of white," and so on. Very often a psychic sees familiar or unfamiliar astral figures wearing white robes. When the Indian White Thunder was out of his body, his two guides wore white robes, which have spiritual significance. At the transfiguration of Jesus, "his raiment became shining, exceeding white as snow."*

The act of dying often generates projections in which details of dress are called to the attention of a friend or relative. The British Society for Psychical Research has investigated many such "crisis apparitions." A British soldier stationed in Armagh, Ireland, in 1886 woke up one night and saw the double of a Major Hubbersty, who looked very pale and fell forward as if dying. The soldier noticed that the major's clothes had a thin red thread weaving through the pattern. A few days later he read in the London *Times* that Major Hubbersty had died the night his double appeared.

In another SPR case, a young Englishman named Charles Tweedale woke up on the night of January 10, 1879, and saw a nebulous face on the panels of his wardrobe. The face came into focus and Tweedale recognized his grandmother, who wore "an old-fashioned frilled or goffered cap." After a few seconds the face faded away. In the morning he told his parents what had happened and learned that his father had also seen his grandmother's double that night, standing at his bedside. A few hours later word arrived that Tweedale's grandmother had died during the night. He heard later that his sister had also seen the double on the same night wearing the same goffered cap.

* Mark 9:3.

The SPR also investigated the case of a Mrs. Paquet, who in 1889 saw the double of her brother standing a few feet away. The brother, a sailor stationed in Chicago, was "in the act of falling forward . . . seemingly impelled by two ropes or a loop of rope drawing against his legs. The vision lasted but a moment, disappearing over a low railing." She cried out, "My God, Ed is drowned!" Later that morning a telegram arrived with news of the drowning. Mrs. Paquet added that she had seen Ed wearing "a heavy blue sailor's suit, no coat . . . his trouser-legs rolled up to show the white lining inside."

Her husband wrote to the SPR later that he went to Chicago and saw that the part of the vessel in the vision was exactly as Mrs. Paquet had pictured it. The crew verified that her brother had bought a pair of pants a few days before the accident and had worn them rolled up, with the white lining showing.

Sometimes it is the living person who visits the sickbed of the dying and wears familiar clothes that can later be identified. A nurse, Frances Redell, was taking care of a young woman deathly ill with typhoid fever, when she heard the doorbell ring and saw the double of the girl's mother, wearing a red shawl over her shoulders and a flannel petticoat with a hole in front. She was carrying a brass candlestick. Miss Redell learned that the description fit the mother exactly and that there were such candlesticks in her home.

The Origin of Astral Accessories

The brass candlestick brings up another knotty question: Where do the metal and wood objects that often accompany the double come from? Sometimes the projector wears jewelry or carries something that is familiar to those who see him. Where did the woman who was worried about her grandson get the electric iron that she showed to her daughter during an early morning projection (see Chapter 1)? Where did the double of Ann Amherst get the lethal pin that she used to stab her friend Mary?

A Colonel Bigge was stationed at Templemore, Ireland, in 1847. One afternoon he was crossing the barracks yard on his way to the mess hall when he saw one of his lieutenants walking about fifteen yards ahead of him. What surprised the colonel was that the lieutenant, out of uniform, was dressed in a bright shooting jacket and carried a fishing rod and landing net. Colonel Bigge followed him into the mess hall and got another shock. The lieutenant disappeared, along with the jacket and fishing gear.

After lunch the colonel went into the barracks yard again and once more saw the lieutenant on his way to the mess hall, dressed as before. This time, however, it was the flesh-and-blood lieutenant just back from a fishing trip. Where did the astral fishing rod and landing net come from, as well as the shooting jacket?

We haven't yet asked how the double's clothes originate. The second body may be a permanent resident inside the physical body, or it may be *the* prime body, possibly a biological-spiritual substance that animates the physical body. But clothes and jewelry, pins and candlesticks are man-made, fashioned from the raw materials of the earth.

Holms poses the dilemma:

> The fact of a spirit or double appearing in clothes is commonly regarded as an unsurmountable difficulty, for it is urged that, while the existence of a spirit body, capable of leaving the material one and visiting a friend, might be credited, it is inconceivable that it could spiritualize a suit of clothes, for these have no physiological relationship with the body, spiritual or material.

The most likely explanation is that astral clothes and the doubles of other objects are thought-forms created by the unconscious mind. The manner in which evening dress, street clothes, and sleeping apparel appear on the second body indicates a specific purpose, just as the projection of the double itself is usually specifically motivated.

Astral clothes seem, however, to have some substance at least in the mind of the observer, just as the second body usually does. Caroline Larsen and many other projectors have seen their astral clothing in the mirror. Even thought-forms may be created as visible objects. The experiments with Ted Serios in thoughtography illustrate this point. Serios, on a number of occasions, has been able to look into the lens of a camera at unexposed film and project pictures from his mind that appear on the film when developed. Where do the pictures come from? They seem to have their origin in Serios' mind.

A case of this kind is that of Miss Scatcherd, cited by Bozzano in *Discarnate Influence in Human Life*. Felicia Scatcherd was asked by Archdeacon Colley to pose for a photograph. Just before the picture was taken, however, she realized that she was in her street clothes and regretted that she wasn't wearing a lace-trimmed blouse back home in her closet. When the photograph was developed, the shadow of the blouse appeared on it.

If persons in their physical bodies can impose their thoughts of clothes on film, their astral minds might have the same power to dress the double either in replicas of the clothes worn by their physical bodies at the time or in other astral clothes that may be appropriate. There have been a few recorded cases in which the projector was naked one moment and clothed the next. As soon as his astrally conscious mind was aware he was nude, his unconscious mind created the clothes.

Evidence from mediums and other sources suggest that dressing the double in astral clothes may occur after death as well as before. There are numerous cases of the dead appearing in clothes they wore at some time during their lives. And the spirits of the dead seem to have the same sense of modesty shown by doubles of the living. An alleged spirit communicating through a medium was somewhat embarrassed at being an "unclothed shade." He then thought of his Turkish dressing gown and the next moment became a "clothed shade."

Holms suggests another possibility that would account for the astral appearance of clothes, fishing nets, pins, or whatever—objects as well as people have their own doubles: "We can easily comprehend it if we accept that everything has an ethereal duplicate and there is no fundamental difference between the double of a medium and his clothes."

Robert Crookall advances the ingenious theory that astral clothes may also derive from "the ideoplastic aura of the vehicle of vitality . . . becoming impressed by a mental image." Since, in Crookall's view, part of the double contains something of the physical in it, the mind of the projector may use this substance as the material for an astral garment. Just as a tailor cuts and shapes a suit from wool, the projector unconsciously fashions the auric or ectoplasmic substance into the apparel he needs on the astral plane.

In *The Survival of the Soul,* Cornillier carries this theory a step further with the notion that the astral tailor may extract elements from fabrics that are already in the physical world. This happens most often in the seance room when a materializing spirit may draw upon whatever is in the room, such as draperies and carpets "to fabricate the costume in which he wishes to appear." The more substantial the astral costume, the thinner and more lusterless the physical materials will appear to the observer. When the Polish medium Frank Kluski materialized clothing, his own physical clothes seemed to wear out more quickly.

The astral carpenter, jeweler, and metal worker might operate the same way. The process of erosion and decay that shortens the life of man-made objects may be hastened by predators in the invisible world. When Ann Amherst stabbed Mary de Lys with her astral pin, a physical pin in her bedroom may have lost some of its sharpness.

Thus we have four theories of how the double makes his own clothes and other astral properties. The one favored by this writer is that all such accessories appearing with the second body are thought-forms created by the double or by the mind that may vitalize both the double and the physical body. A second theory is that the double manipulates the aura, or ectoplasm, or vehicle of vitality, that are its semiphysical components. A third is that the double weaves his astral garments or shapes his woods and metals from materials in the physical world. The last theory is that the doubles of all material objects already exist and merely combine with the human double on the astral plane.

Whatever the explanation, we know that the duplicate body takes along whatever it needs in the way of "extras." When the second body tends toward the asomatic, or misty, aspect, the accessories rarely appear. At the other extreme are the very solid three-dimensional second bodies accompanied by just as tangible clothes and personal possessions that have astonished Church officials and laymen for hundreds of years. Cases of solid doubles moving among people and being recognized as living, breathing human beings while the physical body itself may be elsewhere were first recorded by the Catholic Church and given the term "bilocation."

Let us go back in time again and view the miracle of the solid-body double, first in its religious setting and then in non-Church cases of a more recent period.

As Solid as
You and I

Chapter 8

Doubles That Perform Miracles

It was Holy Thursday in the Church of St. Pierre de Limoges. The priest stood in the pulpit before his congregation, delivering a sermon on brotherly love. He spoke quietly, humbly, and they listened to him with reverence and devotion. Anthony was a good man, and the words came from his heart.

But now something strange happened. The priest stopped talking and seemed lost in thought. Then he drew his cowl over his head and knelt down. The church was still. The congregation knew that something important was taking place, for this was no ordinary man kneeling in front of them, a faraway look in his eyes.

In a monastery on the other side of town the monks, who were chanting, turned as one man to a stall in their chapel that had been empty and saw Anthony step forward. He took his book, read the appointed passage while the monks listened, then seemed to melt away. A moment later he came out of his trance in the Church of St. Pierre de Limoges, then stood up and went on with his sermon.

It happened in the thirteenth century. St. Anthony of Padua had projected his second body to the monastery because he remem-

bered that he was due there at the time he was delivering his sermon. But this was different from other OOBEs, when the duplicate
body, if seen at all, is recognized as an apparition, non-physical in
nature. St. Anthony appeared to the monks as if in his solid physical
body. He walked out of the stall, he picked up the sacred book and
read from it, he was observed in all his actions as though there in
the flesh.

There have been many such cases of bilocation reported by the
Catholic Church since its beginnings. It happens to those holy men
and women who, because they have been granted the power to
perform miracles, will later be sainted. It is probably the most astonishing of OOBEs because of the solidity of the second body and
the fact that it seems to perform all the functions of the physical
body. There are many bilocators in the annals of the Church. One of
them was Alphonsus Liguori, the monk of Arezzo.

Alphonsus, who lived to the age of ninety-one, suffered from a
variety of crippling diseases. In September 1774, when he was sev-
enty-eight years old, he went into a cataleptic trance and remained
motionless in his cell for five days. When he woke up he announced
that he had been at the bedside of the dying Pope Clement XIV
and that the Pope was now dead. The startled monks dismissed this
story as pure fantasy. Rome was at least four days away by horse
and carriage, and there had been no official word of Clement's
condition.

The news came a few days later that the Pope had died. Was this
just clairvoyance, supernormal knowledge of events taking place at
a distance that Liguori saw as in a vision? Liguori claimed that his
second body had been in Rome, and his statement was later con-
firmed by witnesses who were with him as he prayed at the Pope's
bedside—the superiors of the Dominican, Observatine, and Augus-
tinian orders. It was not a collective hallucination. The case was
documented and accepted by the Catholic Church as a true bilocation.

Alphonsus was no "ivory tower" monk. The son of a captain of
the royal galleys, before being ordained in 1726 he had been a
horseman, swordsman, harpsichordist, and an outstanding lawyer.
Saints or not, high spirituality and psychic powers are often found
in men and women of unusual intellect and creativity who are intensely interested in other people and in the destiny of the world.

Ignatius of Loyola, in the sixteenth century, was another bilocator. Once, while living in Rome, he appeared to the rector of the

college in Cologne. The rector, Leonardo Clessilis, had written to Ignatius that he would make the pilgrimage of three hundred leagues by foot to see him, but Ignatius wrote back that Leonardo was needed in Cologne and should not attempt the time-consuming journey. Instead, Ignatius would find a way to visit Leonardo. One day, while the rector was sitting in his study, Ignatius appeared and spoke with him. Leonardo told later how he was filled with joy when the second body of Ignatius materialized.

A less well-documented case from the seventeenth century is that of Maria Coronel de Agreda, whose second body did missionary work in Mexico while her physical body was in Italy. Once she persuaded the people of a native tribe to go to another part of Mexico where a band of Franciscan monks was also doing missionary work. The natives made the long pilgrimage and told the monks about the strange lady who had sent them. When they were shown a picture of a Franciscan nun, they identified her as Maria.

Another link to the bilocation of Maria Coronel de Agreda was Father Alonso de Benavides, who was head of a mission to Mexico in 1630. According to Father Herbert Thurston, who writes about Maria in *Surprising Mystics,* when Father de Benavides went to Italy, he said that an American Indian tribe had described a strange woman who appeared among them and urged them to be baptized. Later he visited Maria in Italy and was convinced that she was the bilocator whom the Indians had seen as a flesh-and-blood person.

The Astral Journeys of Padre Pio

Coming closer to the present time, we have the testimony of a number of persons that Padre Pio, the Capuchin monk who has become a twentieth-century legend, many times projected his solid second body to help those in trouble. Although he was always in or near the monastery of San Giovanni Rotondo, near Poggia, Italy, he was seen as far away as Uruguay, South America.

One of Pio's admirers, Monsignor Damiani of Uruguay, wished to remain in Italy near him, but the priest told him that he would die at home and promised to attend him at his death. Twenty years later, in 1942, the Archbishop of Montevideo, in Uruguay, was summoned by a Capuchin friar to the bedside of the dying Damiani. Here he found a slip of paper reading "Padre Pio came." Several years later the archbishop met Padre Pio and identified him as the

Capuchin friar who had brought him the news that Damiani was dying.

Another Padre Pio story comes from an Italian radio announcer. Once, just before going on the air, the announcer's head ached so violently that he was temporarily paralyzed. A few seconds later Padre Pio came into the studio, put his hand on the man's forehead, and the headache vanished. Astonished as the announcer was, he later decided that it must have been a hallucination. He went to see the priest to tell him what had happened, but before he could open his mouth, Pio put his hand on his visitor's forehead and said, smiling, "Oh, oh, these hallucinations."

Perhaps the most dramatic account of Padre Pio as a bilocator was told by General Luigi Cadorna, commander of the Italian Army in World War I. One night at the front, after a series of discouraging defeats, the general decided in a fit of depression to kill himself. Leaving orders that no one was to be admitted to his tent, he was holding his pistol to his head when he saw the flap of the tent lifted. A monk entered, looked at him for a moment, and said, "Such an action is foolish." Then he left.

Filled with remorse, the general put down his gun, but he was puzzled. Who was the monk? How did he get into the tent? General Cadorna had never seen Padre Pio, but later he heard stories about the priest and decided to visit the monastery. When Pio came out, the general said, "Let me take a good look at you. Yes, it is incredible, but you are the monk."

Stories are legion of sick persons who were cured by visits from the "solid" Padre Pio, even though Pio was in his monastery at the time. It is true that those who are suffering from high fever and delirium, particularly if they have great religious faith, might actually cure themselves and imagine that a saint had helped them. And such was the love and devotion inspired by Padre Pio, it is understandable that many thought they were cured by his astral presence. In a number of cases, however, Padre Pio himself indicated that he was there, and the evidence is very strong that astral projectors do go out at night to heal. (See Chapter 13.)

A Solid Double Comes to Mass

The Catholic Church does not accept miracles without thorough investigation and documentation. W. T. Stead, a British journalist and psychical researcher who lost his life when the *Titanic* sank in 1912, quotes (in *Borderland*) the opinion of a German doctor of divinity who was attached to the Vatican:

> The teaching of the Church is that the phenomenon of bilocation is not natural, but is occasionally permitted by special grace, as in the case of certain well-known saints, or sometimes for other inscrutable reasons which are less advantageous to those who are the recipients of the favor, which is not natural, but distinctly supernatural.

In addition to saints and near-saints who have performed miracles in their solid doubles, many lay followers have projected while spiritually inspired—for what the Church might call "other inscrutable reasons." When such stories come to us from centuries back, however, we are inclined to be skeptical, even when the Church has put its seal of approval on the bilocation. In our own time, too, we may wonder about the gullibility of Italian peasants and even learned men who loved Padre Pio.

But when a case of bilocation happens on our own doorstep, it is time to reconsider. The case I have in mind was told to me by a friend who is a Catholic priest. Although the projector was a lay person and not a priest, it is a very striking example of a solid second body in a religious context.

The priest was standing in front of his New York City church one Sunday morning in 1969, greeting members of the congregation who were arriving for mass. He was surprised but happy to see a man named Walter come up the walk and shake hands with him at the door. Walter was a neatly dressed businessman in his late sixties who had always been a faithful churchgoer until stricken by a serious illness some months before. So far as the priest knew, Walter had been in a hospital all this time.

"It was a million-to-one shot," said Walter, "but I came out of it all right." Then he went inside the church.

A few days later the priest himself had to go to another hospital for a minor operation. Two members of his congregation who were also friends of Walter's visited him, and he told them that he had seen Walter at the church on Sunday.

"But that is impossible," said one of his visitors. "We have just come from the other hospital and although Walter is getting better, he still has to be helped around by the nurses." Then the man added: "It was a million-to-one shot, but he came out of it all right," the same words the priest thought he had heard Walter say a few days before.

The idea of bilocation, of solid second bodies, poses a very difficult question. Granted that a man has a double that on occasion can leave the parent body and be seen as an apparition somewhere else, is it possible for a person to have two physical bodies, both capable of functioning in exactly the same way? If the priest did in fact see and shake hands and speak with Walter, where then was Walter's true physical body—walking into the church or lying in bed in the hospital room?

The priest, a man of unquestioned integrity, told me this story reluctantly. He wondered himself whether he had had a hallucination. As real as psychic events seem at the time they occur, later when we are back in what is called the "real" world, we are apt to question our experience, and if we do not, others will be sure to question it for us.

What is a "hallucination?" If a man is observed in his usual dress in bright daylight walking down the street, talking intelligently, shaking hands, seeing, hearing, touching, tasting, smelling—going through all the actions that identify him as a live human being—then to call him a "hallucination" suggests that, given such objective signs of life and individuality, we may all be "hallucinating" one another.

What, then, was the state of Walter's actual physical body at the time that his solid second body appeared to the priest? Walter was seriously ill, a condition in which separation of the two bodies often occurs. (See Chapters 15 and 16.) But added to that is the factor of motivation. I am not a Catholic, but I understand that failure to attend mass is considered a grave offense, one that may jeopardize the offender's chance to enter heaven. Walter's conscious or unconscious motivation at the time he was ill in the hospital, depleted in strength, perhaps asleep, may have been to appear at the church and be seen by the priest.

A Catholic friend tells me, however, that it is not a sin if the churchgoer is unable through circumstances beyond his control to attend mass. Walter would have had no need to weigh his conscience. My friend points out, however, that the priest may have been the sick man's confessor, and this emotional bond would have been reason enough for Walter not only to appear in his second body but to create the illusion that he was actually there in the flesh. It is understandable that the priest would be reluctant to talk about it.

More Doubles in Church

Whether or not there is consciousness of sin, the need to leave their bodies is very strong in those pious persons who are too ill to attend services. W. T. Stead tells of a woman member of his church who was lying home in bed with a fever one Sunday. During the evening service, her solid double entered the church, walked up the aisle in full view of those present, and took a vacant pew. She picked up a hymn book but did not sing. A verger gave her another hymn book. When the collection box was passed around, she put nothing in it.

When the last hymn was over, she stood up, still holding her book, then laid it down and walked quickly, almost self-consciously, down the aisle, opened the door, and left. She was clearly seen by Stead and several others. She had recently joined the church and had sat in the seat her double occupied.

The woman told Stead later that she had had a strong desire to attend the service but fought it, knowing she was too ill to go. The doctor had given her a medicine that put her to sleep. She slept from 7 to 8:30 P.M. during the period of the service, not knowing that her astral body had been seen in church.

Although the woman had no conscious awareness of projecting, it seems to be a case of wishing strongly to be somewhere, then while ill or asleep, obeying the unconscious impulse to go there. Since she was motivated by religious devotion and perhaps conscience, she appeared in a very solid form so that onlookers would believe she was actually in church in her physical body. This is a well-documented case: the woman was seen not only by Stead, an experienced and responsible investigator, but also four other persons who knew her. The witnesses all signed statements, as did the doctor who attended her and the members of her family who were home with her at the time.

In another church case reported by the French astronomer Camille Flammarion, there was an additional strong motive for the double to appear—the projector's fiancé was pastor of the church.

The young lady was lying in bed deathly ill at the time her fiancé was delivering his sermon. Going into a cataleptic trance, she awoke two hours later and said she had been in church and heard the sermon. Then she died.

After the funeral, her mother asked the girl's fiancé what he had said in the sermon, and it exactly matched the girl's account. The pastor then added: "It is very strange, but in the middle of my sermon, I thought I saw a white figure enter the church, resembling my fiancée. She sat down in an empty place and disappeared toward the end of the service."

There are many more cases of churchgoers who while ill or otherwise indisposed appeared at the service in their solid bodies, also of persons who had OOBEs while physically in church. In *Casebook of Astral Projection* Robert Crookall writes that a girl in San José, Costa Rica, was seen in the church choir holding a hymn book and singing. At the time, however, she was a good distance away and not aware that she had projected.

The Dead Canon Returns

The Church throughout history has exerted a strong pull on the second bodies of both saints and religious laymen. This pull seems also to extend to those who have died, if we can believe that the dead do come back in astral form. William Barrett, the distinguished physicist who was one of the founders of the British Society for Psychical Research, told of a friend, Canon Carmichael, who appeared after his death in the Dublin church of which he had been the incumbent. Several members of the congregation saw him walk up the pulpit stairs, dressed in his familiar surplice and hood, and stand by his successor, the Reverend R. H. Murray, who was delivering a sermon on the subject of survival.

Although Dr. Murray sensed a presence nearby, he did not see the canon. Later, three men and a woman who had been sitting in the congregation gave identical details of the dead man's appearance and behavior. The canon had hitched up his surplice in a customary gesture as he came up the pulpit stairs. He looked younger than at the time of his death. He smiled at his daughter who sat in the audience. And his hood had a red lining.

Since Dr. Murray and other members of the congregation did not see Canon Carmichael, this may not be strictly a case of a solid second body appearing in the natural state of the physical body. It does illustrate, however, the magnetic attraction of the Church for the second bodies of both the living and the dead and indicates that both living and dead may be able to fashion astral clothes that are familiar to their friends and relatives.

Chapter 9

Doubles That Walk, Talk, and Breathe

    Among the thousands of recorded OOBEs, only a small number happen in the solid-body double. The projection of the solid double in a religious context, whether the projector is a member of the clergy or not, seems to be inspired by devotion to the Church and its principles. There are also a few classic cases in which the solid double projected for business, political, or other reasons. In one famous case, however, that of Émile Sagée described in this chapter, the projections were not only without apparent motivation but proved to be an economic liability to the projector.

An interesting aspect of the solid-double cases is that, with the exception of saints and saintlike figures, the projector is rarely aware that he has materialized elsewhere. The more of the semiphysical component that resides in the double, the more clouded the consciousness often becomes, in both the physical and astral selves. The physical body is low in energy at these times—during periods of daydreaming, extreme fatigue, sleep, serious illness, coma, and so on. Even when the saints project their I-Consciousness into solid doubles, they first induce a trance in their physical bodies.

Doubles as Buyers and Sellers

The solid double is often involved in business situations—a customer wishes to buy or pick up some goods, a salesman goes out astrally in search of a buyer. At such times, it would be self-defeating to appear as an apparition and would probably frighten the other party rather than allow him to act as he would in a normal business transaction. In *Borderland* Stead cites a British salesman representing a cigar manufacturer who went to call on a retailer one afternoon in Nottingham. He saw the retailer, a Mr. Southam, on the street near the latter's office, and shook hands with him. Said Mr. Southam: "I'm waiting here for a friend. I don't think I shall want any cigars this journey, but look in before eight o'clock."

The salesman came back at seven-thirty and spoke to Mr. Southam's clerk, who handed him a check for a small order. The salesman expressed his disappointment at not seeing Mr. Southam and explained that they had made an appointment on the street a few hours earlier. The astonished clerk replied: "But that is impossible, as both Mr. and Mrs. Southam have been confined to their apartment for a fortnight and never been out." The Southams were ill and in bed. The salesman recalled that Mr. Southam had looked different than usual and commented upon it. Mr. Southam had then made a curious remark: "Don't you see that I am in my *déshabillé?*"

If this experience had been pure fantasy inspired by the salesman's need for an order, the customer would not have said that he didn't want "any cigars this journey." The sick man may have been debating at the time whether or not to order cigars and, knowing that the salesman was in town, projected to him as a matter of courtesy or hospitality (even though he was in his *déshabillé.* He did not project consciously, but his solid double acted out his intention. Regardless of his reasons for projecting or his lack of awareness that he had projected, however, the man's solid appearance, his speech, and his handshake made his presence a reality to the salesman.

In another classic case reported by Stead, a customer, also ill and in fact dying, called at a photographer's shop to pick up some pictures he had sat for earlier. Although it happened in 1891, the Thompson-Dickinson case is very well documented through the testimony of several witnesses.

On Saturday, January 3, of that year, Mr. Dickinson, the photographer, opened his shop at eight A.M. and while he was getting ready for the day's work, a man entered, looking quite pale and distraught. He identified himself as Mr. Thompson and asked if his pictures were ready. Dickinson checked the date of the order but the photos had not been developed yet. He told Thompson to return later that day, but Thompson shook his head wearily and said, "I have been traveling all night and I cannot call again." Then he turned and left, and Dickinson noted that he appeared very upset about the pictures.

When Dickinson's assistant came to work later, she said that Thompson's father had called for the photos the day before. Dickinson then asked her to get the negative, and he recognized the face of the man who had just left.

On the following Friday Thompson's father came again and asked for the pictures. The younger Thompson, he said, had died the previous Saturday, the day he ostensibly appeared at the shop and spoke with Dickinson. He had been in a coma all day and had called loudly for his pictures before dying on Saturday afternoon.

Young Thompson's concern about his photos was apparently the motivating factor that sent him out of his body in a functioning physical double to the photographer's shop. It is idle to speculate about what the photos represented to him, although an object can symbolize something in the psyche. Coma, however, is highly conducive to astral travel, as will be seen later in cases of the second body leaving just before or at the time of death. What makes the Thompson case so remarkable, as in all solid-body cases, is the lifelike appearance and behavior of the double.

Another classic incident of the solid second body in a business situation was reported in the *Proceedings* of the British Society for Psychical Research. A Mr. R. P. Roberts, personally known and vouched for by members of the Society's Literary Committee that investigated the case, was an apprentice in a London dry-goods shop. It was his habit to go home for lunch every day at twelve noon and return at twelve-thirty P.M. One day he was home eating his lunch when he noticed with a start that it was already twelve-thirty, although he was in the middle of his meal. Alarmed because he did not want to be late for work, he looked at the clock again and saw that it was only twelve-fifteen.

While Roberts was looking at the clock, his double walked into the store, went behind the counter, and hung up his hat. His employer, Mrs. Owen, was upset at his entrance and turned to her husband and a customer, remarking loudly that Roberts had come back at a time when he was not wanted. No sooner had she spoken than he took his hat off the hook and left the shop. Mrs. Owen noticed that Roberts didn't appear to hear the remark and that he looked "quite absent-minded and vague."

When Roberts returned to work at twelve-thirty, Mrs. Owen demanded that he explain his strange behavior. The astonished clerk protested that he had never left home and was in fact in the middle of his meal at twelve-fifteen. The other three insisted that he had been there, the customer adding that she had followed Roberts down the street at twelve-fifteen and had seen him enter the store.

Roberts' aunt, who had eaten lunch with him, swore that he did not leave the table until about twelve twenty-five, when he finished his meal. The clue to the mystery was that just before Roberts was seen in the shop, another customer had come into the store and asked for an article that only the clerk could locate, as it was part of his stock. Mrs. Owen had thought irritably that if Roberts had been behind the counter instead of at home eating lunch, he could have completed the sale. Roberts, sitting at the dinner table, unconsciously felt her displeasure and saw the time on the clock momentarily as twelve-thirty.

He said later: "At the moment when I felt, with a startling sensation, that I ought to be at the shop, and when Mr. and Mrs. Owen were extremely anxious that I should be there, I appeared to them, looking, as they said, 'as if in a dream or in a state of somnambulism.'"

For Roberts to appear as merely an apparition in this case would not have been enough to satisfy either his employers or his own conscience. So for a few seconds he projected in his solid double to the store, satisfied his employers that he would have been there to take care of the other customer if possible, then returned to his meal.

A Solid Double in the Classroom

There were some fifty witnesses to the solid double of Mlle. Émile Sagée, a schoolteacher of the last century. Mlle. Sagée was a woman of thirty-two who taught at an exclusive school for young ladies at Livonia in Central Europe, the Pensionnat de Neuwelcke.

She was well liked by the directors of the school and by her young
charges and was considered an excellent teacher.

It was the students who first noticed something strange about
Mlle. Sagée—there seemed to be two of her. When they reported
this to the other teachers and the directors of the school, it was
dismissed as childish imagination. It was only when all thirteen
girls in one class saw two identical teachers in front of them that the
directors became alarmed. Either it was a collective hallucination or
there really were two Émile Sagées.

The conscientious Mlle. Sagée was writing a passage on the
blackboard when her double appeared at her side and wrote with
the same motions. (It was not reported whether an identical passage in the same handwriting was on the blackboard beside the
other writing.) Then about a week later one of the girls, standing
with the teacher, looked into the mirror and again saw two Mlle.
Sagées standing there. The child fainted.

From that time on the teacher and her double were seen not only
by the students but also the serving girls. Once, while she was eating, her double stood behind her making the same eating motions,
as if mocking the physical Mlle. Sagée. The waitress was under-
standably agitated.

Now the teacher's two bodies began to appear at greater distances from each other. One day forty-two pupils were playing in a
large room on the first floor, while Mlle. Sagée sat in an armchair
and watched them. One of the girls happened to look out the window and screamed when she saw the same Mlle. Sagée picking
flowers in the garden. Which was the real Sagée? Two of the girls
boldly touched the figure in the chair and said it felt like muslin or
crepe.

While the second or psuedo-Sagée sat in the armchair, the girls
noticed that the flower-picking Sagée was moving as if in a trance.
But when the figure in the armchair suddenly disappeared, the
Sagée in the garden became more animated, more her usual self.
Although the true Sagée was the one in the garden, the children insisted that there were two identical Sagées, one inside the room, the
other outside picking flowers.

During the thirteen months that Mlle. Sagée taught at the school,
there were many such occurrences. It was noted that her double
generally appeared when she was preoccupied in thought or was
not as physically vigorous as usual. The weaker and more trancelike

her physical body, the clearer and more solid her double appeared. It would seem that the two bodies borrowed from a common source and one gained in energy and density as the other was depleted.

When the school directors asked Mlle. Sagée about these strange goings-on, she claimed she was not aware of them. She was just as distressed over the phenomenon as the directors were. The girls didn't seem to mind. Many of them thought it was great fun, but their parents thought otherwise. Gradually the children were withdrawn from the school and transferred to other fashionable schools where the teachers were not psychic freaks.

Although Mlle. Sagée was considered an outstanding teacher, the directors felt that it was economically necessary to dismiss her, which they did with apologies. It then came out that the same thing had happened in other schools where she had taught, nineteen in all. Since no school would hire Mlle. Sagée again, she went to live with a sister-in-law who had several children. The children saw her and her double many times but they enjoyed, as they said, having two Aunt Émiles.

Generally there is a motivation for a psychic happening, whether an OOBE or some other manifestation of the paranormal. But since Mlle. Sagée only brought trouble on herself when she projected, there was no practical or spiritual reason for her doing so. Mlle. Sagée may have been born with what Robert Crookall calls a "mediumistic constitution"—in which the physical and astral bodies are loosely connected and may separate far more readily than in other projectors. As with other solid-double projectors, Mlle. Sagée's second body contained an unusual amount of her physical self, so much of it that the two bodies were identical in appearance and often in their actions.

The details of the Sagée case were first reported by a member of the school staff, Mlle. de Güldenstubbe. The case has been described in several books, including Battersby's *Man Outside Himself*.

Doubles in Politics

From school, shop, and office we move to the political arena. Here the motivation of the political projector is quite clear: he wishes not only to be present in Congress, Parliament, or another legislative body, but to be an unmistakably solid figure who can be seen as such by his colleagues and who can even cast his vote when necessary.

Take the case of Dr. Mark Macdonnell, member of the British House of Commons. He was seriously ill at home when an important measure came before the House for a vote. For two days Macdonnell's solid double appeared in the House and managed to cast his vote, which is on record.

Another politician whose physical body was ill in bed not only appeared in his solid body but was photographed along with his fellow members of the Legislative Council of British Columbia. On January 13, 1865, Charles Good was in his bedroom at home, yet a newspaper photo of the Council showed Good's face along with the others.

When Good recovered later, he was astonished when he saw himself in the picture, which is now on display in the provincial parliament buildings in Victoria, B.C. Allen Spraggett, discussing this case in *The Unexplained*, comments that Good appears somewhat transparent on the photo. He speculates that "Good had a strong desire to attend the Legislative Council session . . . He was gravely ill, possibly in a coma."

Another political projection was that of Sir Carne Rasch, also in the House of Commons. The projection took place in 1908 when Rasch was home with a bad attack of influenza. At this time the House was bitterly divided over an issue, and Rasch wanted very much to be present. Three members of the House testified that they saw Rasch sitting in his usual place. One of them, Sir Gilbert Parker, said: "When Rasch accepted my nod with what looked very like a glare, and met my kindly inquiry with silence, I was a little surprised." Another member of the House noticed that Sir Carne looked quite pale.

The Double Who Drank Coffee

In another solid-double case, two men sat at a table in an English coffeehouse, one of them in his physical body, the other a psychic who had projected three thousand miles.

A woman in Philadelphia had become anxious about the continued absence of her husband, a sea captain. Having had no word from him in several months, she visited a psychic in Philadelphia and asked if he could help. The psychic went into another room and shut the door. The woman waited patiently, then peeked through the keyhole and saw him lying quietly on a sofa, ostensibly in a trance.

Finally the psychic came out of the room and told the woman that he had located her husband in London in a coffeehouse. The husband had told the psychic that he would be back soon and explained why he hadn't written. When the husband came home, he verified all that the psychic had told his wife, and when he was introduced to the psychic, he identified him as the man he had spoken with in London.

If true, this story would clinch the case for OOBEs without the shadow of a doubt. To project at will from Philadelphia to London in a solidly physical second self, and there to converse with a man in a coffeehouse and within minutes give evidence of the projection that is later verified in all details—too good to be true! But did it happen? Robert Dale Owen, whose books are source materials for many contemporary writers on the paranormal, points out in *Footfalls on the Boundary of Another World* that the story came originally from the German Jung Stilling but that Stilling himself heard it in a roundabout way:

> It was brought from America by a German who had emigrated to the United States . . . He related it, on his return to Germany, to a friend of Stilling's from whom Stilling had it. But no names or exact dates are given; and it is not even stated whether the German emigrant obtained the incident directly either from the sea-captain or his wife.

Since we know about other projections of the solid second body, the coffeehouse story may be accurate. The evidence is skimpy, however, and it should be put in the category of doubtful cases. We have enough impressive evidence that the solid second body—a living, breathing organism identical in appearance and behavior to the physical body—has been seen and heard by witnesses and even photographed.

Chapter 10

A Review
and Preview

Let's take time out to review what we have explored about the out-of-body experience. We have learned that astral travel has been common in all countries throughout history and that primitive tribes even today accept the OOBE as a natural happening. We know that, although it is a universal phenomenon, the manner of projection and the beliefs about it are somewhat shaped by the culture in which it happens.

We have examined the kinds of evidence for out-of-body travel: the awareness of the I-Consciousness that it is in another vehicle; the knowledge of details and events out of range of the physical senses; the testimony of witnesses; the ability of the double to sometimes lift and move objects; the reported conversations between the double and his host and hostess.

We have seen that in a good percentage of cases the duplicate body rises, sometimes rotates out of the physical body, most often through the head, to a horizontal position above the passive body, then uprights itself, and that the process takes place in reverse when the second body returns. There is almost always a momentary blanking out of consciousness when the double leaves. Many projectors say also that their physical body is cataleptic during this process.

There is a cord that connects the two bodies and thins out as the astral body moves further away, but it can be lengthened indefinitely. Fear, excessive noise, or some other disturbance can cause the double to slam back into the physical body with an unpleasant shock effect, and it is better to return slowly. We read that the double may move in various ways—walk, glide, float, fly—and that it may stay near the physical body or travel great distances at lightning speed.

We have considered the appearance and nature of the double and found that it may range from just a wispy presence to a very solid three-dimensional body that walks, talks, and breathes exactly as the physical body does. We have learned that the astral traveler may give off his own light and that he sometimes sees himself in the mirror, often appearing much younger than his chronological age and bigger than his physical body. He is generally stronger, too, although lighter and freer in his movements. Although he is often frightened during his first OOBE, he loses his fear when it is repeated and not only enjoys it thoroughly but is usually reluctant to go back to his physical body.

We have wondered how the double can appear in clothes and have leaned to the theory that he creates them as thought-forms that are visible to witnesses. He can also create other objects as thought-forms, although not consciously—electric irons, brass candlesticks, fishing gear, pins, whatever he may need on his astral mission. We have evidence also that spirits of the dead may sometimes return to familiar surroundings wearing clothes that are recognized by friends and relatives.

We suspect that the double is a composite, made up of a soul body and a semiphysical component such as ectoplasm and that the proportion of this physical substance determines whether the double may pass through or be impeded by matter, and whether it can touch and move objects. We know that many countries and philosophical systems believe in as many as seven or more bodies of varying density within one individual. We have speculated somewhat tentatively that the fundamental principle of the second body may be light or electricity.

In some cases we have found that, although the I-Consciousness did not accompany a double that was seen by one or more witnesses, the projector did wish very strongly to be somewhere, then fell asleep and learned later that his double was actually there. Generally this happens when the person is dozing or dreaming and he may not remember what took place. We suggested that most astral projections happen during sleep, and later we will see cases in which the projector *woke up in his dream* to find it a reality and learned a technique of becoming conscious when he was acting out his dream in the second body.

The Reasons People Project

It is the belief of this writer that almost no paranormal event is without motivation. In cases of telepathy, there is usually an emotional bond between sender and receiver that opens up their psychic lines of communication. Members of the same family, close friends, sweethearts carry on a silent dialogue even when separated great distances, and the generating force is love and affection. When someone is ill, emotionally disturbed, or in danger, he may send out psychic signals that are picked up by his loved ones and even by strangers who wish to help those in trouble.

So, too, most OOBEs are motivated by a person-to-person bond. The grandmother who appeared to her daughter with the electric iron was anxious about her grandson. The woman who projected to her two sons in school was concerned about them. The woman who flew to the home of her deceased cousin, Mrs. Napier who went to her dying father, the man who visited his son at night—each OOBE was generated by family affection. Because Lucian Landau needed her help, Eileen's double came in to check his pulse and temperature. The Englishman who sought advice took an astral trip to see his friend in Egypt.

Loyalty to the group, tribe, or country also generates OOBEs. Elisha's double spied on the Syrian king and brought much classified information to the Hebrews. Ngema Nzago traveled to the meeting place of his fellow magicians because of a feeling of solidarity with them and a desire to help his tribe. Sorceresses and witch doctors take astral trips to find lost objects and missing people and to solve crimes—all for the benefit of the tribe. The man in the icebound ship went on a rescue mission to the other ship because of his bond with his fellow passengers.

The spiritual motivation is strong and finds expression in many kinds of OOBEs. Alphonsus Liguori wished to be at the bedside of the dying Pope. St. Anthony could not disappoint the monks who were expecting him. Maria Coronel de Agreda traveled thousands of miles from Italy to Mexico to help the natives. Padre Pio went out to heal the sick, administer to the dying, and even cure a radio announcer's headache.

Projectors leave their bodies to seek help or give it, often in a spiritual context. Many claim that they have been assisted out of their bodies by the spirits of the dead, as White Thunder was guided by the two Indians in white robes. And, like White Thunder, they find themselves on higher planes of existence where they meet dead relatives and friends or receive advice from unknown entities.

There are many reasons for projecting—personal, practical, spiritual, humanitarian—just as people are motivated to follow many paths in their physical bodies. We have seen how the conscience of a clerk propelled him back to his dry-goods shop during his lunch hour, how a businessman rose in his double from a sickbed and met the salesman he was unable to contact in his physical body. Politicians project from their sickbeds so that they can represent their constituents in legislative bodies.

Even something as prosaic as getting home in time for dinner may release the astral body ahead of the physical body, which, after all, must do the eating. An Edinburgh man, napping in a chair at his club one afternoon, realized that he would be late for dinner and found himself rushing home in his second body. He went through all the usual motions, opening the door with his key and going upstairs to change his clothes. While he was on the stairway, his father came out in the hall and looked at him.

He woke up at this point and went home in his physical body. Here he found his father and brother searching the house for him and calling his name. His astonished father said that at twelve o'clock he had gone into the hall, heard the front door shut, and had seen the young man run upstairs, look back at his father, and then disappear. The father claimed that the door had been locked and that his son's double had opened it with his key.

And what could be more practical, if rather offbeat, than to go house hunting in the double? Another offbeat projection with a practical purpose was that of a young East Indian described in *Moreton's History of Apparitions*, who got the shocking news that his father was about to disinherit him. Having no time to lose in conventional travel, he flew in his double to the lawyer's office and paralyzed the proceedings with one word: "Hold!"

Physical and Mental Conditions

Yet even when the motivation is strong, the projection generally cannot happen unless body and mind are ready for it. Strangely enough, both a state of relaxation and a state of stress may help to induce a projection. In the former, the projector may be dozing off, asleep, dreaming, suffering from illness or exhaustion, or under the influence of an anesthetic. He may be daydreaming, in a mild or deep hypnotic trance, not attentive to the world around him. Body and mind are quiescent. Sometimes a mood brings on projection: when Caroline Larsen was lying in bed and listening to the music, she may have felt nostalgia for her lost youth.

The grandmother with the electric iron was asleep when she made her astral journey. So were White Thunder and the ship passenger whose double wrote on a slateboard. The lady who went house hunting did so while asleep. Giuseppe Costa and Dr. Ostby woke up in their doubles while their physical bodies slept. Eileen watched over Lucian while she continued to sleep. Ann stuck her astral pin into Mary without fear of reprisal, since she was asleep at the time with her door closed.

Gladys Osborne Leonard was relaxing in bed when she found herself out of her body. Bert Slater was extremely tired as he lay near his wagon with his battered hat under his head. Sophie Swoboda was lying down with a headache when she projected. Walter was seriously ill in a hospital when his solid body appeared and shook hands with the priest. Carne Rasch, Mark Macdonnell, and Charles Good were all ill in bed when they projected to their legislative bodies. Young Mr. Thompson was in a coma when he showed up at the photographer's shop and asked for his pictures, as was Curma the senator when he thought he had died and gone on to the next dimension.

A hypnotic or cataleptic trance often comes on without warning before a spontaneous OOBE, but many projectors deliberately induce it, as the saints did. Primitive chieftains such as Ngema Nzago, shamans, sorceresses, witch doctors all begin with ceremonies and rituals designed to put their minds and bodies into astral readiness. They often take such drugs as *yagé* to alter their physical and mental chemistry and make projection easier.

Do hallucinogenic drugs loosen the connection between physical and astral bodies? Many OOBEs have been reported during "trips," and some researchers believe that the very nature of consciousness expansion by LSD is that of astral travel. Robert Crookall thinks that "the psychedelic experience *is* an out-of-body experience." Aldous Huxley, who was instrumental in making the youth of the 1960s drug-conscious, wrote that LSD did not seem to improve ESP but that it promoted "traveling clairvoyance."

In *The Enigma of Out-of-Body Travel,* Susy Smith tells about a New York psychologist who had a partial OOBE after taking LSD. His double "almost completely detached" from his physical body and he had the illusion of looking down from a great height. The psychologist stressed that his mind was much clearer and he had a more vivid feeling of reality than in his physical body. As in so many other out-of-body experiences, what happened convinced him that he would survive bodily death.

In *Casebook of Astral Projection,* Robert Crookall cities two instances in which the ingestion of mescalin, another hallucinatory drug, and cannabis, an extract of Indian hemp, were followed by OOBEs. In the mescalin case the projector had more acute senses —seeing, hearing, etc.—than in his physical body and he called his experience the most thought-provoking of his life. The other case, reported originally by Rosalind Heywood, was of an anthropologist named Turnbull who visited India and was given cannabis in a drink called "bhang." He felt himself traveling "through the clouds" and over the Himalaya Mountains, returning to his body, like so many other projectors, "with regret."

Does alcohol promote OOBEs? No statistics are available, but J. Hewat McKenzie, founder of the College of Psychic Science in London, once drank a large quantity of whiskey to see what the psychic effects would be. Walking down one side of the street, he saw himself standing on the other side. Crossing over to rejoin his other body, he looked back and saw himself still walking on the side he had just left. Although he had hoped for an OOBE, he couldn't figure out which was his physical body and which his duplicate self, since they were alike in every respect. When he arrived home, somehow the two bodies had come together.

Stress of Body and Mind

At the other extreme projection may be generated by extreme stress of body and mind. This could happen during illness when there is not only physical depletion but pain and tension that may alternate with passivity and relaxation. Drugs may also bring on mental and physical tension as well as relaxation, depending on what kind of drug is used and the body-mind response to it. Purely stress situations occur, however, when danger threatens—threats of drowning, suffocation, an imminent accident.

Fear alone, although the body comes to no harm, may generate an OOBE. During World War II a woman in London who had to endure daily bombing raids went into a state of terror whenever she heard the sirens. At such times she would run downstairs to the basement shelter from her upper-floor apartment and wait there until the "all clear" was sounded.

One day, as she heard the sirens, she felt herself go out of her body and float near the ceiling. It was too late to run to the stairs, and she listened with a curious sense of detachment to the planes screaming overhead and the sound of bombs falling. When the raid was over she went back into her physical body lying on the bed. After that she was no longer afraid of death and faced each new raid with a calmness she had never before known.

The Double Absorbs Cosmic Energy

The Sagée case is, at first glance, a puzzling one. Although we can understand that Mlle. Sagée may have had a constitutionally loose connection between the bodies, she not only had no motive for her projections but was also personally distressed and economically deprived because of them. It seemed, however, that Mlle. Sagée projected when her physical body was debilitated and it is possible, although we have no evidence, that she was physically weak and prone to illness.

When the body is below par, it is thought that the double moves out to pick up energy it then transmits to the parent body over the connecting cord. Sylvan Muldoon believed that the purpose of sleep was to restore vigor to the physical body through a disconnection of the astral self. During sleep, according to this theory, the two bodies are slightly out of coincidence. The double is then able to absorb a kind of cosmic energy which it transfers to the sleeping self. The same thing would happen, of course, during illness and other times when the body is below par.

Cornillier writes in *The Survival of the Soul:* "What causes sleep is a disunion between the astral (fluidic) body and the phsycial body. The purpose of this disunion is to liberate sufficiently the astral body, so that it may go to gather from the ambience the vital force contained in the magnetic and cosmic currents, whose emission or passage is intensified and facilitated by the night. In this way the stock of force that is spent in daily activity is constantly renewed."

The next six chapters will follow this plan: because of the importance of person-to-person relationships in OOBEs, the first three will go more fully into the kind of links between people that motivate out-of-body experiences—links between members of a family, friends, lovers, and those who need each other's help for mental and physical healing. The three chapters that follow will explore certain body-mind conditions that set the stage for OOBEs: illness at home or in the hospital, accidents in war and peace, and the stress of danger.

The "Why" of
Astral Projection

Chapter 11

Astral Reunion of Families

Where do astral projectors go most often when they leave their bodies? They go where their affections take them—to members of their families, their friends, their sweethearts. A special kind of OOB relationship exists between those in love, sometimes even before they meet physically, that will be explored in the next chapter. This section will be devoted to astral visits of relatives—mothers to sons, fathers to daughters, husbands to wives, and so on.

The Cradle of ESP

No psychic relationship is stronger than that between mother and child. Psychiatrist Jan Ehrenwald theorizes that the ability of a mother to sense the needs of her infant may be telepathic. He has called infancy, before speech develops, the "cradle of ESP"—extrasensory perception—and believes that there is a constant telepathic exchange between mother and child that has a "survival value." As the child gets older and learns how to communicate through speech and to fend for himself, the psychic link with his mother weakens, but it never dies throughout his lifetime.

When the mother is physically incapacitated, she sometimes responds to the ESP message by traveling to the child in her second body. Susy Smith in *Out-of-Body Experiences for the Millions* tells of a mother who was ill in bed and too weak to go to her six-week-old infant in the next room. She concentrated very hard for almost a minute, then felt herself being lifted from her body and wafted through the air to the baby's room.

Here she noticed that the infant had "turned himself completely over and was lying up against the bars of his crib." She didn't think so small a child could do this, and when she returned to her body, she managed to get out of bed physically and walk to his room. Sure enough, the baby was on his side up against the bars of the crib. The woman called her husband and told him what had happened. He thought she had been dreaming, but she showed him two marks on the baby's cheeks and forehead from the pressure of the bars.

Sylvan Muldoon describes another projection of a mother to her child in *The Case For Astral Projection*. A German mother took a trip with her husband, leaving her infant in her sister-in-law's care. Concerned about the baby, she left her body and floated back home, entering the house and going into the infant's room. She stood for a moment at the side of the cradle, then bent down and blessed the baby, reciting a verse from the Bible. Her sister-in-law saw her and screamed. The loud sound caused her double to snap back into her physical body, and she was with her husband again.

Later, when the couple returned from their trip, the woman's sister-in-law admitted that she had seen the double and screamed. She said the double stood beside the cradle, blessed the baby, and recited the Bible verse. Thus the projector was conscious of being in a second body and traveling to her home, she brought back clairvoyant evidence, and she was seen and heard by a witness, her sister-in-law.

We do not know if infants project to their mothers, although it is reasonable to assume that they do if it works the other way. There are many known cases, however, of very young children having OOBEs from about the age of four (see Chapter 20). Perhaps the most dramatic instance of a psychic bond between mother and child that resulted in the child's OOBE was told by the Reverend Max Hoffmann. When Hoffmann was five years old, living with his parents in Germany, he contracted cholera, apparently died, and was buried. He projected his double from the grave to his mother's bedside and implored her to dig up his body. She saw him in a dream telling her that his right hand was positioned under the right cheek of his physical body in the grave.

Max's mother begged his father to exhume the body, but he refused to consider it. Three nights in succession she dreamed that Max came to her, insisted that he was still alive, and described the position of his body in the coffin. Finally the grave was opened, and after a doctor had given him first aid, Max opened his eyes and smiled at his parents. He had been lying in the grave just as his double had said, and there were marks on his right cheek from the fingers of his right hand.

Max Hoffmann later became a well-known medium. The question arises of how the child managed to stay alive during the three days he was buried. He might have been in the cataleptic state so common in OOBEs and in suspended animation. Although these details are not mentioned, he was probably buried in this condition after there appeared to be no signs of life. Instances will be given later of doctors who pronounced their patients dead only to have them wake up and describe what happened after their physical bodies apparently stopped functioning.

Lonely Mothers, Homesick Sons

The psychic bond between mother and son or daughter continues to operate throughout childhood and young adulthood. An English mother was worried about her son at school and had a strong urge to see him. Knowing about astral projection, she made a determined effort to get out of her body. After several partial projections, she suddenly felt herself shoot straight out through her head. She described herself as "moving without walking," and eventually was standing outside a large oak door. She walked straight through it.

Later she came to a wide road and noticed "a path of dirty-looking water and back of that even dirtier docks." She was unable to find her son but she knew she was in the vicinity of his college. When he came home, she accurately described the college town, although she had never been there before. Here the I-Consciousness functioned in the second body and the double brought back clairvoyant information, yet she was unsuccessful in reaching her son.

It is possible that something caused her to return abruptly to her body. Or perhaps a psychological block prevented her from completing her astral trip. These are just conjectures, but they point up the importance of knowing as much as possible about the projector and what motivates her.

This story appeared in Crookall's *More Astral Projections,* which also cited the case of an English mother whose loneliness for her daughter caused her to project to a ship sailing the Atlantic. In a letter to Crookall she wrote that her newly married daughter had just left on the *Queen Mary* with her husband to take up permanent residence in the United States. The first day they were at sea, the mother sat in her kitchen thinking about the girl. Suddenly she left her body and flew over the ocean until she came to the ship. She went into a cabin and saw the young lady lying on her bunk and looking quite ill.

She took her daughter's hand and asked what was wrong. The girl said she had been seasick and had been wishing her mother was there. The mother told her to wash her face, get dressed, and go on deck and she would recover. Then she left the cabin and flew back to her kitchen. During this time her physical body had been sitting in an armchair. The hands of the clock, which had pointed to 3 P.M. when she left, were now at 3:05.

A short time later she received a letter from her daughter verifying what had happened. The girl had been seasick, had retired to her bunk, and had seen her mother come in and sit on the bunk and say the very words recalled by the mother. The girl had followed her mother's advice and gone out on deck, where she felt refreshed, and she enjoyed the rest of the trip without illness. The time had been 3 P.M. Crookall doublechecked the story by writing to the daughter, who replied: "Everything happened just as mother described it."

Young men and older men away from home have been impelled by loneliness to project back over long distances. In *Casebook of Astral Projection* Robert Crookall tells of a man who lived in Los Angeles, 1,350 miles from his mother's home in Omaha, Nebraska. Relaxing after lunch one day, he began to drift off and suddenly was in his mother's living room. He saw her sitting on the sofa and went over and lay his head in her lap. Two days later he received an airmail letter from his mother stating that she had seen him come into her room at the time he was napping. She also verified the clairvoyant details—the position of the furniture, the dress she was wearing, and so on.

Soldiers and sailors in service on land and sea often solve the problem of homesickness by projecting their second bodies. An English soldier stationed in Germany found himself out of his body "hurtling through space." He caught glimpses of land and water and then was standing in his living room at home. His mother was knitting, her Alsatian dog sleeping beside her. She didn't see him, but the dog woke up and ran over, barking excitedly. A few days later his mother wrote that she had indeed been sitting and knitting and that the dog had awakened and was "barking, running and jumping at the back of the settee."

Fathers Out-of-the-Body

There is much psychic interplay between fathers and their sons and daughters. In *Mysterious Worlds* Dennis Bardens reports the experiences of writer John Eyre, who had many astral projections while practicing yoga, a discipline that breaks down mental barriers and often triggers psychic communication with others. Said Eyre: "The emotional state of universality led me to send out from me a mood, an emotion of love and affection to people I knew, people I knew were sick, and particularly to my two children, from whom I was separated at the time."

Eyre's seventeen-year-old son began to see his father's second body just before he went to sleep. The boy saw him without the glasses he always wore, but since Mr. Eyre was lying in bed with his glasses off the son received his exact facial image. Parenthetically, I must tell about a young lady I knew who once saw my double walking down a New York street but without the glasses I wear most of the time. I checked back and remembered that I had been taking a nap when she saw me and, like Mr. Eyre, would not have been wearing glasses. Yet, if I had been conscious of being in my second body, I might have created a pair of astral glasses so that friends would recognize me.

A woman in South Africa wrote to Robert Crookall in 1961 that she had seen her father's double when she was a schoolgirl. The family was entertaining friends on the patio and the girl's mother had asked her to prepare tea. As she went into the house, her father was leaning back in a deck chair and talking. Walking by the bath-room in the house, she was amazed to see her father's double wash-ing his hands in the sink. At the same time she could hear his voice coming from the patio. Then the double vanished.

It is interesting to speculate why the girl's father projected at this particular time. In other cases of family OOBEs, the motiva-tions are fairly clear—the loneliness of a mother for her son or daughter (and vice versa), a son's homesickness, anxiety about an infant, affection between members of a family who are separated in space. But what caused a man to project while he was presum-ably enjoying a conversation with friends? Was he thinking at the time that he would like to break away and wash his hands, espe-cially since tea was to be served? Did he want his daughter to know he was washing his hands? Was the action symbolic?

Brother-to-Brother Projection

An OOBE motivated by the death of his brother in 1908 is de-scribed by writer Frank Hives in *Glimpses into Infinity*. Hives was in Nigeria at the time, while his brother was living in New Zealand. One night Hives returned home after an exhausting day, lay down for a nap, and flew off in his double until he reached an English meadow adjoining a churchyard. Although the ground was cov-ered with snow, he was still in tropical dress—bush shirt, khaki shorts, and puttees.

Hives glided into the churchyard and saw relatives and friends, all dressed in black and looking very sad. Four persons were carry-ing a coffin which was placed in an open grave. Hives bent down and saw the name of his brother on a metal plate on top of the coffin. He was puzzled. What would his brother be doing in Eng-land? Then Hives was drawn back to his physical body in Nigeria.

The next evening Hives wrote a letter to his sister, who lived in England, describing what he had seen in his second body, and asked for confirmation. She wrote back that their brother, visiting in England, had caught a chill that turned into pneumonia, result-ing in his death. He was buried in the churchyard on the same day that Hives appeared at the funeral. His sister also gave the names of those attending the funeral, all of whom had been seen by Hives's double.

Husband-to-Wife, Wife-to-Husband

It is quite natural, of course, for husbands and wives to project astrally to each other and sometimes to go off together in their doubles. In 1913 a captain on a gunboat off the east coast of the United States was very lonely for his wife in Kansas. One night at 2 A.M. he lay thinking about her and decided to visit her astrally if he could. Traveling at great speed over the eastern states, he soon found himself lying in bed beside her. At the same moment she felt his arm around her shoulder. They compared notes later and discovered that they were aware of each other at the same time.

Wives also miss their absent husbands. One wife went looking astrally for her husband who was away on business, although she had no idea where he had gone. She thought of various towns but could not locate him and finally decided to concentrate on him instead of on where he might be. She saw him walking down an alley and into a strange house, where he entered a room, undressed, and got into bed. Actually, her husband had just returned to his hotel by way of an alley, and had gone to bed. He said later that he had seen the figure of his wife standing by the bed.

Probably the most famous instance of a wife "visiting" her husband was the Wilmot case, carefully investigated by the British Society for Psychical Research. Mr. Wilmot, who lived in Bridgeport, Connecticut, was returning on a ship from England in the year 1862. Mrs. Wilmot was at home in Bridgeport. There was a storm at sea, which finally began to die down after several days. One morning Wilmot dreamed that his wife entered the stateroom, clad only in her nightdress. As she approached him, she hesitated for a moment. Then she leaned over and kissed him and quietly left the stateroom.

Wilmot woke up to the sound of laughter and looked at his cabinmate in the upper bunk. The other man was grinning: "You're a pretty fellow to have a lady come and visit you this way." It may have been a dream to Wilmot, but his cabinmate had been awake all the time and watched Mrs. Wilmot's movements.

When Wilmot arrived home from his trip, his wife asked him, "Did you receive a visit from me a week ago Tuesday?"

"A visit from you? We were more than a thousand miles at sea."

"I know it. But it seems to me that I visited you."

She then said that she had been worried because of the storm and had lain awake a long time thinking about her husband. At 4 A.M. she left her body, crossed the sea, and came to "a low, black steamship." She went up the side, then walked along the deck and into the stateroom. Here she embraced and kissed her husband.

An interesting bit of evidence is that Mrs. Wilmot noticed that the upper bunk, unlike those in most staterooms, was set back some distance from the lower. She saw the man in the upper bunk looking directly at her. She said that she then hesitated, as both men had observed, before she kissed Mr. Wilmot.

The case is impressive from many points of view. The I-Consciousness was present, the double brought back many unusual and verifiable facts about the ship and cabin, which she had never seen, and there were two witnesses. In addition, Mr. Wilmot felt her embrace and kiss. The motivation is clear—Mrs. Wilmot's anxiety for her husband because of the storm.

In many family OOBEs one member needs the other because of illness or danger, and these will be explored along with friend-to-friend and stranger-to-stranger OOBEs in which the projector goes out to seek help for himself or to help others. Meanwhile, let's enjoy astral romances, when love or the promise of love gives wings to the second body.

Chapter 12

Romance in the Second Body

"Healthily tired in body, blissfully expectant in mind, I would lie on my back, with my hands duly crossed under my head, and sleep would soon steal over me like balm; and before I had forgotten who or what or where I really was, I would reach the goal on which my will was intent, and waking up, find my body in another place, in another garb, on a couch by an enchanted window . . .

"Then would I stretch my limbs and slip myself free of my outer life, as a new-born butterfly from the durance of its self-spun cocoon, with an unutterable sense of youth and strength and freshness and felicity; and opening my eyes I would see on the adjacent couch the form of Mary, also supine, but motionless and inanimate as a statue . . .

"Everything [from the past] was as lifelike, as real to us both, as it had been to either at the actual time of its occurrence, with an added freshness and charm that never belong to mortal existence . . . a couple of hours in the Yosemite Valley, leisurely strolling about and gazing at the giant pines—a never-palling source of delight to both of us—breathing the fragrant fresh air, looking at our fellow tourists and listening to their talk, with the agreeable consciousness that, solid and substantial as we were to each other, we were quite inaudible, invisible, and intangible to them . . ."

The above passages are from George du Maurier's *Peter Ibbet-son*, the story of a man imprisoned for life who spends each night in his second body with the double of the woman he loves, and what they cannot have in reality becomes possible in another, per-haps a greater, reality. So strong an appeal did the theme of *Peter Ibbetson* have for its readers that it was later adapted into an opera, for which Deems Taylor wrote the music.

Romantic? Yes indeed, and probably vicariously satisfying to thousands of men and women permanently separated from their sweethearts or forced to live their lives with just imaginary sweet-hearts. Although *Peter Ibbetson* is romantic fiction, however, more and more cases of real life astral romance have been coming to light in recent years. Many a young (and older) man has met a young (and older) woman in an out-of-body experience even before meeting and loving her in the flesh. *Peter Ibbetson* contains more than one truth about the second body: the possibility of dual pro-jection, of visiting scenes from the past (retrocognition), of de-veloping a practical technique for "dreaming true"—that is, fashion-ing a dream that becomes the setting of an actual experience in the duplicate body.

"Haven't We Met Before—Out of My Body?"

Lonely men often go out in their doubles on scouting trips in search of pleasant young women they can later track down in their physical bodies. It happened once to Sylvan Muldoon on a beauti-ful moonlit night in 1924, the kind of evening conducive to romantic thoughts. Muldoon had gone for a walk but came back feeling very restless and threw himself, clothes and all, on his bed.

His body became rigid, and as an experienced projector, he knew what was coming. He moved up in the horizontal position, then floated for about ten feet. Finally standing upright, his astral body walked outside and was immediately transported at great speed to the inside of a house. Four persons were in the living room, one of them an attractive seventeen-year-old girl, but none of the four was familiar to Muldoon. Without willing it, he moved in front of the girl, who was sewing a black dress.

Six weeks later Sylvan was walking down the street in his physical body when he saw a car stop and a young lady get out of it and go into a house. It was the girl he had seen astrally, but this was not the house his double had visited. He waited for her to come out, wondering what he would say. Girls sometimes are amused by an original approach, but "Pardon me, haven't we met before—when I was out of my body?" would not have gone over so well. Muldoon, somewhat embarrassed, blurted out, "Excuse me, but where do you live?"

The girl snapped, quite properly, "None of your business!" and started to get into the car. But Muldoon continued talking to her and explained what had happened. The girl still thought he was somewhat "kooky" but she caught his sincerity, and when he described her home and the members of her family, she was so impressed that she invited him to visit her.

In the *Projection of the Astral Body* Muldoon writes, rather gleefully, "One thing led to another! I began to like her. I have seen her many times since." He discovered that her home, a farmhouse, was fifteen miles from his own and that all the details he had seen astrally were correct. Muldoon and the young lady became good friends and conducted many experiments together in astral projection.

Oliver Fox, who wrote about his OOBEs in *Astral Projection*, also went searching for romance in his second body, but he was not as lucky. He did meet a very desirable young woman in the astral realm, but he couldn't locate her later. Fox was in somewhat the same restless mood as Muldoon, but his projection was deliberate, although he was not sure of his destination. After walking in his double, he was "suddenly caught in an astral current" and carried away at lightning speed.

He came to a beautiful outdoor setting and saw children playing and drinking tea beneath the trees. Walking further, he reached a red-brick house, its front door open. He went inside and walked up the stairway on a plush carpet. Through an open door on the second floor he saw a young lady, "dressed in claret-colored velvet . . . tidying her hair before a mirror." Fox writes wistfully of the girl's "rich auburn tresses . . . gleaming redly in the glamorous light."

He took careful note, as Muldoon did, of many objects in the room—the crumpled cover of the bed, a water basin on the washstand, and other details. Several of his normal senses seemed to be operating. He smelled the "pleasant fragrance" of the girl's hair, even felt the "softness of her velvet dress." When he laid his hand on her shoulder, she jumped. Startled, Fox was jerked back into his physical body.

Unlike Muldoon and other astral travelers in search of romance, Oliver Fox never met the very appealing young woman with the rich auburn tresses. We must ask, of course, whether in her subliminal mind the young lady wanted to meet him. Although she could not see his astral body, she evidently did sense his presence and felt his touch, and she may not have approved of him. A projector looking for romance may pick the wrong time, even the wrong person.

Doubles That Vibrate in Harmony

What about men and women, boys and girls, who are sweethearts in the present or who at least have an affectionate relationship? Do they have astral as well as physical dates? Muldoon and Fox wrote about their out-of-body meetings with their steady girl friends. Yram, the Frenchman who was the third of a triumvirate of famous projectors that included Muldoon and Fox, had probably the most enduring of second-body romances with the young lady who later became his wife.

After first meeting her physically, Yram was forced through circumstances to be separated from her by hundreds of miles. He decided he would use his astral talents to keep the romance alive. Without even knowing what town his sweetheart lived in, he managed to fly to her every night. Fortunately, she was psychic herself and although she couldn't see him, she always knew when he was there. According to Yram in *Practical Astral Projection,* "she had the sensation of finding herself near a focus of energy from which she constantly received waves of great intensity." If she was busy when he paid astral court, she would ask him mentally to leave and return later.

It was during one of his second-body visits that he asked her to marry him and she accepted—all through mental exchanges. This is the only marriage proposal that I know of made by a duplicate body. So closely attuned were Yram and his sweetheart that after marriage they began to project together, the first time when he suggested that she "take a trip" with him. Shedding their physical bodies easily, they flew off together, astral hands clasped. Shades of Peter Ibbetson!

Yram writes: "Her love penetrated into my being under the guise of a general warmth, while a feeling of absolute confidence filled my spirit. On the other hand, my aura penetrated hers and I had the sensation as if of melting into her . . . In no other experience have I had so wide awake a consciousness, no love so powerful, nor a calm and serenity so profound . . . If you want to be united truly, eternally, with those you love, you must vibrate in harmony with them on all the planes, and in every kind of activity. The more intimate the communion of thoughts and desires, the less will be the separation."

There are many examples of OOB experiments between pairs who, if not passionate lovers, at least "vibrate in harmony" and are unusually successful in projecting to each other. In *The Projection of the Astral Body*, Muldoon gives this suggestion: "Arrange with someone of whom you are fond, and who in turn is affectionately disposed toward you. Both should awaken at a given hour in the night, and, lying awake, conscious but drowsy, allow your conscious passive Wills to operate upon the desire."

Muldoon proposed an experiment to a girl friend who, though skeptical at first, agreed to try it. They were to wake up at two o'clock in the morning and visualize Muldoon leaving his body and traveling astrally to her bedroom. Muldoon did successfully project his double to her many times, but she was never aware of his presence.

Then, without telling her in advance what he was going to do, he tried something else when he was in her room. He went to her dresser, put his hand on her hairbrush, then walked over to her bed, doing this several times during the projection. She appeared to be asleep.

The next day he asked her if she had seen him in her room. She replied that she had not, but she had dreamed that he was trying to brush her hair and that he kept running back and forth looking for the comb, while she kept telling him that it was on the dresser. On a later occasion, just to confuse the astral issue, it was Muldoon who dreamed he was in the girl's room but had no conscious knowledge of being there. The next day she told him that at long last she had seen him in her room.

Oliver Fox also had a skeptical girl friend named Elsie, who objected strenuously to his OOB experiments. She felt that he was being sacrilegious and that God would punish him for his nocturnal excursions. Being somewhat of a male chauvinist, he told her airily that she really knew nothing about the subject and should not give an opinion on it. Elsie was no shrinking vine, however, even for the year 1905, and she challenged him. Far from not knowing what astral projection was, she announced that *she* would show *him* how it was done.

Oliver laughed.

"Very well," she said, "I'll prove it. It's wicked, but I don't care. I'll come to your room tonight and you shall see me there."

"All right," he replied, not in the least impressed "Come if you can."

Sometime that night Oliver woke up with a sensation of "tingling nerves." Before him was a large, egg-shaped cloud of intensely brilliant bluish-white light. In the middle of it was Elsie, hair loose, wearing her nightdress. She stood by a chest of drawers on the right side of Oliver's bed and seemed quite solid to him. Elsie—or her double—looked calmly at Oliver. He stared at her for awhile and finally rose on one elbow and called her name. She vanished.

The following evening he met a very excited and triumphant Elsie, who said, "I did come to you. I *really* did. I went to sleep, willing that I would, and all at once I was *there*." Then she described the room which, since she was a well-behaved post-Victorian young lady, she had never seen before: the relative positions of the door, window, fireplace, washstand, chest of drawers, and dressing table. She noted also that the window had a number of small panes instead of the customary large ones. She described Oliver's bed and his position in it when she saw him. Other items she observed were a black Japanese box covered with raised red figures, an old-fashioned pincushion, and a leather-covered desk lined with gilt.

Elsie said that she ran her fingers along a projecting ridge on the top of the chest of drawers. Oliver acknowledged all details but this one—there was no projecting ridge. Elsie insisted that there was and that she had felt it. When Oliver went home he discovered that she was right. The ridge was on the front side of the dresser, and he had not noticed it before.

All the ingredients of a valid OOBE are here: the I-Consciousness of the projector, the accurate description of Oliver's room and the objects in it, Oliver as a witness, Elsie's appearance in an egg-shaped mist before her double came into focus, her contact with the chest of drawers. An interesting sequel to this story is that later Oliver projected to Elsie's room and she woke up to see him looking quite real, fully dressed but without a hat, standing by her bed. Hearing her mother come up the stairs to wake her up, she was paralyzed with fright. But just as the doorknob turned, Oliver faded away, saving her the embarrassment of being discovered with a lover in her room, insubstantial though he was.

Astral Romances, Mid-Victorian Style

Twenty years earlier another man, convinced that it was useless to argue with young ladies about the pros and cons of astral travel, decided one night to project to his girl friend without first telling her. The number of men and women in the Victorian era who seemed determined to invade each other's bedroom in the middle of the night astrally if not physically makes us realize that there was much more enterprise in love affairs those days than the history books have told us. It is curious to note, in fact, that Elsie had no qualms about appearing in Oliver's room in her nightdress, while he was more circumspect when he paid her a return visit.

This time it was a man of the cloth, the Reverend Clarence Godfrey, who planned the daring project. At 3:30 A.M. on November 16, 1886, his young friend woke up with a strange feeling, her throat dry. She lighted her candle and went downstairs to fetch a glass of water from the icebox. She wrote later: "I returned to my room, where I saw Mr. Godfrey standing before the window. He wore his usual dress. I raised the candle, looked at him for three or four seconds, and he disappeared."

Those were the early days of the British Society for Psychical Research, and if a minister did that sort of thing, it was at least for a scientific purpose. Frank Podmore, an SPR investigator and one of its chief skeptics, asked Godfrey to set another day for an attempted projection. This time Godfrey's girl friend heard and felt as well as saw him. He entered her bedroom and shouted, "Wake!" She woke up feeling his astral hand on her forehead.

The SPR reports a case from the same period in which another gentleman decided to pay a surprise "visit" to a young woman,

Miss Verity. In November 1881 the projector, S. Beard, proudly wrote: "Having been reading of the great power which the human Will is capable of exercising, I determined with the whole force of my being that I would be present in spirit in the front bedroom of the second floor of a house . . . in which slept two young ladies . . . aged respectively twenty-five and eleven years."

Beard tried to project at 1 A.M. on Sunday. The following Thursday he went to see the two girls, saying nothing about his experiment. The elder Miss Verity then told him that on the previous Sunday she had been "much terrified" when she woke up and saw him standing at her bedside, and she had screamed. Her young sister then woke up and saw Beard's double. Both girls placed the time at 1 A.M.

Edmund Gurney, another SPR investigator, asked Beard to let him know the next time he tried to project. Beard waited three years while the girls got over the shock of his first visit, then told Gurney that he was going to do it again on March 22, 1884. On April 3 Gurney received a letter from Miss Verity: "On Saturday night, March 22, 1884, at about midnight, I had a distinct impression that Mr. Beard was present in my room, and I distinctly saw him, being quite awake. He came toward me and stroked my hair . . . The appearance in my room was most vivid and quite unmistakable."

Beard also informed Gurney that Miss Verity's nerves had been "much shaken, and she had been obliged to send for a doctor in the morning." If one is tempted to scold Beard for giving the young lady such a fright on two occasions, there is also the suspicion that she enjoyed the experiment, since their friendship persisted in spite of her nerves being "much shaken."

Podmore, Gurney, and F. W. H. Myers investigated many such cases of OOBEs involving men and women who were either very good friends or sweethearts and reported them in the two-volume *Phantasms of the Living*. In one case, an accident to the man motivated his appearance to his sweetheart. She wrote later that she had been sitting and reading when "Suddenly I *felt*, but did not *see*, someone come into my room . . . To my astonishment, I felt a *kiss* on my forehead—a lingering, loving pressure. I looked up, without the least sensation of fear, and saw my lover standing behind my chair, stooping as if to kiss me again. His face was very white and inexpressibly sad."

Later she received a note from her sweetheart saying that on the night of her experience, he was almost crushed to death by a horse. Believing he would die, he said to himself, "May, my little May! Don't let me die without seeing her again," and then lost consciousness.

In a similar case reported in *Phantasms*, it was the girl who appeared to the man at the scene of his accident. Just after he was kicked by a horse, he saw the girl's double looking pale and anxious. The next day she told him: "Why, I expected you all yesterday afternoon. I thought I saw you looking so pale, and your face all bleeding." She said later that she saw him "immediately after lunch, when he did in fact have his accident."

A Secretary Projects to Her Boss

To bring our astral romances up to date, I have the story of Sheila Saperton, a psychic of Huntington, Long Island. Sheila's was a one-sided romance, however, motivated by her desire to project to the home of the attractive man who had just hired her as his secretary. Sheila had never seen his apartment but one night while asleep she found herself there, sitting on one end of a coffee table, a blond girl sitting on the other end. She was surprised at the appearance of the wallpaper—it was in strips that were slanting rather than straight, with a design of small animal figures.

She later learned from her employer that he was living with a blonde, a fact unknown to her the night she projected. He also admitted that his wallpaper was just as Sheila had seen it, in slanted strips with animal figures. As of this writing no romance has developed, but Sheila's motivation was certainly clear—to find out more about her boss, what kind of apartment he lived in, and who his girl friends might be. She found out.

There are many interesting aspects to the out-of-body romances discussed in this chapter, from the daring Victorian experiments to the contemporary visit of a young secretary to her boss's apartment. The investigations of the British Society for Psychical Research gave much impetus to the attempted projections of nineteenth- and twentieth-century men to their girl friends. In many of these cases both parties involved gave depositions to the SPR. The careful records of their own OOBEs kept by Oliver Fox and Sylvan Muldoon are also impressive and make the accounts of their astral romances believable.

The I-Consciousness, the surprising number of clairvoyant details noted and later verified, the testimony of witnesses are present in many of these cases. Several of the girls reported not only seeing but also hearing the projector, while some were kissed and felt their hair being stroked. The common factor in nearly all the experiences described was the affection and friendship between the man and woman involved, whether the projection was experimental or it just happened. Those who saw their future sweethearts astrally before they met them physically forged an emotional bond before the life experience itself began.

When George du Maurier wrote *Peter Ibbetson,* he not only stirred romantic fancies in the minds of many actual or would-be lovers, but also described an event that contains as much truth as poetry.

Chapter 13

Doubles That Help and Heal

One of the most compelling motives for going out of the body is to help others or to seek help from them. Projectors visit others to heal them in body and mind, to help them face danger, sometimes to offer spiritual comfort or give advice. Conversely, they may be asking for help themselves. Because we have emotional ties to relatives and friends, it is usually to them that we direct our thoughts and send our doubles in healing and helping situations. Often, however, a projector is called to give mental, physical, or spiritual assistance to a stranger in need.

Family Calls for Help

Sylvan Muldoon writes that when he was a boy, he became ill as he lay in bed late one night. He tried to call out to his mother who was sleeping on the floor above with his little brother, but she didn't hear him. He crawled out of bed toward the stairs, but fainted from weakness. At this point his double emerged and glided easily up the stairs. When he reached his mother's bedroom he could not wake her up. In some way, however, he caused her mattress to rise up, throwing her and his brother out of bed. His mission accomplished, he flashed back into his physical body, and the next moment his mother came running down the stairs to tell him how the spirits had upset her bed.

When danger threatens, husbands and wives hurry to each other in their doubles and ask for assistance. Cromwell Varley, a psychic investigator who also helped to build the transatlantic cable, had many paranormal experiences but perhaps the most dramatic occurred when he nearly died. In 1869 he described this incident in a lecture to the London Dialectical Society.

Chronically ill with throat spasms, Varley kept a bottle of chloroform at his bedside which he saturated with a sponge and inhaled for relief. One night he was so uncomfortable that he put the sponge in his mouth, then rolled over on his back and passed out. Coming out of his body, he saw himself lying unconscious, the sponge still in his mouth. His wife was upstairs nursing a sick child. Unable to talk with her, by an extreme effort of the will he impressed his danger on her mind. She came running down the stairs and removed the sponge.

In *Casebook of Astral Projection* Crookall tells how the husband was the rescuer when his wife fainted in the bathtub, her body face down in the water. While he was in the living room reading, she left her body, came out, and tapped him on the shoulder. Although he was not consciously aware of her presence, he felt compelled to run to the bathroom, where he pulled his wife out of the water and gave her artificial respiration. She said later that she hovered over, watching every move he made.

I heard of a similar case in 1973 when I was on the Bob Grant morning radio show on WMCA in New York City. A young woman called in and told me that one day while she was in the living room of her home talking to a friend, an invisible presence began tugging at her arm. She felt at once that her two-year-old boy was in danger and rushed to the bathroom, where he was lying face down in the water. She was able to rescue him in time. It is difficult to say who or what was pulling at her sleeve, but there are many such instances, one of them the Max Hoffmann case, in which telepathy and/or a second body have enabled a mother to save her child from danger or death.

In many family cases it is the helper who goes out of his body rather than the one who seeks help. Crookall describes the experience of a Mrs. Combs, who found herself floating out of her bedroom window when she heard someone moaning early one morning. The next moment she saw her husband lying unconscious on an unfamiliar street. As her double bent over him, an ambulance arrived and took him to the hospital. In a flash she was in the hospital corridor, where the image of her husband emerged out of a "greyish-white fog," his face twisted with pain and his left arm in a cast.

Mrs. Combs woke up with the conviction that something had happened to her husband. Almost immediately the phone rang and she learned that he had had an accident and was in the hospital with a fractured arm. When she saw the hospital ward, she recognized it as the one in her out-of-body vision. Her husband had fallen out of a window in his hotel at the time she heard him moaning in her dream.

A young photographer who lives in New Jersey told me about the time he gave his brother a psychic healing via the double. While he was in New York City one weekend, his parents called him and asked him to drive to a town near Atlantic City, where his brother was ill and in great pain. Instead of driving out, the photographer stayed physically in New York and went to Atlantic City in his second body. Standing at the foot of his brother's bed, he stretched out his astral arms. His brother's pain went away and he fell asleep.

Friends on a Rescue Mission

Friends often project to friends when they wish to give help or to receive it. When Paul Lachlan Peck was recuperating after his automobile accident (see Chapter 1), he woke up at 3 A.M. one night, feeling depressed and apprehensive. When he took his own pulse, there was no beat. He got out of bed and tried to turn on the light, but his hand passed right through it. Now quite alarmed, he went to the door to call for help, but only a gutteral sound came out of his throat.

Peck wanted to call his friend Jim and ask him to come over but he couldn't remember Jim's number. He flashed to Jim's apartment, read the number on the dial of the telephone, then returned to his physical body and made the call. He noticed on his astral trip that

Jim had been sitting up and studying, wearing tattered jeans and a T-shirt. When Jim arrived a half hour later, he was in different clothes but admitted that he had been awake studying and wearing the clothes that Peck saw.

Joy Snell, an English psychic who was also a nurse, tells in *The Ministry of Angels* of many OOBEs in which she helped her friends. She writes that she woke up suddenly one night when her room filled with light. At her bedside was the double of her closest friend, Maggie. Her friend spoke to her: "Joy, I have a secret to tell you. I know I am going over to the other world before long and I want you to be with me at the last and help to comfort my mother when I am gone."

A week later Joy was called to her friend's home. Maggie had a bad cold but it didn't seem serious. Joy said nothing about Maggie's visit, sensing that the other girl was not aware she had gone out of her body. Three days later Maggie became critically ill and died in Joy's arms before a doctor could come.

Maggie's visit would suggest that she had subconscious knowledge of her impending death and was able to convey this knowledge to her friend without ever being aware of it. In other "crisis apparitions" occurring when death is imminent, the second body is seen by friends and relatives as a way to announce the death of the physical body. Rarely, however, does the double speak in these situations.

Another story of a double seeking help from a friend involved several members of a family—a mother, a father, and their little girl —in addition to the friend. The mother knew she was dying and that it was important for her to convey this information to her friend hundreds of miles away.

The story first appeared in Adolphe d'Assier's *Posthumous Humanity*, a book that tells many interesting and delightful true tales of projectors living and dead in nineteenth-century France. The man, wife, and daughter were an Alsatian family sailing across the Atlantic to Rio de Janeiro, Brazil. The wife became ill and grew steadily worse. Realizing that she would die, the woman worried about her little girl. What would become of her? Where could her father find a home for her?

Shortly before her death the woman went into a trance, and her double journeyed to Rio de Janeiro, to the house of her friend Fritz. Fritz was standing in the doorway. The dying woman silently pointed to a form she had created of her little girl and was holding in her arms. Then she went back to the ship and came out of her trance smiling.

"I die happy now," she said to her husband. "I have seen Fritz. I am sure that on your arrival he will recognize her [the girl] and take care of her."

When Herr Schmidt, the Alsatian, arrived in Rio de Janeiro, he was carrying the little girl in his arms. Fritz cried, "My poor friend, I know all! Your wife died on the voyage, and before dying she came to show me her little girl, so that I might take care of her. See, I have marked the date and hour." It was the exact time that the woman had been unconscious, just before she woke up prior to dying.

When Frau Schmidt appeared to him, Fritz explained, she looked at him imploringly and held the child out to him. He thought she was extremely pale and emaciated and sensed that she was dying. Her message was clear to him.

Astral Aid for a Stranger

Many persons go on astral missions of mercy to help strangers. Paul Neary, a psychic who divides his time between New York City and Atlanta, Georgia, has often gone out at night to alleviate someone's pain. Once he was "called" by a man Neary had never met who was suffering from cancer. The man met him later and said that Neary had come to him in the middle of the night and cured him of his ailment. Padre Pio's astral journeys were for the benefit of all mankind.

There is an altruistic British doctor who makes house calls via his second body, if we are to believe Crookall's account in *Casebook of Astral Projection*. A Major Pole, ill on his houseboat on the Nile River in Egypt, in some way sent a psychic appeal that was picked up by a Scottish doctor. The doctor suddenly materialized on the boat and laid his hat on the table. As he wrote out a prescription, he explained that he often got psychic calls for help and would project his double if a great distance was involved, first locking his office door so that no one would disturb his physical body.

When Major Pole returned to England, he asked on a BBC broadcast if his medical benefactor would reveal his identity. The doctor called him and said that he was the physician who made astral house calls.

Many persons claim that they leave their bodies at night to give spiritual comfort to strangers in distress. There are several such cases in Crookall's *During Sleep*. In one a Mrs. Clara Clayton projected to a mother and baby when the agitated mother kept calling for her deceased husband. Mrs. Clayton's double helped the woman leave her physical body and become reunited temporarily with her husband.

In *More Astral Projections* Crookall tells of a Mr. Hickson, who journeyed in his sleep to comfort strangers and help them make decisions. Once he visited a woman who was about to commit a rash act. The man's double spoke soothingly to her—either in actual voice or through mental impressions—and advised her against it. When she met Hickson later on a boat to Australia, the first time she had seen him physically, she cried out, "My mentor!"

Each night when Ed Corsino comes home from his job as a stockbroker in New York City, he puts out of mind the problems of a workaday world and tunes into the spiritual realm. His motivation is to help those who are ill through psychic healing.

First he lies down or sits in a chair and puts himself into a light trance. Then he thinks of someone he knows who is suffering from cancer or another ailment and asks for help from the invisible world. He feels that in some way help does reach the body and soul of the person he is trying to heal, who is often miles away. He doesn't quite believe that he goes out of his body, but there is some evidence that this is what happens.

Once, when he and his wife were seated with his in-laws in church, his mother-in-law complained of an arthritic pain in her fingers. Corsino, who usually heals at a distance, sometimes does contact healing—laying on of the hands. During the services, he held his mother-in-law's hand. When the services were over, Corsino's wife, aware that he had been in something of a trance, asked him "where he had gone." Corsino pointed to a chair in the balcony overhead and said that he had been sitting there watching his physical body heal his mother-in-law.

Ed often does contact healing on his wife, who has suffered for years with a bad back. It seems to work, for she usually feels much better after the healing. While he is holding his hand on her back, he visualizes himself at another point in the room, looking at himself and his wife as he heals her. He told me that when he was in church, there was no other place to "go out" on the main floor where he was sitting, so he had to send himself to the balcony.

Corsino learned the healing technique of "going out" when he was in England visiting the psychic surgeon George Chapman. Chapman, who has no medical education, claims that he is a medium through whom Dr. William Lang, an opthalmologist who died in 1935, performs operations on living persons. When Chapman goes into a trance at the start of the working day, Dr. Lang takes over his body and operates on his patients, using invisible surgical instruments handed to him by invisible helpers—his son Basil, who predeceased him, and a dead nurse.

Dr. Lang works not on the physical but the etheric, or second, body, which apparently hovers just above the physical during the operation. Ed Corsino had gone to him because his eyesight was poor following an operation some time back for a detached retina. Medical doctors had told Corsino that he could expect no improvement beyond 20/60 vision with corrective lenses. After the astral operation, however, performed in ten minutes without anesthesia or pain, the dead doctor told Ed that his eyesight would be better in three months. Three months later he could make out the figures on the 20/40 line of an eye chart with corrective lenses.

Dr. Lang gave Ed this technique for psychic healing: "Look at yourself in a mirror until you are in the mirror and looking back at your physical body. When doing contact healing, imagine yourself standing away looking back at yourself in this manner. Then let us [the spirits] take over your body and do the work for you." After Ed did this exercise several times, he found that he could see himself during the healing session from a point about six feet away.

Ed is not sure if the spirits take over his body, as they do in psychic surgery, but he does feel that something spiritual is happening, in both contact and absent healing. His wife and I believe that something akin to astral projection is taking place. Mrs. Corsino once had an OOBE herself while experimenting with a drug. She found herself up at the ceiling looking down on her physical body.

Whether Ed is out of his body or merely imagining himself out and looking back, he has had remarkable results in a few absent healing cases. A woman in her sixties had an operation for cancer and was given one week to live. Three months later, after Ed began absent treatment, she was still alive, very cheerful and optimistic about the future, and some of the cancer had disappeared. A brain-damaged boy of thirteen began to improve after Corsino's treatment started. Born with a blood clot on his brain, unable to speak clearly and forced to walk on crutches, he put aside his crutches three weeks after Ed sent healing thoughts to him each night and began to walk without help, although awkwardly. His speech since that time has greatly improved.

Ed Corsino is not his real name, but he is a real person. When spiritual healing takes place, whether or not an OOBE is involved, names are unimportant.

In the last few chapters we have discussed the relationships between people—family, friends, sweethearts, strangers—that motivate projections: the desire to be together, the need to heal or be healed physically or spiritually, the need for help when danger threatens. Now let us examine the physical and psychological conditions that put the body in a state of readiness for OOBEs.

When Body and
Mind Are Ready

Chapter 14

Escape from Fear and Pain

The double is often forcibly ejected from the body when there is a threat of sudden death or painful injury. It happens also when pain and suffering become so intense, they can no longer be endured. Sometimes other motives are present. When the double of Paul Lachlan Peck emerged just before his accident, he not only avoided shock to his physical body but was able to give himself a psychic healing. It was probably the stress factor, however, that caused the bodies to separate.

When physical or mental conditions generate an OOBE, another person does not have to be involved as in cases of family affection or helping-and-healing situations. Accidents, the danger of drowning, the stress of war, or—when the physical body is passive—illness and exhaustion can cause a mechanical separation. Since out-of-body experiences do not occur in a vacuum, however, other motivations and other persons often become part of the total situation.

The Indestructible Double

In accident cases the second body may, as Peck's did, shoot out a split second before the impact. Crookall cites the case of "R.E.," who said that just before he was hit by a car, "the true conscious part" of him seemed to jump out of his body. He adds that, once he had left his body, he was indifferent to its fate. He watched as a "dispassionate observer" while the doctor filled a syringe and inserted it into his arm. A moment later he was pulled back into his body.

In what Sylvan Muldoon calls "The Marcinowski Case," a Dr. Marcinowski had an OOBE just before a bicycle he was riding crashed into an obstacle. As soon as his double left, his fear left with it, and he could see the back of his physical body and head and the rear wheel of the bicycle as it turned over. Dr. Marcinowski claimed that he was able, from his astral position, to alter slightly the direction of the bicycle and thus averted a skull fracture. If true, this would be a remarkable case of astral mind-over-matter.

In another case reported by Crookall in *More Astral Projections* the accident itself was averted but the second body was ready to escape if necessary. A man was crossing the street when he saw a truck bearing down on him. At this moment he sensed his double standing beside his physical body and felt that it could not be hurt—it was "separate and indestructible." As the truck swerved away from him at the last second, he stood there unperturbed.

Other astral projectors are not so lucky, and they escape after the accident—soon enough, however, so that physical suffering is at least temporarily averted. The British television star Hughie Green left his body after an accident and watched the ambulance arrive and the drivers pull his body from the wreckage.

One of Celia Green's correspondents was in a motorcycle accident and blacked out for a moment from a blow on the head. The next moment his double was in the middle of the road, watching the motorcycle topple over and "my body tumbling toward me." As in nearly every other case, he felt detached and without pain, and he calmly noted the details of the accident. The rear wheel was spinning and the motor was ticking over. He also saw a man get out of a car, stop the motor, and lift the motorcycle off his unconscious body.

In *Life, Now and Forever* Arthur J. Wills tells the story of an Englishman who was thrown from his horse some years ago and was in his double for five hours while his physical body was unconscious. During that time he witnessed everything that happened and subsequently told it in detail to the astonished persons who were present. He saw his body lying on the ground, two strange men picking it up and carrying it into a house and the doctors trying to bring him back to consciousness. He had the typical feeling of peace and contentment, of not wishing to return to the motionless figure lying on the bed.

Later he gave an accurate description of the men who had picked him up and who left before he regained consciousness. He told the doctor exactly what injuries he had sustained. This experience convinced him, as OOBEs convinced others, that he would survive bodily death.

Escape from the Body in Wartime

There have been many OOBEs during wars, generated by the stress of battle and the physical suffering inflicted by gunfire. A dramatic projection during the Civil War is described by J. Arthur Hill in *Man Is a Spirit*. An artilleryman was sitting on the ammunition chest of his gun when it was hit by an enemy bullet and exploded. As his physical body was hurled to the ground, his double rose high above it, and he saw the two bodies connected by "a slender cord of a clear silvery appearance."

Two medical officers examined his body and pronounced him dead, but the stretcher-bearers noticed a flicker of life and carried him off the battlefield. At this point he "came down the silver cord" and rejoined his body. Although he had been blinded, his right arm had been torn from his shoulder, and there were forty-eight wounds on his face and chest, his second body was intact, without pain or injuries.

The *Journal* of the British Society for Psychical Research reported many such stress-generated projections during World Wars I and II. On August 3, 1944, an officer in a tank was thrown twenty feet when the tank was hit by German shellfire. As he lay there, his clothes on fire, he was conscious of being two persons, one "lying on the ground in a field . . . waving my limbs about wildly, at the same time uttering moans and gibbering with fear," the other "hearing them [the sounds] as though coming from another person." His double floated about twenty feet above the ground and could see his physical body writhing below, the tank enveloped in smoke.

The officer's double calmly gave instructions to his physical body: "It's no use gibbering like that—roll over and over to put the flames out." The physical body began to roll, finally falling into a ditch partially filled with water. As the flames went out, the officer returned to his body.

This OOBE is interesting in many ways. As in the Peck and Marcinowski cases, the double was able to save the physical body. Also, this is one of the relatively few OOBEs in which the physical body was not passive or unconscious while the double was out. In another such case described by Crookall, a British soldier in Burma was also thrown from a tank when it was hit by Japanese gunfire. The soldier lay for some time in the undergrowth wondering how he could get out without being fired upon. Suddenly his double rose high above his body with all fear gone, feeling calm and detached. Although the I-Consciousness was in the double, his physical body got up and walked slowly through the roadblock, while the double thought: "He'll have a bullet in his back any time now."

The physical body got past the roadblock and found a tank that had broken through. When the double returned, the fear and terror that had been delayed took over once more. Although there was no injury as in other accident cases, the projection seemed to be generated by the need to dispel fear and get through the roadblock.

During a World War I battle at Ypres, Belgium, the double of a British soldier escaped after he was hit by a bullet. Rather than hover over his injured body, he decided to visit his family back in England. Feeling "vitally alive and free," he flew home and floated into the house just in time to see his mother become ill and collapse on the stairs. A glass bowl she was carrying rolled down the staircase and rang "like a bell" as it bounced along the tile floor. She had not seen her son's double.

Later the soldier returned to England in his physical body, suffering the ill effects of poison gas. As he lay in bed one afternoon he heard his mother telling his sister about the day she fell on the stairs. "We never let him know . . . When I collapsed the bowl must have rolled downstairs." The soldier recalled his projection and came to understand that his physical body was not really himself but only a "cloak" or "skin" that he wore over his true self.

The timing of the soldier's OOBE brings up this question: Did he project because he was hit by a bullet or because of the illness that suddenly struck his mother? Time is a mysterious dimension in psychic phenomena, and it may be that in some way the two events were connected.

Suspended in Space and Time

Another kind of OOBE generated by the threat of death is described by Raynor Johnson in *The Imprisoned Splendour*. A mountaineer, F. S. Smythe, was climbing in the Dolomite Alps when a shower of rocks caused the rope he was holding to pull him over a precipice, where he hung frozen with fear. Certain that he would die, he began to sense that a great change was taking place, "the change called death," but that the end was not to be feared, that it was "the climax, not the anti-climax, of life." He was suspended not only in space but also in time.

Smythe felt a sense of detachment—"indifference to what happened to my body . . . I seemed to stand aside from my body. I was not falling, for the reason that I was not in a dimension where it was possible to fall." His body was severely bruised by hurtling rocks and his hands were lacerated as he clung to a ledge, but his I-Consciousness was apart from these injuries, apart from the physical body itself. After he was rescued, Smythe said he was convinced that "consciousness survives beyond the grave."

There are many accidents in caves, mines, and trenches when a workman is submerged by debris and in danger of suffocation and death. In one instance a trench collapsed and buried a man who had been welding two pipes together. His double escaped and floated above his body. Thinking about his family, he flew with the speed of thought to the kitchen of his home, where his wife was peeling potatoes. He tried to beam a thought to her—"I need your help"—but she didn't hear him. A fellow welder caught his telepathic message, however, and he was rescued.

"A Frightening, Agonizing Cry"

"When on the verge of drowning there may be much mental agitation; there is no way of escape, to plan, to struggle is useless, and so all mental energy is directed to introspection. It is probably due to this that the spirits of the drowning seem peculiarly ready to manifest at a distance."

The above lines written by A. Campbell Holms are from *The*

Facts of Psychic Science and Philosophy. In addition to the "mental
agitation" in drowning cases, there is also the extreme bodily tension
that is another factor in stress-generated OOBEs. *Phantasms of the
Living* describes forty cases of those who drowned or almost
drowned who appeared in their doubles to friends or relatives. In
one a thirteen-year-old-boy was thrown into the water near Java
when his boat capsized. He distinctly saw his mother and three
sisters at home in England, and he called out to them. All four,
sitting in their living room at the time, heard "a frightening, agoniz-
ing cry." When the boy came home later from his sea voyage, he
told them what had happened. His cry came at the exact moment
his mother and sisters heard it in England.

Dr. Marcinowski, who projected during his bicycle accident,
also told about a lady who had an OOBE during a near-drowning.
As reported by Muldoon in *The Phenomena of Astral Projection,*
she "shot forth into the air" and could see her physical body below
as it struggled against the waves. She felt detached and indifferent to it.

Astral Projection in Prison

Peter Ibbetson, the man who left his body in prison each night
while he traveled through space and time with his sweetheart,
was a fictional character. At least two others who have had out-of-
body experiences in prison were real persons, and it is clear that
extreme mental and physical distress allowed their doubles to
escape.

Ed Morrell, who wrote about his OOBEs in *The Twenty-Fifth
Man,* served a term in an Arizona prison about fifty years ago.
Sadistic guards not only beat him but immobilized him in two
strait jackets, tightly pulled over his body to prevent the slightest
movement. Then they doused water over him, causing the strait
jackets to shrink and intensify the torture.

One night, as Morrell lay on the prison floor panting and choking
for breath, the pain suddenly left, and his mind seemed to move out
of his body. He felt himself pass through the prison walls and glide
upward, deliciously free in body and mind. He floated above the
treetops, then traveled at great speed to many cities. He returned
to his body in the morning feeling quite refreshed, although he
was still in the strait jackets. And each morning the prison guards

would be flabbergasted and frustrated at his cheerfulness and the good condition of his physical body.

In his astral travels Morrell saw many events that were verified later, including a shipwreck. Once he met the governor of Arizona and learned the date of his release from prison. Many times he had previews of persons he was to meet later when he was out of prison. One of them was the young lady who became his wife.

The guards, puzzled by their failure to break Morrell's spirit, often came into his cell during the night and flashed a light in his face. Since he was out traveling in his second body, his physical body was asleep and resting comfortably. The guards then devised new tortures. Once he was left in his strait jackets for 196 consecutive hours, yet he kept going out on his astral excursions and returned to a body that always seemed to renew itself.

An interesting sequel to the Ed Morrell story was that after projecting nightly during his four years in prison, after his release he was unable to leave his body. Now in good health, free of pain, and happily married, the mental and physical conditions that had allowed him to escape from his physical body were no longer there. And escape was no longer necessary.

A more recent case of OOBEs in prison was that of Isidore Zimmerman, who spent twenty-four years in several New York prisons, sentenced first to the electric chair and then to life imprisonment for a murder he did not commit.

Zimmerman told me his story on March 7, 1974, just before he was interviewed by Barry Farber of radio station WOR in New York City. Arrested in 1938 at the age of nineteen, he was kept for two months on Death Row, fearful at the thought of dying and filled with despair because he knew he was innocent. He wrote a letter to Governor Herbert Lehman asking for exoneration and said that he would rather die than accept a pardon or commutation of his sentence.

The governor refused to pardon Zimmerman but commuted his sentence, and the next twenty-four years were taken up with his fight to be declared innocent. Finally, in 1962, the state admitted that Zimmerman had been wrongfully incarcerated. He was exonerated and set free.

During these years Zimmerman lived through intense mental stress and, like Morrell, suffered physically at the hands of prison guards. Yet the agony of being in prison for a crime he did not commit was softened by many paranormal experiences. In one, while he was on Death Row, the spirit of Zimmerman's dead brother appeared on the wall of his cell, then came off the wall and spoke to him. His brother told him that death was not to be feared and that in the afterlife people lived in love and harmony.

Zimmerman saw his brother twice and a feeling of calmness replaced his fear of death. For many years thereafter, however, he had to cope with the stress of his legal battles and the cruelty of the prison guards. He was beaten so severely that six times he appeared to be dead. Then one day, during a beating, he rose slowly out of his body and hovered overhead.

Now no longer in pain, he watched the beating with a sense of detachment and a feeling of pity for "that poor fellow" on the cot below. The action took place in slow motion, as if he were in a different time dimension. One guard was kicking him in the groin, but the foot moved up deliberately, mechanically. The other guard hit him with a club, which went down and up and down again in a slow, robotlike rhythm. His physical body was a dummy, the guards puppets pulled by invisible strings.

After that Zimmerman had many more OOBEs during the beatings. When he tried desperately to get out of his body, however, he was not successful until he reached a point when the physical pain was no longer endurable, what Zimmerman called "a certain kind of suffering." It seemed, as in Morrell's case, that a mechanical separation occurred at this level of stress.

A skeptic might argue that in Zimmerman's condition—and this would also be true of Ed Morrell—his suffering was so extreme and his sense of reality so distorted that the out-of-body state was an illusion, a defense mechanism to shield himself from pain. Zimmerman, however, sometimes traveled astrally around the jail grounds and brought back clairvoyant evidence that he had had an OOBE, just as Morrell did. Once he saw what a guard was doing in another part of the building and told him later. Another time he heard a conversation between two guards beyond the range of his physical senses.

In stress situations, no setting is more conducive to an OOBE than a prison cell. The prisoner's mind and soul cry out to escape from his bodily as well as his actual prison. The purely fictional experience of Peter Ibbetson and the very real and painful experiences of Ed Morrell and Isidore Zimmerman have probably been repeated many times in penitentiaries.

In Isidore Zimmerman's case, the added strain of knowing he was innocent prepared him not only for his out-of-body experiences but also for a spiritual development that began with the appearance of his dead brother in his cell on Death Row and is still going on today.

Chapter 15

Astral Projections of Doctors and Their Patients

Sylvan Muldoon, Oliver Fox, and Vincent Turvey believed that the physical body must always be below par before OOBEs could happen. All three, however, were ill most of their lives and thought that bodily depletion was the most important factor in their ability to project. Eileen Garrett was inclined to agree with them: "I have had many out-of-body experiences. They almost always occur when I am ill or depleted."

On the other hand, Crookall has stated that four of five projections occur when the body is healthy. This statistic would include, however, projections during the dozing-off or sleeping period, when all physical bodies need to be replenished. In cases of both illness and fatigue, there seems to be a looser connection between the two bodies that enables the double to leave more easily and pick up energy that will invigorate the parent body.

My research indicates that involuntary projections come more readily when the body is below par, while projections done by will power are most successful during periods of good health. Paul Lachlan Peck, for example, could go out when he wished to before his accident but not later, when he was recovering from neck and knee injuries. During his convalescence, however, he often found himself outside his body without willing it.

The energy necessary to eject the second body by an effort of the will seems to be lacking during illness. Even then, projection may occur if the problem is turned over to the subliminal mind. When the woman cited by W. T. Stead tried to project to church from her sickbed, she was unsuccessful. When she gave up and went to sleep, her two bodies separated naturally and her desire to be in church was fulfilled.

In *The Case for Astral Projection,* Muldoon mentions a New Zealand woman who tried while ill to visit friends at a seance. She hoped that they would see her and that she could speak with them. Apparently unable to do so, she fell asleep and slept soundly all night. In the morning she received phone calls from the members of the circle who said she had appeared dressed as in bed, wearing her nightgown and jewelry. She spoke to the sitters, then faded away.

The Doctors' Dilemma

If they wished, doctors could testify to the great number of projections during illness, but they have enough trouble trying to keep physical bodies functioning without worrying about a duplicate body that has its own set of rules. Yet there have been so many paranormal happenings in their presence—whether they were visiting their patients at home or in the hospital—that many doctors have begun to wonder if there isn't more to a human being than just his anatomy.

Many times a patient unconscious with fever, in a coma, even seemingly dead, has opened his eyes and announced brightly that he went for a visit in another body. Then the previously comatose, sometimes "dead" man would further confound the doctor by telling everything that happened in the sick room when he was supposed to be unconscious.

In *The Meaning of Immortality in Human Experience,* philosopher William Ernest Hocking describes the OOBE of a woman who was deathly ill with pneumonia and seemingly unaware of her surroundings. The doctor and her husband were at her bedside. When her husband left the room, she got out of her body and followed him.

"He crossed the hall," writes Hocking, "closing the door, and went into his library. She saw him pace to and fro, then take down a book from the shelf, open it and gaze at the page without reading on. She saw the page. He put the book back and returned to her bedside. She was there; she had not moved; she heard him plead with her, in the hope that his words might reach her consciousness, to try to come back to life."

The woman recovered and remembered being out of her body. One day, while her husband was in the library, she took the book she had seen him with off the shelf and showed him the page he had been reading.

When astral travel happens to the doctor himself, he may begin to believe in it. In 1937 a former professor of anatomy, in a speech to the British Royal Society of Medicine, suggested that there just might be something to this second body business. He spoke cautiously, using medical terms that his colleagues would understand, such as "acute gastroenteritis," "typhosus," and "fibrillating," then gradually introduced such exotic abstractions as "time-dimensions of space," "psychic stream," and "the fourth-dimensional universe."

Actually, Sir Auckland (later Baron) Geddes was trying to tell the other doctors that a physician friend of his had gone out of his body. In later years, however, the consensus was that Geddes had been describing his own experience.

Geddes (if it was truly he who had the OOBE) had suffered a severe stomach attack during the night and by morning realized that he had the symptoms of acute poisoning. In great pain, he could not get to the phone to call for help. Settling back to die, he suddenly found himself outside his body and looking down on it. The next moment he was floating over his house and garden, then off to a bird's-eye view of London and Scotland.

Now completely free of pain and suffering, Geddes thoroughly enjoyed what was happening—until he was rudely snapped back into his physical body. A friend had come into the room and, seeing his condition, got in touch with a doctor who hurried over and revived him with an injection. Like so many astral travelers who find their second bodies far superior to the ones they have lived with, he was very much annoyed at being called back from his "trip."

"What are we to make of it?" Geddes asked at the conclusion

of his lecture. "Of one thing only can we be quite sure—it was not fake. Without that certainty I should not have brought it to your notice." Then he ended his speech on a rather bold note: "It brings telepathy, clairvoyance, spiritualism, and indeed all the parapsychic manifestations into the domain of the picturable."

"Dead" for Four Hours

Another medical doctor had one of the most dramatic projections during illness ever recorded. In 1889 Dr. A. S. Wiltse of Skiddy, Kansas, lay dying with typhoid fever, surrounded by grieving relatives and friends. Having nothing better to do, he observed the details of his demise with much professional interest. His illness took a turn, however, for which his medical education had not prepared him.

Writing later in both the *St. Louis Medical and Surgical Journal* (November 1889) and the *Proceedings* of the British Society for Psychical Research (Vol. 8, p. 180), Dr. Wiltse gave the following clinical description:

> The pupil of my eye contracted, my perceptions became feeble, my voice weakened, and I felt myself overpowered by a general sense of heaviness. I made a violent effort to stretch out my limbs. I crossed my arms on my chest, then joining my stiffened fingers, fell suddenly into complete unconsciousness.

That should have been the end of his report. There was no perceptible pulse or heartbeat, his temperature was falling, his body was apparently settling into rigor mortis. Once the attending doctor thought he detected a faint breath, but when he stuck a needle into various parts of Wiltse's body, there was no response. The churchbell in the village of Skiddy tolled out the mournful news that Dr. Wiltse was dead.

After four hours of apparent "death," Wiltse woke up, surprised that he was still alive. But no, he couldn't be alive because the women in the room were crying, the men looking grim, the doctor staring at him as if he were a corpse.

"Moreover," wrote Dr. Wiltse, "my body and I no longer had any interests in common . . . I looked in astonishment and joy for the first time upon myself—the me, the real ego, while the not-me closed it upon all sides like a sepulchre of clay. I have died, as men term death, and yet I am as much a man as ever. I watched the interesting process of the separation of body and soul."

Now Dr. Wiltse experienced the classic OOB process. He felt a rocking motion, as if he were in a cradle, then heard the "snapping of innumerable small cords" in his feet. His double began to move upward from his feet to his head until all consciousness of self was in the head. Then he passed around the brain "as if it were hollow" and emerged through the sutures of the skull. His second body then "floated up and down laterally like a soap-bubble attached to the bowl of a pipe." Finally his double fell to the floor, then stood up "expanded to the full stature of a man."

He noticed that his second body was nude. Embarrassed, he glided to the door, where two men were standing, but when he got there he was wearing a new suit of clothes. As he swung around, his astral left arm touched the arm of one of the men, passing right through it. The man did not notice him. Nor did anyone else, for as his "corpse" lay on the bed, the women kept crying and the men spoke in whispers to each other. Wiltse waved his hands, gesticulated, bowed, did all he could to get their attention—to no avail.

How pleasant it was to die! "I am here," he thought with a sense of wonder, "and I am more alive than ever." He was delighted with his new body. It was taller than the one he had just left, just the height he had always regretted his physical body lacked. He liked his suit—of a kind of Scotch cloth, not expensive but quite a good fit.

As Dr. Wiltse walked jauntily through the open doorway, he noticed that a thread was trailing from the back of his coat. No, it wasn't a thread but a thin line that went all the way into the house and ended in his physical body, at the base of the neck in front. Strange, but nothing to be concerned about.

It was raining as Wiltse walked down the street, and he picked his way carefully past the many puddles of water. Soon, he thought, some kind of entity would arrive and escort him to a postphysical environment. But no one came—no spirit, no angel, not even a demon. Somehow, it didn't seem right. He began to feel rather lonely, neither in the world nor completely out of it.

Suddenly he was lifted into the air by an invisible pair of hands high above the tops of green trees. Floating for a short distance, he saw "three prodigious rocks" on the road below. Then overhead came "a great and dark cloud" filled with "living, moving bolts of fire." He was aware of an unseen presence that said he was on the road to the eternal world. The three rocks below were the boundary between physical life and the life beyond.

He was given the choice to go forward or turn back.

"But once you pass the rocks," he heard the voice say, "you can no more return into the body. If your work is complete on earth, you may pass beyond the rocks. If, however, you conclude that . . . it is not done, you can return into the body."

Dr. Wiltse had no trouble choosing. But as he started to cross the boundary line, a small black cloud appeared before him and covered his face. Lapsing into unconsciousness, he opened his eyes in his physical body.

The temptation is to regard Dr. Wiltse's experience as a dream or a subjective vision, but many questions are unanswered. How could he remain without the vital signs of life for four hours? (He later estimated that he was medically dead for half an hour, but even this would be considered impossible by most doctors.) His OOBE followed a familiar pattern in projections—the rocking motion, the double going out through the head, the horizontal position above the physical body, etc. He saw the connecting cord between the two bodies. He had the I-Consciousness of the astral traveler who knows he is in another vehicle. And he brought back clairvoyant evidence of this consciousness—it was established later that everything in the room was exactly as he saw it, including the two men standing at the door.

Dr. Wiltse's story was carefully investigated by two of the top researchers of the British Society for Psychical Research—F. W. H. Myers and Richard Hodgson. Wiltse's meticulous account of what happened inspired confidence in him as a keen observer of his own astral experience.

When Is the Moment of Death?

The Wiltse case brings up the question of when a man or woman is actually dead. In many OOB cases the physical body shows all the symptoms of death—catalepsy, the absence of breath, pulse, or heartbeat—while the second body may be roaming around, fully aware of what is happening. Crookall describes in *The Study and*

Practice of Astral Projection how another doctor, George Kelley, had also apparently died after a serious illness. Kelley heard the attending doctor pronounce him dead, had a sensation of momentary darkness, then left his body.

Seeing the spirit of his wife's dead sister in the room, Kelley touched his wife and tried to explain that he was going away with her sister, but she paid no attention to him. Then he found himself in a strange park, where men and woman stood around "beautiful in their glistening soul bodies." He was conscious of a bright, ethereal light. After another moment of unconsciousness, he was back in his physical body and woke up, to the great joy of his wife but the bewilderment of the doctor. He said later that "the knowledge I gained at that time assured me of a future life."

In *Life, Now and Forever* Wills tells of a woman who was pronounced dead in the presence of three doctors and a nurse. Several hours later her son arrived and watched her as she lay motionless in bed. Suddenly she opened her eyes, sat up, and greeted him. He remained with her all night, and when the nurse arrived in the morning she found her "dead" patient very much alive. When she told the nurse and the doctors that she had been in her second body, the doctors concluded that she had been temporarily insane. Too bad they could not have consulted with Drs. Wiltse, Kelley, and Geddes before making their diagnosis—first of death and later of insanity.

An item in the Bergen (N.J.) *Record* of Sunday, July 22, 1973, quotes Dr. J. F. Burton, medical examiner of Pontiac, Michigan, as admitting that the signs of death are not always reliable. Rigor mortis, for example, may develop in less than an hour or be delayed for several hours or perhaps not set in until just before burial. Our instruments are not yet sensitive enough to detect very subtle signs of life in the patient.

If an electroencephalograph (EEG) were available in all cases of apparent death, the absence of brain wave patterns would give what might be the definitive answer, but this is rarely done, and the decision is left to the judgment of the attending physician. Even when the EEG is available, however, there have been lawsuits that questioned the definition of death as the cessation of mental function. In a later chapter evidence will be given that the moment of death occurs when the connecting cord is severed, but it will take some time before the medical profession even considers this a possibility.

It is believed that if oxygen does not reach the brain for a period of six minutes, the patient will suffer irreversible brain damage if he recovers. Yet Dr. Wiltse claims that he was medically dead and without breath for at least half an hour. An American soldier in World War II, George Ritchie, was not only without oxygen for nine minutes but came back from the dead and told the story of an out-of-body experience that changed the course of his life.

"The Search for Myself"

The story of Private George Ritchie first appeared in *Guideposts* and was later included in the book *Life After Death*. It happened in December 1943, when Ritchie had just completed basic training at Camp Barkeley, Texas, and had been assigned to medical school in Richmond, Virginia, for training as an Army doctor.

Ritchie was to be picked up on December 20 at 4 A.M. and taken in a jeep to the railroad station for his trip to Richmond. The day before, however, he developed a chest cold and went over to the base hospital to have it treated. About 9 P.M. he felt uncomfortably warm and began to lose consciousness. He was put into an ambulance and taken to the X-ray room, where he passed out.

George woke up in a strange room, his first thought that he must make the train to Richmond. He jumped out of bed and looked for his uniform, but it was not there. Then he saw a body on the bed he had just left. The man appeared to be dead, but to Ritchie's horror he was wearing George's own fraternity ring.

George ran out into the hall. He must get to Richmond and medical school. He called out to an orderly passing by, but the orderly didn't see or hear him—in fact, passed right through him. He got out of the hospital building and seemed to fly toward Richmond, the earth moving very fast beneath his feet. Once he stopped by a telephone pole and put his hand on the guy wire, but could not feel it.

Suddenly Ritchie remembered the body on the bed in the room he had left. It must be his own body and he must return to it. In a flash he found himself back at the hospital but he couldn't find his body. He ran from ward to ward and peered at the faces on the beds but his own face was not among them. He looked at the hands of the patients but didn't see his ring anywhere.

Finally he came to a small room and recognized his bed. But the body on the bed was covered with a white sheet. He tried to pull the sheet back but could not hold it. Then he saw a limp arm hanging over the side of the bed, his fraternity ring on one of the fingers.

The melancholy thought came to him that he was dead. Suddenly the room was filled with light, but it was no ordinary light.

"There is no word in our language," Ritchie wrote in his *Guideposts* article, "to describe brilliance that intense. The light which entered that room was Christ: I knew because a thought was put deep within me. 'You are in the presence of the Son of God.'"

George saw his whole life pass in review—"every event and thought and conversation, as palpable as a series of pictures." Then he began to experience other realms: one with very unhappy people who had left the earth but were still earthbound, a second superimposed on the earth but with philosophers and artists seeking for truth, and a third world far removed from the earth with a city and its inhabitants giving off brilliant light.

Suddenly George woke up in his "dead" body.

After weeks of slow recuperation, Ritchie was released from the hospital, physically healthy once more and with a new spiritual outlook. Before he left, however, he saw his medical chart. It read: "Pvt. George Ritchie, died December 20, 1943, double lobar pneumonia." He had been medically dead for nine minutes, but during those nine minutes he was probably more alive than at any time in his physical life. The doctor on the case said that George's return to life without brain or other damage was "the most baffling circumstance" of his career.

The editors of *Guideposts* add that they have documentary evidence of Ritchie's experience—affidavits from the Army doctor and nurse who attended him, stating that he was pronounced dead on the morning of December 20, 1943.

Today Dr. Ritchie is a psychiatrist in Charlottesville, Virginia, with a special interest in the problems of adolescents. In 1957 he founded the Christian Youth Corps of America, which later became the Universal Youth Corps and indirectly led to the concept of the Peace Corps introduced by Senator Hubert Humphrey and activated by the Kennedy administration.

Dr. Ritchie believes that he was allowed to return from the dead so that he could "learn about man and then serve God." And it is certain that if one of his patients ever leaves the body during a period of illness, the doctor will understand why it happened.

Chapter 16

Astral Projection in the Hospital

In what kind of place—room, building, institution, indoors or out-of-doors—is an OOBE most likely to happen? We have seen many astral projections generated in the home, mostly in the bedroom, sometimes in the living room. Many OOBEs have taken place in a church or monastery or elsewhere when religious devotion is the motivating force. There are OOBEs on the battlefield, in prison, in the mountains or in water, on city streets when danger threatens. No environment, however, is more suited to an out-of-body experience than that of a hospital ward. Here the strong odor of chemicals, the feeling of disease and death in the air, the subdued entrances and exits of medical personnel and religious figures create an atmosphere in which some of the most dramatic and meaningful OOBEs occur.

Just lying on a hospital bed and praying to escape from pain may bring on an out-of-body experience. One patient was so ill and wracked by such a high fever that glass partitions were placed around her bed. At one point her double escaped and floated up to the corner of her cubicle, where she stayed for eight days. Feeling very much alive and now without pain, she observed her body on the bed, watching the nurses bathe it and listening to their hushed comments. She had circular vision—she could see at a glance through all four partitions.

Although the concern of most hospital patients is with themselves and their ills, sometimes a compassionate man or woman will be astrally drawn to a fellow patient whose suffering may be greater than his own. A woman was lying in bed prior to an operation, so weak that she was unable to move. Another woman was brought in from surgery and given a bed at the far end of the ward. This woman's crying and moaning awoke such pity in the first woman that she longed to help if she could, but her bed was too far away.

One night, while she was thinking of the postoperative patient, her double sat up, got out of bed, and walked across the ward. After speaking words of comfort to the distraught woman, she said, "I must leave you now or my body will be cold." Then she walked back to her own physical body, which lay passively in bed, and entered it through the mouth.

When her sister visited her a few days later, she expressed a desire to see the other patient, who had quieted down and was no longer moaning. Her sister wheeled her across the room and the other patient flashed a glance of recognition, saying, "Oh, I know you—you are the one who came in here to cheer me up that night after the operation when I was so ill." Yet the "helper" had been too ill herself to move her physical body.

Leaving the Body During Surgery

When drugs are taken or anesthetics administered in the hospital, OOBEs are even more likely to occur, often with striking results. An example is a World War I case reported in the *Journal* of the British Society for Psychical Research of a soldier seriously ill with dysentery. When it appeared that he might die, he was given a rectal injection of saline solution. Rising from his body in a horizontal position about three or four feet up, he could see his physical body lying on its stomach. He also heard the conversation of two orderlies and saw a military officer present who had not been there before.

When the soldier woke up, he said that he had watched the orderlies make the injection and had listened to their conversation. Then he asked who the strange officer was. The amazed orderlies protested that he could not possibly have known all this because he was completely unconscious during the injection. An interesting facet of this case was the way the soldier's double left—face downward in the same position as his physical body.

In many cases of an OOBE during surgery, the I-Consciousness of the patient is quite strong. The double not only watches the operation in progress but notices details, often of things that go wrong, and reports it later. In one case the nurse lost her cap during the operation, and later the patient told her what had happened.

The second body of a patient in surgery is usually quite fascinated by what is going on and will pay particular attention to the part of the physical body that is exposed. Sometimes the double hovers over the table on which the instruments are laid and examines them closely. In two cases something unusual happened to a surgical instrument, and the patient later told the amazed doctor about it.

In a letter to the London *Daily Sketch,* a woman described how, during an operation, her double saw the doctor drop his instrument and the nurse pick it up and put it in the sterilizer. She also noticed that her physical face had accidentally been burned. When she regained consciousness she told the nurse and the doctor about the instrument falling, then asked for a mirror so that she could examine the burn.

In *The Enigma of Out-of-Body Travel,* Susy Smith quotes from an article written by a doctor on the staff of Lenox Hill Hospital in New York City. The writer of the article, Dr. Russell MacRobert, told how the chief surgeon of the hospital operated on the ear of a clergyman. So painful was the ear that the patient was given an extra dose of anesthetic. As the surgeon was about to operate, he discovered that a special instrument he needed was missing, and he was so annoyed that he cursed, pulled off his gloves, and went down the hall to fetch his instrument bag. He brought back the tool he needed, gave it to the nurse to be sterilized, then got into a fresh gown, put on fresh gloves, and proceeded with the operation.

Unknown to the doctor, he had company on his trip down the hall. It was the astral body of the clergyman, who watched the doctor get his special instrument and floated back to the operating room with him. After the operation, which the patient observed with keen interest, he not only repeated every remark that had been made by the doctor and nurses, but told the nurses exactly where they had been standing at all times. He then said he had been with the doctor on his trip down the hall and chided him for swearing in the presence of a minister.

Many doctors, some of them skeptical at first, have written about the OOBEs of their surgery patients. In *A Surgeon Remembers*, George Sava tells of an out-of-body case that made a profound impression on him. Not only was the I-Consciousness of the patient unusually strong, but she brought back from her astral experience such detailed evidence that the surgeon called it a miracle.

After the operation of Mrs. Frances Gail, an urgent phone call informed Dr. Sava that she couldn't be awakened. The doctor hurried back to the hospital, and it appeared that Mrs. Gail was dying. He worked frantically to revive her, and when she woke up, she told him an astounding story. She had been out of her body and, like Dr. Wiltse and other projectors, preferred to go on to the next world rather than return to the inefficient organism that lay on the hospital bed. What brought her back was realizing that her friends would be unhappy if she died.

"I have come back at their call," said Mrs. Gail.

So far it seemed to be no more than an inner struggle whether to live or die. But Mrs. Gail's next words made the doctor think otherwise.

"You didn't carry out the operation you first intended, did you, Mr. Sava? . . . You kept my body lying there under the anesthetic while you and the others discussed whether it was strong enough to withstand what you proposed to do. You took away some pieces of bone. You were chiefly troubled about the anesthetic and said to the anesthetist: 'Do you think she can stand three hours of it? Heart all right?' The anesthetist just nodded and said, 'She's okay, especially considering she's no chicken.' Is that right?"

The doctor could only nod dumbly. Everything Mrs. Gail told him was exactly how it had happened—the discussion about the operation, the pieces of bone, the comment "She's no chicken." How could Mrs. Gail have known all this? She had been in a deep state of unconsciousness and could not be awakened for quite awhile.

Dr. Sava realized that this was no ordinary case. Her recovery was against "the longest odds." Then he made an observation that would account for the reluctance of most doctors to accept the out-of-body theory: "It is indeed a disquieting thought that, if Mrs. Gail is correct in her beliefs, every time one operates, one's activities are under observation from the patient's astral body hovering overhead . . . a fascinating but frightening possibility."

The second body of the patient under anesthesia doesn't always stay in the operating room and watch the doctor perform. Sometimes the double wanders off in search of family and friends. In one case mentioned by Crookall, the patient not only traveled some distance from the operating room but brought back clairvoyant evidence of where she had been. During the operation she felt herself go out of her body in the form of "a wispy puff of cotton." The "wispy puff" then shaped itself into her duplicate body.

She glanced casually at her physical body lying on the operating table, then floated out to the corridor and saw her husband sitting there. Wondering where her daughter was, she immediately found herself in a gift shop and saw her daughter looking over some "get-well" cards. The young woman read one of the cards but thought the sentiment was too flippant and bought another one. Her mother heard her read every word of both cards, then suddenly snapped back into her body in the hospital.

When the young woman came in after the operation, holding the "get-well" card, her mother repeated the verse word for word before reading it. Then she recited the words on the card her daughter had rejected. The astonished girl admitted that the patient had read the cards verbatim.

Doctors and Nurses as Witnesses

Are doubles in the operating room ever seen by the surgeon? I am not aware of any such case, and it is just as well. Aside from the likelihood that the doctor would go into shock and probably stab the patient, he might also wonder if he was working on the right body. Yet there was a doctor who in one day saw the astral bodies of three patients leave their physical bodies during surgery. Fortunately, he was not the operating surgeon but an observer.

Dr. R. B. Hout wrote in the June 1936 issue of *Prediction* magazine that at the time he was in the surgical clinic of a Chicago hospital. The patient in each case, unconscious after an inhalation of ether, floated above the operating table while the physical body lay inert. As the anesthesia deepened, the double moved farther away and seemed to have more freedom of action. While the incision was being closed at the end of one operation, the double came close to the body but had not yet entered it when the patient was wheeled into the recovery room.

In one of the three cases the double floated horizontally, while in another it was upright and moved about in an active and spirited manner. Dr. Hout also noticed other etheric forms standing around and observing the surgeon's operating technique. Their cords, attached to no physical bodies, were drifting about like "silvery curls of smoke." Hout wisely did not call the surgeon's attention to the presence of so many discarnate entities making themselves at home in the operating room.

Nurses, too, have often seen the doubles of surgical patients rise out of their physical bodies and join the observers. In one case a nurse herself left her body while assisting in the operation. To her surprise, Myrtle Hendry found herself on the other side of the table, looking over the doctor's shoulder and watching her own body behave in its customary professional manner as it handed the doctor his instruments.

When the operation was over, she floated up over the table and rejoined her physical body. In a letter Miss Hendry wrote to Sylvan Muldoon, she claimed that she had been completely without awareness in her physical body, even though it was performing as usual, with her I-Consciousness in her double. There is an interesting psychological aspect to this case. The nurse stated that whenever she was near this particular doctor, she would feel lightheaded and perhaps go into a trance.

This case must be ranked as one of the offbeat kind (see Chapter 18). The physical body is ordinarily passive and even cataleptic when the second body is out. It might have been fatal to the patient, however, if the nurse's physical body had frozen. Possibly there was a kind of astral mind-over-matter at work, the nurse directing the movements of her physical body from her double.

Knowledge of a Deeper Reality

The conviction of immortality is especially strong following OOBEs during operations. Sometimes it comes just from a feeling of lightness and freedom, the absence of pain, and the delight with an attractive and agile new body in place of the rather unappetizing one on the operating table. The projector often believes that he has met deceased relatives and friends while in his double and he comes back certain of an afterlife, as Drs. Kelley, Wiltse, and Ritchie did when they returned from apparent death.

In *The Case for Astral Projection*, Muldoon tells of a New Jersey woman who found herself standing next to the surgeon and observing her own body "lying limp on the table." She looked up through the glass ceiling of the operating room and saw her dead grandmother, who took her astral hand and passed through the ceiling with her. As they flew over the city, the "dead" woman pointed out the roof of the patient's home. Then she said, "Now it is time for you to return." The patient remarked later that she no longer had any fear of dying.

Many times while on the operating table, a man or woman experiences a deeper reality in the double. Many projectors feel that they have penetrated beyond the physical world to a higher plane of existence. In *Invading the Invisible* James Edgerton describes how his son had an auditory experience of this kind during an operation. Young Edgerton inhaled the anesthetic three times and on the second breath "seemed suddenly to shift to a body other than physical."

Edgerton sat up in his double and saw within his physical shell a new body "glistening brilliantly" as it slid out of his "fleshy envelope." At this point he heard a beautiful sustained tone corresponding to middle E on the piano that started very low in volume and increased until it "seemed to fill the universe." A voice then told Edgerton that he was passing through the experience of violent death but that he was with friends and "everything would be all right." He said later that this experience absolutely convinced him that there is a future personal life.

Other projectors under anesthesia have traveled, like Dr. Kelley, to realms where there was bright sunshine and nature brilliantly transformed and were met by kindly souls they could not identify. Sometimes the realm visited is unearthly in another, less appetizing sense, and the astral traveler wanders through fog, mist, and water, with threatening figures around him. A good percentage of those who project during operations seem to visit the more pleasant realms.

Psychologist Joseph Jastrow, in his book *The Subconscious*, notes that many well-known figures, among them the chemist Sir Humphry Davy and writer J. A. Symonds, while under anesthesia had "the metaphysical conviction of piercing the secret of reality." Jastrow, by no means a believer in astral projection, admitted that anesthesia dreams are often accompanied by "an extra-bodily feeling" which one subject described as "the extraordinary impression that my spiritual being stood outside my body, regarding that deserted body lying on the bed."

Chapter 17

"I Am
in Two Worlds"

"My dear Geraldine: It is strange how my thoughts have gone out to you in this dreadful time. I am in two worlds. I am not dead but I may be soon. I can't talk to anyone. I want to tell them things: how I was with B [her son killed in World War II]. He took me into a world so brilliant I can't describe it. This is just a little visit to beg you, if you go to Ireland, not to lose sight of my darling [daughter] . . . Explain to her, if I am taken, that I am only gone on a journey . . . Now that queer cord is beginning to pull at me. I saw my body lying there and I am still bound to it by a silvery cord —a bit frayed, you know."

The above lines were written on a sheet of paper by a woman at home in London—but they seemed to come from another woman lying near death in a Dublin hospital. Mrs. N. Webb had suffered a brain injury in an accident and had been through a delicate operation. The message was received through automatic writing by the British medium Geraldine Cummins, who was in a trance at the time. In automatic writing the hand of the medium or psychic holds a pencil over a pad of paper and writes without direction from the conscious mind. The double of the communicator may be present controlling the arm movements of the medium.

Was Mrs. Webb out of her body or was this just a telepathic message processed in the medium's unconscious mind and dramatized as though coming directly from the hospital patient? Practicing mediums and sometimes other persons try to communicate with the dead and are often surprised when messages are received from the living as though they are present but invisible. Such messages frequently come through automatic writing or the Ouija board, sometimes by way of a disembodied voice, at other times when the double ostensibly takes control of the medium's body and speaks through her vocal cords. The dialogue, written or spoken, is often so natural that a conscious intelligence seems to be operating. Yet generally the communicator is surprised to hear later that she was present, in mind if not in body.

The more we examine the paranormal, the clearer it becomes that the mind functions dynamically on a subconscious level, that our conscious life is only the thin surface over an ocean of thoughts, feelings, motivations, and experiences that are the greater part of reality. Although one of the most important kinds of evidence for OOBEs is the awareness of the projector that he is in another body, there is also impressive evidence such as automatic writing that the double may travel without conscious knowledge, when the physical body is ill, asleep, in a coma, or otherwise preoccupied. This was apparently the case with Mrs. Webb.

Much if not most of the messages received through automatic writing are probably psychogenic rather than paranormal—that is, they originate in the subliminal mind of the person whose hand is writing or spelling out the message. There are occasions, however, when the alleged communicator is doing something or thinking of something or is unconsciously disturbed by something while in a certain mental or physical state that would motivate her to send a telepathic message or even be present in her double.

On the day that Miss Cummins did the automatic writing, she received a letter from a friend of Mrs. Webb's, reading in part: "She is very, very far away these days, and I feel that she is half . . . with the others, and only comes back with an effort." Mrs. Webb had had a serious operation and was in a hospital atmosphere conducive to projection. Her physical body was depleted, she was probably being given drugs, and she was sleeping much of the time while in a passive, dreamy state the rest of the time. She was also close to death, a condition that generates many projections.

She had a need to communicate with Miss Cummins, who was her friend, and ask her to take care of her daughter. Her "letter" speaks of meeting with the dead and of being in "a world so brilliant" that she could not describe it, the kind of realm often visited by patients either at home or in the hospital who are gravely ill. She saw her own body lying in bed and felt the pull of her connecting cord.

Most mediums have "controls"—persons or entities from the spirit world who act as intermediaries for other dead persons wishing to communicate with living friends or relatives. Sometimes the control is startled when a living soul (double) comes through. Miss Cummins' control, Astor, who also wrote messages through her hand, first announced that a strange woman was present, and then Mrs. Webb presumably took over the medium's arm and hand.

After Mrs. Webb's writing stopped, Astor said: "I do not think she has passed over because the cord of life was there. But she is in and out of her body and it is possible that she may live." Astor said later: "She has pulled at the cord of life, fretting about her daughter. Now she is at peace and is likely, therefore, gradually to recover."

Unless both the control and the message received from Mrs. Webb were products of Miss Cummins' subliminal imagination, a very dramatic projection took place from the hospital room to the home of the medium. Geraldine Cummins described the case in *Mind in Life and Death.*

The Double Signs His Name

In another automatic writing case, a conversation took place between individuals separated by three thousand miles. Not only was the exchange of ideas as rational as though both were physically in the same room, but the handwriting matched that of the absent (or present?) person.

Frederick Bligh Bond, who had previously learned the secrets of Glastonbury Abbey in England through automatic writing, was sitting with medium Margery Crandon in Boston one evening in the 1920s when they attempted an experiment. Bond had no special dead or living person in mind as Margery held the pencil over a sheet of paper, but soon a message came through giving veiled references to Glastonbury that were understood by Bond but unfamiliar to the medium. The message concluded with: "I am from the Isle of Apples. I will keep my eye upon you. (Signed) Flohr."

Bond knew that the "Isle of Apples" meant Glastonbury, but he did not recognize the name "Flohr." Finally Margery wrote "Flower," the name of a man Bond had been associated with in business. This dialogue followed, Bond speaking, Flower writing (quoted from *Psychic Research*):

BOND: Tell me, Flower, are you talking to me in your sleep?
FLOWER: Not so.
BOND: Well, you must be traveling in your dreams. Now, Flower, listen to me. I want you to remember all about this dream when you awake. You have been dreaming true.
FLOWER: Yes.
BOND: And be sure to write it down. You will promise me this? . . . Will you make an effort to remember everything?
FLOWER: I will if I can.
BOND: Now, once more, give me your name. The lady holding the pencil does not know it. I want you to sign your full name through her hand.

Margery then wrote "Harold A. Flower," the man's full name and, according to Bond, "in a style of writing which seemed to me characteristic of the writer." Bond made a careful tracing of the signature and mailed a copy of the message to Flower, who answered that at the time of the experiment he had been in London, sitting up late at night and talking about architecture with his brother-in-law. He had mentioned Bond's name several times during the night. Flower recognized his signature but thought that Bond had copied it from another document. He told Bond also that the name "Flohr" was the original German spelling of his family name, a fact unknown to Bond or to Margery, who had never met Flower.

With five hours difference in time between Boston and London, it would have been around 3 or 4 A.M. in England when the writing came through. Bond theorized that, although Flower was still awake, he might have been drowsy and in a state of readiness for astral travel. And since Flower's thoughts had turned to Bond, it is

likely that Margery's mediumship exerted a pull on his double. Yet
Flower had no conscious awareness of traveling three thousand
miles across the ocean to "rap" with his friend through Margery's
hand.

The Double Negotiates a Loan

Even more unusual were the spoken-written dialogues between
psychic investigator W. T. Stead and several friends not present
in their physical bodies. Stead produced evidence that the absent
friend was thinking of something at the time or did something
later connected with the "conversation" that took place.

Stead had told a friend, Miss Summers, that he would try to
bring her double to him through automatic writing. One day he
sat with his hand over a piece of paper and asked her out loud to
write something. The pencil began to move over the paper (quoted
from *Proceedings,* SPR, Vol. 9):

> STEAD: (*speaking*) Are you really writing, or is it only my
> subliminal consciousness?
> SUMMERS: (*writing*) I will try and prove to you that I am
> really writing. There is an object in my hand just now which I
> will bring to your office. I am sitting at my table. It is a small
> present that I want to make to you. It is an old thistle.
> STEAD: What! A thistle?
> SUMMERS: Yes, an old thistle; it played a part in my life that
> made it dear to me. I will give it to you tomorrow.

Stead was puzzled by the nature of the gift, but he eagerly
awaited Miss Summers' visit the next day. If she did not come, the
experiment would be a failure. If she came and said nothing about
the thistle, the results would also be negative. Miss Summers did
show up, but when Stead asked her if she had brought a present
for him, she said no. Then she added that she had thought of bringing a piece of scented soap but rejected the idea as silly.

Disappointed, Stead told her about the thistle but immediately
perked up when she said that a thistle was stamped on the piece
of soap. She had thought of bringing the soap at about the time
that Stead's hand was writing. Although she had had no conscious

awareness of being with Stead, a subliminal conversation did take place that may have involved the second body.

Professor Ernesto Bozzano, writing about the incident, points out that although Miss Summers was apparently awake at the time, it is possible that she was in a passive state—dreamy, distracted, even drowsy. It is possible also that when Stead began the experiment, she put herself into this state in order to communicate with him through automatic writing.

On a later occasion Stead held pencil over paper and asked the absent Miss Summers aloud what she was doing. His hand wrote that she needed money for rent but she hadn't told him because she knew he would offer her a loan. Stead said that he would send her the money, and his hand then wrote: "No, I won't take it. I will send it back if you do. I don't like to seem mercenary."

Stead sent the money the next day, and Miss Summers was appalled that he knew about her problem. Such a meaningful exchange of words with one of the parties physically absent suggests that some form of intelligence was present and active. That Miss Summers communicated her need without being consciously aware she was doing so suggests also that she may have hoped on a deeper level that Stead would send the money.

What activated the exchange of thoughts between Stead and his friend? First, there was the desire of both to communicate through automatic writing. Second, there was the bond of friendship that is often a generator of both telepathy and out-of-body experiences. Third, Miss Summers' financial need may have been so great that she psychically prodded Stead into doing the automatic writing. We can further assume, although we do not know for certain, that Miss Summers was in a changed state of consciousness, at least temporarily, while the projection and the writing were going on.

Stead also wrote automatically once when another friend needed money. The man had previously turned down Stead's offer of help. About two o'clock the next morning, when Stead knew his friend would be sleeping, he sat down with paper and pencil, and the following spoken-written dialogue took place (quoted from *Proceedings,* SPR, Vol. 9):

STEAD: (*speaking*) You did not like to tell me your exact financial position face to face, but now you can do so through my hand . . . How much money do you owe?

FRIEND: (*writing*) My debts are ninety pounds.

STEAD: Is that all?

FRIEND: Yes; and how I am to pay them I do not know.

STEAD: How much do you want for that piece of property you wish to sell?

FRIEND: What I hope is, say, a hundred pounds for that. It seems a good deal, but I must get money somehow.

STEAD: What does it cost you to live?

FRIEND: I do not think I could possibly live under two hundred pounds a year . . . Where can I get this? I cannot tell.

The next day Stead told his friend what had been revealed through automatic writing. The man was shocked but now willing to discuss his affairs in more detail. Later he wrote to the British Society for Psychical Research that Stead had learned the exact details of his problem through automatic writing.

As in the Summers case, it appears that subliminally the man wished that Stead knew all the facts and could help him but consciously he was too proud to say anything. These experiments tell us that our true motivations are buried in our unconscious minds but that they surface during out-of-body experiences and other psychic situations.

Is automatic writing a form of astral mind-over-matter? If the double is indeed present, it may use psychic energy to move the hand of the writer, who detaches his arm and hand from the control of his mind. Or, as many controls claim to do with trance mediums, the projectors may take physical possession of part or all of the medium's body.

The Double in the Seance Room

Closely allied to the automatic writing type of projection is voice communication through mediums. Trance mediums sometimes allow spirits to speak through their vocal cords. During some seances, however, the voice may be heard independently in another part of the room. In the "direct-voice" phenomenon the dialogue between the person who seeks information from the medium and the absent communicator is purely in spoken words and even more lifelike than when one of the parties is writing. An outstanding case of this kind was that of Gordon Davis, who was believed to be dead when his voice was heard but was actually alive some distance away. This case, from *Proceedings,* SPR, 1925–26, has been cited by both skeptics and believers in the survival theory as proof of their position.

The medium was Blanche Cooper, in whose presence the voices of spirits could be heard speaking as though coming out of the air. Professor Soal, a mathematician who was at the seance, knew Davis and identified him by his voice, accent, and personality. He thought, however, that Davis had been killed in World War I and that this might be the discarnate spirit of Davis rather than a projection from his living physical body. Even more startling was that Davis, if it was he, also thought he was dead and asked Soal to send a comforting message to his family.

Later Soal met the living Davis and told his astonished friend that his voice had been heard in the seance room. Davis recalled no conscious projection and consulted a diary of his daily activities. Twice when Davis was presumably present in his double, he was actually in his office, talking with business clients.

How do we explain what happened? Automatic writing and direct voice cases suggest that a person may not only project his double but carry on an intelligent conversation and furnish details of his life unknown to the medium and others present. That Davis was there in his second body could be inferred from the fact that his voice and personality were recognized by his friend. When we speak with a friend on the telephone, we do not demand that we see him physically before we are sure it is he. It is enough that we recognize his voice and way of speaking and he talks to us of familiar matters. If he later denied he had been on the phone, we would be utterly baffled.

Was Gordon Davis in an altered state of consciousness—sleeping, dozing, convalescing, etc.—that would favor a projection? He was physically well and in his office when he apparently spoke with Dr. Soal in the seance room. Bozzano points out, however, that Davis was heard only for about a minute and that he could have been dozing or wandering mentally or in one of many subtle changes of mood that practically everyone experiences in one day.

This explanation may not suffice, since we have no way of knowing exactly what Davis was doing or what his state of mind was during his direct-voice communication. There are other interesting facts, however, that point to an OOBE. Blanche Cooper's control, through whom allegedly dead persons had communicated, said that Davis was coming through very strongly, too powerfully for the control, who would not let him speak when he was present the second time but merely relayed the message from him. The control said that living spirits (doubles) seemed to have much more physical energy than spirits.

Another significant point was that Davis described in detail a house he was not living in at the time, had never seen, but moved into later. He said, for example, that the house had "a funny, dark, tunnel." Soal visited the house and noticed, along with other features Davis had mentioned, that there was a long dark passageway resembling a tunnel.

Why did Davis think he was dead? His subconscious self probably played a role that would satisfy those who had gathered at the seance to get messages from the dead. Role-playing is common in hypnotic trances, when the subject will perform any part the hypnotist assigns him, and it accounts for many cases of hypnotic regression in which the subject sees himself in a previous life as a famous personality. Certainly the conscious Davis would not have been play-acting.

Gordon Davis dropped in at the Soal-Cooper seance uninvited and didn't learn until later that he had been on an astral trip while sitting in his office. Florence Marryat, a writer and psychic of the nineteenth century, was once brought against her will to a seance through the efforts of the members of the circle. Mrs. Marryat, who wrote *There Is No Death*, also had precognition in the astral body. Although she had been sleeping at the time and was not aware that she was out of her body, her double was quite agitated and begged, through raps on the table, to be allowed to go back home.

"Let me go back!" she spelled out. "There is a great danger hanging over my children! I must go back to my children." The next day while her brother-in-law was showing a gun to her son, it went off accidentally, the bullet missing her eldest girl by a couple of inches. While sleeping, of course, it was quite likely that Mrs. Marryat had both an OOBE and a premonition.

Conscious Projection to a Seance

Has a living person ever *consciously* manifested himself to a medium through automatic writing, direct voice, or control of the medium's physical organism? There are a few cases. In *Encyclopedia of Psychic Science* Nandor Fodor quotes a statement made by Sir Lawrence J. Jones in 1928 while speaking at a meeting of the British Society for Psychical Research. Jones said that his nine-year-old daughter had four times projected during sleep to a medium and taken over her body. A Mrs. Laura Finch on several occasions was the control of medium Alfred Vout Peters while she was physically in Paris and Peters was in London. Those present recognized her voice and personality as she spoke through the medium's organism.

Vincent Turvey also claimed that he often consciously projected to a seance room and controlled persons in the circle, sometimes telling them beforehand that he would do so and other times projecting without warning. According to Fodor, Turvey "could hear and see and to achieve physical effects he appeared to draw from the medium's wrists and knees a sort of red sticky matter."

If the living double can project to the seance room, why can't it be seen as well as heard or known through automatic writing? There are a number of claims that this has happened, one example being the woman in New Zealand (see Chapter 15). In another strange case, cited by Muldoon in *The Projection of the Astral Body*, a little girl sleeping in a hammock outside the seance room materialized inside while the circle was trying to call up the dead daughter of one of its members. The girl's double said that she was the spirit of the dead child. When she woke up she remembered nothing of her appearance in the second body. It would seem that as she slept she was moved to answer the needs of those inside and did so in this dramatic though unsuitable manner.

Where Does the Medium's Double Go?

Where do trance mediums go when their bodies are taken over by either a dead spirit or a living double? Elwood Babbitt, a medium in Wendell Depot, Massachusetts, says he wanders off into other realms, often back through time, when his dead control, Dr. Frederick Fisher, occupies his body (see Chapter 24). In *The Facts of Psychic Science,* Holms tells what happened to Mrs. Conant, a nineteenth-century medium, when her control took over.

Once, during a seance in 1857, Mrs. Conant was controlled for an hour, 10 to 11 P.M., by the spirit of a dead Indian boy. After awhile the members of the circle became restive and asked the spirit to leave. He explained that he couldn't do so because Mrs. Conant had not yet returned from her astral travels. A rather strained silence followed until the medium finally woke up in her physical body.

The next day a friend of Mrs. Conant's told her that she had come into his bedroom about 11 P.M. and bowed her head. Fearing that she had died, he asked her if she had passed to the spirit world. Mrs. Conant shook her head and faded away. The man noticed that she was wearing an unusual hair-do and learned later that a woman friend had dressed her hair in an unusual manner on the night of the seance.

Muldoon asked a Seattle, Washington, medium what happened when he went into his trance. The medium replied that as he felt himself moving away, he looked back and saw his physical body sitting in the chair with "a magnetic connection between the two bodies."

The most famous of trance mediums and perhaps of all mediums, Leonora Piper, went out of her body when it was taken over by her control. Richard Hodgson, of the British Society for Psychical Research, described the process as follows (quoted from *Proceedings,* SPR, Vol. 13):

> She seems to be partly conscious, as it were, of two worlds . . . [Her] normal or supraliminal consciousness becomes in some way dormant, and . . . her subliminal consciousness withdraws completely from the control of her body anl takes her supraliminal consciousness with it . . . The hand [in automatic writing] behaves at times as though one consciousness withdrew from the hand to make room for another.

Mrs. Piper mentioned "snapping noises" and the connecting cord: "They [the spirits] were talking to me. I came in on a cord—a silver cord." Her controls, Phinuit and George Pelham, stated that they could see the medium leaving and returning to her physical body. Phinuit said, "When I came in, I met the medium going out."

This chapter has dealt with the evidence for OOBEs in cases of automatic writing, direct voice, trance mediumship, and other phenomena occurring mostly in the presence of mediums. We started with Mrs. Webb, who "wrote" to Geraldine Cummins that she was "in two worlds." Mrs. Piper, the medium, also seemed to be in two worlds, one of the spirit, the other of living beings. Let us close this section with the story of a woman, who, like Mrs. Webb, lay near death in a hospital ward. Mrs. E. S. Smith was fated to stay permanently in the second of her two worlds.

Before she died, however, her husband, a doctor, contacted her through automatic writing. While she was in a coma, the day before her death, a message came from her through his hand. In *Life, Now and Forever*, Wills quotes Dr. Smith: "We were able to plan out the business affairs and arrangements for the disposal of the body . . . She could not only write through me, but we could also talk to one another."

A startling disclosure was that Dr. Smith received a message from his dead father saying that his wife had already died even though she was breathing and medically alive in the hospital. Once more we must ask when is a person dead? Or—more to the point—is he ever really dead? Does he always live in two worlds at the same time?

Chapter 18

Offbeat
Astral Happenings

There are many OOBEs that do not fit neatly into the categories described in previous chapters—exceptions to the general pattern, unusual circumstances, special kinds of projections such as the "arrival" phenomenon. There are times when the I-Consciousness shifts back and forth between the physical and astral selves, other times when the double is experienced only from the point of view of the physical body. Occasionally, consciousness has been outside both bodies, sometimes in what seems to be a third body.

The physical body is not always passive or cataleptic while the double is out. When Eileen Garrett projected to Iceland (see Chapter 1), she sat in a chair in New York City and described what was happening. In one of the war cases, the physical body was thrashing around while the double tried to control it. The soldier whose physical body walked through enemy lines was watched by his double hovering over. There is a class of projections that happen accidentally during some sort of rhythmical activity—walking, talking, writing, dancing—or in a fast-moving vehicle such as a plane or automobile. There may be no motivation in the rhythm situations, just a mechanical loosening of the two bodies along with a change of mood induced by the activity.

The Arrival Phenomenon

There is, however, an apparent motivation in "arrival" cases, also known as "premonitions of approach." A host expects a visitor who appears in his double ahead of the scheduled time and then disappears. The flesh-and-blood guest shows up a bit later, unaware that he has given advance notice of his coming. The arrival phantom is called the *vardogr* in Norway, a country known for this type of OOBE. According to Thorstein Wereide, who writes about "Norway's Human Doubles" in *Tomorrow* magazine (Winter 1955), the *vardogr* is heard as well as seen—there are steps on the stairs, the outside door is unlocked, boots are kicked off. When the host investigates he finds the hall empty but knows that his friend will soon be there. One woman was so accustomed to seeing and hearing the *vardogr* of her gentleman guest that its arrival was her signal to prepare dinner.

In *The Enigma of Out-of-Body Travel* Susy Smith tells the story of a New York businessman who went to Norway for the first time and was greeted everywhere as a familiar friend by persons he had never seen before. The hotel clerk said it was a pleasure to have him back, while a Norwegian dealer's first words were "Delighted to see you again, Mr. Gorique." Gorique had been thinking about his trip in the preceding months and evidently projected his double without conscious awareness.

The host may not know that he is about to have a visitor, astral or physical. *Phantasms of the Living* reports one of the strangest cases of this kind, which happened in England and involved the double of a horse and carriage. A Reverend W. Mountford, staying with the Coe family about a hundred years ago, saw a carriage drive up with his host's brother and sister-in-law inside. Instead of stopping, however, the horse galloped right by. Ten minutes later, the real-life horse and carriage arrived with its flesh-and-blood occupants, who said they had suddenly decided to visit the Coes at the time their doubles were seen by Mountford.

Were the phantom horse and carriage thought-forms created by the visitors to signal that they were coming? Did the horse telepathically know that he was going to make the trip and then obligingly accompany the man and wife on the astral rehearsal of their journey? Unlike cases in which the person is unaware of projecting and still acts or speaks intelligently, as in automatic writing, the *vardogr*'s behavior is mechanical and ghostlike and may be a mental projection rather than an OOBE.

The famous nineteenth-century medium D. D. Home was once due to meet the writer Count Tolstoy at a railroad station in St. Petersburg. His double got off the train and walked away, taking no notice of the amazed Tolstoy and his wife. When Home did arrive at the station three hours later, no one was there to greet him. A note was waiting at his hotel expressing the disappointment of the countess because Home had ignored her at the station.

Why are there so many arrival cases in Norway? Crookall speculates that "the high altitude . . . with diminished supply of oxygen, favors the release of the double." It is possible, too, that the sense of loneliness and isolation in large sections of the country induced by the sparse population and absence of the sun for many months of the year may predispose Norwegians to this type of OOBE. Since human contacts are fewer, they may be more psychically charged than in countries of high-density population.

When Projectors See Their Doubles

Why does the I-Consciousness sometimes stay in the physical body, permitting the projector to see his own double at another point in space? According to Muldoon and other investigators, this generally happens when the double is still close by, within "cord range," in Muldoon's words, or up to from ten to fifteen feet away from the physical body. Sometimes the double in these cases appears as a symbol, often of death. In *The Mystery of the Human Double* Ralph Shirley tells about a professor of mathematics who went to his library to look up a disputed point in a theological discussion and saw his double sitting there reading the Bible. One of the double's fingers was pointing to this passage: "Set thine house in order, for thou shalt die." The professor died suddenly the next evening.

Projectors out for a stroll are sometimes accompanied by their own doubles. A woman wrote to Crookall that while she was walking one day, she sensed that someone was following her. She turned around and saw her double. The projector may turn a corner and meet his double coming down the block. There are also the three-body cases, when the projector is aware of having two doubles in addition to his physical body. One of Muldoon's correspondents numbered his bodies 1, 2, and 3. In one projection his conscious-ness was in body No. 2, observing his double, No. 3, walking, and his physical body, No. 1, off to one side.

The Rhythm of Projection

Walking is one of the rhythmical activities in which out-of-body experiences may occur, with the I-Consciousness in the double most of the time. Philosopher C. J. Ducasse gives the case of a woman walking down the street who felt herself "rising higher and higher, up to the height of the second floor of the surrounding buildings, and then had an urge to look back; whereupon she saw her [physical] body walking about one block behind. That body was apparently able to see 'her,' for she noticed the look of be-wilderment on its face."

Why did this woman go out of her body at this time? In the absence of more facts about the case, it can at least be said that the monotonous action of legs moving and arms swinging may have in some way caused separation of the bodies and/or induced a kind of psychological dissociation that can bring on OOBEs.

Aniela Jaffe, the Jungian analyst who studied cases of doubles in Switzerland, found one man who was able to escape physical pain by leaving his body through rhythmic movement. As he walked down the street, he saw his physical self walking in front of him and realized that the pain had left him. He ran to catch up with himself and as he touched his physical body, it seemed to dissolve and he was back in it. At the same moment his pain returned.

In another walking case the physical body was able to indulge in what Celia Green calls "complex activities" while the astonished double looked on. One of Muldoon's correspondents was going to the market when her I-Consciousness shifted into her double walk-ing a short distance behind. She followed her physical body into the store and watched it give the order, then open her purse and hand the money to the clerk. Her double, lingering behind, heard the conversation between her physical self and the clerk.

Another instance of complex activity was that of the nurse mentioned earlier who found herself on the other side of the operating table watching herself hand instruments to the surgeon. Celia Green writes in *Out-of-the-Body Experiences* about a dentist who "extracted a tooth while in an ecsomatic condition." He claimed that his physical body performed with its usual skill even though his I-Consciousness had deserted it. Although there is a possible motive in the case of the nurse, who admitted that the surgeon's presence made her feel lightheaded, the dentist's reason for leaving his body is not clear. It would seem that concentration upon a task might prevent rather than facilitate an OOBE unless there were a compelling psychological motive present. Neither the nurse nor the dentist case, however, is illustrative of "rhythm" OOBEs.

Writing or typing is another kind of rhythmic movement in which an OOBE may occur. One of the leading nineteenth-century mediums, Stainton Moses, was sitting at his desk one day jotting down notes when he found himself standing in his double. Since Moses frequently did automatic writing, the physical action at this time may have stirred up his paranormal senses. Green mentions a young woman who projected while she was in a business office typing. She described the exact position of her double—four feet above her physical body, eight feet behind, and two feet to the left. Another projecting typist (or was it the same one? Green does not say) saw her physical body stop typing and stay "motionless, leaning forward slightly over the typewriter."

Perhaps the typist projected because her thoughts were not on what she was doing, and she preferred being elsewhere. Without more information, however, this is mere conjecture. Whatever her motivation, or even if there was none, the mechanical act of typing may have induced a kind of hypnotic trance and the resultant OOBE.

Oobes in Theater and Concert Hall

Appearing before an audience—talking, acting, singing, playing an instrument—or even being in the audience absorbed in a performance often generates OOBEs. Both Crookall and Green cite cases of clergymen suddenly finding themselves at the back of the church during their sermons, watching themselves as they spoke in the pulpit. It is possible that the sound of his own voice, especially listening to its rhythm, may lull a speaker into an OOB-prone state. This frequently happens to performing artists and may be generated in part by the state of self-absorption brought on by their performance.

One of Celia Green's correspondents was singing in a concert when she found herself at the back of the hall listening to her own performance and judging it very critically. She stated later that she had felt quite impersonal toward the creature who was singing. The voice wasn't bad, she thought, but it was not giving enough interpretation to the music—not enough light and shade. The double felt that that voice belonged to someone else and she evaluated it as a critic would.

In another of Green's cases, a piano player left his body on the stool, where it continued playing, while he hovered over it "criticizing and directing control of all operations and knowing the result, musically, was certainly an improvement." The pianist added that he felt his playing had reached heights never before achieved when his I-Consciousness was in his physical body. The double sent directions to the fingers, which executed them perfectly.

In a New York *Times* interview with columnist John Corry, pianist Byron Janis said: "I know there have been times [during a performance] when I was an onlooker, looking at myself, at what I was doing, absolutely outside of myself. I was absolutely listening to what I was playing."

Artists would like both their critical and creative senses to work simultaneously, but this is not always possible. To divide oneself into critic and creator, each operating at the highest level during a performance, is to reach an ideal state artistically. What better way to achieve this than for the body to continue performing while the critical double stands outside and directs each movement? A psychologist might say that the desire of the artist to separate these functions creates the illusion that he is out of his body and thus satisfies a strong need. Astral projectors do not need to create illusions, however, and it is highly likely that the performers mentioned did leave their bodies, motivated by a strong desire to improve their performance, their out-of-body state induced by the rhythmic pattern of the voice and piano.

The spectator may also find his double moving out. Green gives two cases of this kind. One man was listening attentively to the overture before a play began and suddenly was "floating above the great dome of the theatre . . . I saw the roof of the theatre and thought how dirty it looked in the misty night air . . . the whole roof structure needed a good cleaning . . ." The other projector was sitting in the balcony of a movie theater when he felt himself float out over the edge and look back at his physical body in the seat.

Music seems to be a generator of many paranormal experiences, whether one is performing or listening. Caroline Larsen left her body while listening to the music of her husband's chamber group. A young woman in Ohio used music as a "contact point" when she projected several hundred miles to her parents' home in Pennsylvania (see Chapter 22). In *The Phenomena of Astral Projection* Muldoon and Carrington describe how a church organist vacated her body while playing and let another entity take over and continue playing with her fingers. "All the time," she wrote, "my spirit is standing just outside my body . . . A cord connects me—my spirit and my body."

OOBEs in Moving Vehicles

Although the walking - talking - writing - typing - playing - singing OOBEs are frequently generated by need as well as by physical activity, unusually rapid movement alone is enough to free the second body. This often happens in certain kinds of feverish dancing, the whirling dervishes coming to mind. As mentioned earlier, the shamans of primitive tribes induce through frenzied dancing a physical and mental state that allows them to project and travel long distances.

Mechanical separation is also common in high-speed vehicles—airplanes, trains, racing cars, motorcycles. A letter from parapsychologist Renée Haynes, appearing in the SPR *Journal* of March 1961, reads in part:

A middle-aged guest mentioned at lunch that both he and his wife had at one time done a good deal of motor racing, so I asked him if he had ever known of this phenomenon [OOBEs while racing cars]. He said that it was very well known . . . you could ask almost any racing driver. It happened suddenly, in a breath, a heartbeat. After it had happened, you could "see" yourself at the wheel, driving. At the same time your actual body became identified with the car. You felt a rattle, a vibration of anything out of order as if it were a pain in your own bones, your own stomach . . .

In the SPR *Journal* of December 1961 a letter from William T. Richardson discusses OOBEs during air travel:

> Disassociation of mind with the physical world is apparently a fairly common phenomenon experienced by pilots, particularly those who fly at great heights and speeds. This sensation of "out-of-body" is a momentary experience of detachment, a glimpse of oneself as though from without. Not only have I had such an experience, but others sharing the common background of solitary flight have told me of their experiences with similar sensations . . .

Crookall believes that this type of OOBE is caused by lack of oxygen and links it to other cases generated by restricted breathing —anesthesia, suffocation, drowning. Whatever the cause, in his letter Richardson suggests checking with flight surgeons to see how many more of such cases have been reported by pilots.

Celia Green gives many cases of OOBEs while riding in an automobile, bus, or motorcycle. In one case the driver of an auto found himself above the car, traveling along with it, yet with the physical body continuing to operate the car with normal skill. A projector on a motorbike said that "the drone of the engine and vibrations seemed to lull me into a stupor." Suddenly he was hovering over a hill and he thought, "I shouldn't be here, get back on that bike!" and the next instant he was in the saddle again.

As in all paranormal experiences, there are patterns that emerge from an examination of OOB cases, but also offbeat astral happenings that deviate from these patterns or, as with the arrival phenomenon, must be put in a special class. The human being is a complex entity, often contradictory in thought and action, and cannot easily be subject to analysis. If we find mysteries and anomalies in the out-of-body pattern, we also find it in the practical day-to-day behavior of men and women.

The Projectors
Tell Their
Stories

Chapter 19

Celebrities and Their Doubles

Out-of-body experiences are universal, and many great men and women of history, along with the near-great, have had astral encounters in one form or another. Statesmen, philosophers, kings, writers, religionists, scientists have seen their doubles or traveled in them or knew of others who had projected. St. Augustine wrote about OOBE's. So did Aristotle, Plato, Goethe, and Shelley, and in our own time Admiral Richard Byrd and Ernest Hemingway.

The logical Aristotle, who debunked the occult practices of his day, said that he had talked with a man who had seen his own double walking down the street. When Socrates was asked by Critias where he wished to be buried, the philosopher gently corrected him: "You will not bury 'me'; you will only bury 'my body.' 'I' shall be elsewhere." Plato wrote: "When death approaches a man, the mortal part of him dies, but the immortal part departs safe and incorruptible."

Poets, Playwrights, and Novelists

Many writers and philosophers have not only expressed their belief in a second and perhaps more bodies along with their physical shells, but have also had OOBEs or witnessed the OOBEs of others. Tolstoy saw D. D. Home get off the train and disappear. The Swedish playwright August Strindberg said he often traveled in his duplicate body. Edgar Allan Poe and Dostoevski saw their own doubles. Poet Walter De la Mare woke up in his astral body while under anesthesia in a dentist's office.

Guy de Maupassant had an eccentric double that frequently annoyed him while he was at his desk working. Once in 1889 he was writing when he heard the door open. He turned around and saw his double enter, sit down in front of him, and bury its face in its hands, as though in deep thought. Then the double began to dictate what Maupassant was writing.

In commenting on this case, Robert Crookall points out that Maupassant was nearing "general paralysis," a condition in which the second body would tend to separate more easily from the physical body. It is also interesting to note that in cases of brain damage or other mental aberrations, the patient is more likely to see his own double than to be in it. (See Chapter 30.)

Percy Bysshe Shelley once saw his own double, but his vivid imagination may have been responsible. As Stead tells it in *Borderland,* he began yelling and screaming, and when his hosts ran in to see what was wrong, they found him staring at the wall and muttering that his other self had tried to spirit him away. A cloaked figure had appeared at Shelley's bedside and signaled that the poet should follow him. When they reached the living room, the mystery figure lifted the hood of his cloak, revealing Shelley's own face. The double said, in Italian, "*Siete soddisfatto?*" (Are you satisfied?)— then disappeared. On another occasion Shelley's friends, one of them Lord Byron, saw his astral body walking in the woods. Other friends said that the poet was with them at the time.

Goethe had two striking OOB encounters, seeing his own double in one and observing the double of a friend in the other. One day, while coming home with a companion during a rainstorm, he met another friend who was wearing his (Goethe's) nightclothes. This was so astonishing that Goethe exclaimed: "Frederick, what has become of you . . . wearing a dressing gown, nightcap, and slippers on a public road?" The embarrassed Frederick immediately disappeared.

Goethe was convinced that his friend had died, but when he

reached his house, he found Frederick sitting in the living room, wearing the very garments Goethe had seen on his double. Frederick explained that he had arrived soaked from the rain and had changed into Goethe's clothes. Then, exhausted from his journey, he had fallen asleep and dreamed that he went out to meet the poet.

When Goethe was twenty-one years old, he not only met his own double on the road, but it was a double from eight years in the future. Goethe wrote: "I was riding on the footpath toward Drusenheim and . . . saw myself coming to meet myself on the same road, on horseback, but in clothes such as I had never worn. They were of light grey mingled with gold. As soon as I roused myself from this daydream, the vision disappeared. Eight years later I found myself on the identical spot, intending to visit Frederica [his sweetheart] once more, and wearing the same clothes which I had seen in my vision."

Note that Frederick was asleep during his experience, exhausted from his trip in the rain, and Goethe was daydreaming when he saw himself in the future. An emotional element was present in both cases—the friend-to-friend relationship of Goethe to Frederick, and the poet's romance with Frederica. Goethe writes that just before he saw his double from the future, he had been returning from a visit with his beloved, the same Frederica, and feeling sad at the parting.

Mark Twain Sees a Live Ghost

Mark Twain, another writer fascinated by the supernormal, once saw a man—or was it the man's double?—disappear before his eyes. He was standing in front of his house one afternoon when a stranger approached him. Twain had no desire to talk with the man and hoped that he would ring the bell and discuss his business inside the house.

"I was looking straight at that man," Twain wrote later, "and he got to within ten feet of the door and to within twenty feet of me—and suddenly he disappeared . . . I was unspeakably delighted. I had seen an apparition at last, with my own eyes, in broad daylight. I made up my mind to write an account of it to the Society [for Psychical Research]."

Twain carefully examined every inch of the ground to be certain the man couldn't have escaped by natural means. No trace of the stranger anywhere. He then ran into his house to get paper and pencil and record the incident while it was still fresh—and there, in the living room, sat his apparition. The man had evidently rung the bell, and the servant had let him in.

Mark Twain may actually have seen the man's double, since there was no reason for him to disappear while Twain was watching him so closely. He may have arrived earlier while the writer's attention was elsewhere, and his double may have retraced his steps to the front door. In any event, what Twain wanted was a genuine apparition, not an astral body, and he didn't send an account of the incident to the Society for Psychical Research.

Astral Projections of Novelists

Ernest Hemingway had an out-of-body experience when he was at the front with an ambulance unit in Italy during World War I. He was handing out bars of chocolate to some Italian soldiers when a mortar shell exploded near him. He said later: "I felt my soul or something coming right out of my body, like you'd pull a silk handkerchief out of a pocket by one corner. It flew around and then came back and went in again, and I wasn't dead anymore."

Many writers have incorporated their out-of-body experiences into novels. Hemingway used this incident in *A Farewell to Arms*. A British writer, William Gerhardi, wrote about his astral projections in *Resurrection*. The first time it happened to Gerhardi himself, he had gone to bed in a state of exhaustion and dreamed of pulling a broken tooth out of his mouth. He woke up with a start and stretched out his arm to press the switch on the bookshelf over his bed but found himself "grasping the void" and "suspended precariously in midair, on a level with the bookcase." The room was in darkness but all around him was "a milky pellucid light, like steam."

Gerhardi wrote that he was then pushed out horizontally and placed on his feet. He looked back and saw "a coil of light . . . like a luminous garden hose." This light (the cord) extended back to his body sleeping on the bed. Gerhardi staggered in his double toward the door and tried to turn the handle, but felt no grip. Then he passed through the door. As he went by his bathroom he saw his second body in the mirror, dressed in his nightclothes. After wandering through the house, he felt himself fly out through the front door, then suddenly snap back into his sleeping physical body.

Gerhardi had five later projections with interesting results. In one he obtained proof that he had been in a friend's apartment. In another he visited strangers and described them accurately to someone who knew them. Once he passed right through a man walking on a road.

One of the projections had a melancholy ending. Gerhardi met the double of his friend Bonzo, and they decided to visit Bonzo's house. They were distressed when they found that Bonzo's physical body was no longer breathing. The cord had been severed, and he had died. Gerhardi said good-by to the saddened Bonzo and went back to check on the state of his own physical body. He found it in good condition, rigid but still alive. Gerhardi writes: "My double lowered with expert precaution into a vessel which . . . was now myself. I was lying, stiff, cataleptic, unable to see or move a muscle."

In the morning he called Bonzo's home and heard the butler sobbing on the phone. Bonzo was dead. His wrist had been broken the day before, and while it was being set he expired under anesthesia. Gerhardi had not known of his friend's injury.

Literary Doubles at Death

Writers seem to be fascinated with the process of dying, and many have projected or witnessed the projections of other writers from their deathbeds. When Aldous Huxley was present during the last hours of D. H. Lawrence, the dying man described to him how his double was coming out of his physical body and standing in one corner of the room looking back.

The American writer Horace Traubel lay dying in September 1919, with his friend Colonel L. Moore Cosgrave at his bedside. About 3 A.M. both men noticed a point of light in the room that grew larger and larger and finally contracted into a human face. They recognized their old friend Walt Whitman, who had died twenty-seven years before. Whitman's complete body materialized and stood beside the bed wearing clothes that Whitman had worn in his lifetime—a rough tweed jacket and an old felt hat. Whitman smiled, then faded away. Psychic researcher Walter F. Prince wrote about the Whitman ghost in *Noted Witnesses to Psychic Occurrences*.

During the last illness of the French poet Alfred de Musset, his two nurses saw him feebly struggling to get to a bell near the mantelpiece and ring for his servant. He was too weak to get out of his chair, but the nurses were astounded when the bell moved, as if by an invisible hand, and the servant came in answer. Had De Musset's double, in perfect health as doubles seem to be, separated from his body because of the looseness of the connection caused by physical depletion and rung the bell that summoned the servant?

Jung Puts on an Astral Show for Freud

Do psychiatrists have OOBEs? If they do, they generally keep it to themselves. Although Sigmund Freud never admitted going out of his body, his other paranormal experiences and those of his patients inclined him to a belief in telepathy and clairvoyance. Carl Jung, at one time heir apparent to Freud's psychoanalytic mantle, was less cautious about discussing his psychic adventures. One confrontation between the two giants of psychiatry could have involved the second body.

Freud and Jung were arguing the merits of the paranormal hypothesis when Jung had "a curious sensation" in his diaphragm, which was becoming red hot. Suddenly there was an explosive sound in the book case, startling both men. The quick-thinking Jung said, "See, that is an example of so-called catalytic exteriorization phenomena."

"Oh come," said Freud, "that is sheer bosh."

"It is not," Jung countered. "You are mistaken, Herr Professor, and to prove my point I now predict that in a moment there will be another such loud report."

A moment later there was a second explosion. What happened? Jung may have been able to project some form of energy into the bookcase analogous to the energy generated in poltergeist phenomena. Another theory is that Jung somehow managed to "exteriorize" his second body and cause the explosion. Today, Randi and other magicians who claim they can duplicate psychic photography and other paranormal happenings would label it a trick. Whatever the explanation, Dr. Freud was stumped for one of the few times in his career.

Jung reported other strange incidents. Once, when he came into the room, a dining table split apart. Two weeks later a bread knife broke into several pieces. Later another knife in Jung's strongbox split four ways. These mind-over-matter happenings in the presence of a famous and respected psychiatrist give credibility to the psychic fork-bending and other such feats by many psychics of the 1970s.

Jung, whose grandparents were "ghost seers," thought at times that his home was visited by spirits.

"There was an ominous atmosphere all around me," he wrote. "I had the strange feeling that the air was filled with ghostly entities . . . My eldest daughter saw a white figure passing through the room. My second daughter . . . related that twice in the night her blanket had been snatched away."

In 1920, when Jung was spending weekends at the country home of friends in England, he kept hearing strange sounds, and one night he "glimpsed the disembodied half of a woman's face on the pillow next to him, one fully open eye staring at him." He spent the rest of the night sitting up with the light on.

Another time, after the funeral of a friend, Jung was lying in bed thinking about the deceased when suddenly he saw an apparition of the man in the room. He felt compelled to get out of bed and follow the figure on the road that led to the dead man's house. Once inside, the figure climbed on a chair and pointed out the second of five books which stood on the second shelf from the top. The next morning Jung visited his friend's widow and asked permission to go into the library. On the second shelf from the top there were five works of Emile Zola's. The second volume was *The Legacy of the Dead.*

One of Jung's patients had an out-of-body experience. She felt herself near the ceiling looking down on her physical body on the bed. Jung himself may have had an OOBE while in bed. Once when ill, he nearly died. The nurse told him later that his body had been surrounded by a "bright glow." Crookall believes that Jung had a loose vehicle of vitality.

Astronomers, Physicists, and Other Scientists

Some well-known scientists have conducted experiments in astral projection while others have been out of the body themselves. The French astronomer Camille Flammarion, an avid investigator of psychic phenomena, did an OOB experiment involving four persons. He sat in one house with a man who tried to project his double at midnight to a friend's home twelve miles away. In the first experiment the friend saw the double, but his sister did not, although she was in the same room. In a subsequent projection, not only did the friend and his sister see the double, but their dog, who was asleep on the rug, woke up and ran to the corner of the room, where he crouched in terror.

Professor J. H. M. Whiteman, a physicist and mathematician who teaches at Cape Town University in South Africa, claims that he has left his body two thousand times since he was a boy. Whiteman is also a mystic and believes that astral projection could be, in its purest form, a spiritual experience.

Perhaps the leading scientist-mystic in history was Emanuel Swedenborg, the Swedish philosopher. So great was Swedenborg's influence that a religion was later organized based on his out-of-body observations of what he called heaven and hell. Swedenborg, who lived in the eighteenth century, profoundly affected many nineteenth-century philosophers and writers, among them Blake, Coleridge, Emerson, Henry James, Baudelaire, and Balzac, who wrote two novels based on the mystical teachings of the Swedish seer—*Séraphita* and *Louis Lambert*.

For most of his life a leading scientist of his day, Swedenborg began in his fifties to have the kind of dreams and visions that come to saints and mystics. He decided that it was his duty to visit the spiritual world and give a detailed account of what he found there. In his *Spiritual Diary* Swedenborg claimed that after going into a trance, he could visit Paradise and that he had spoken with Plato and Aristotle. Swedenborg's trances would sometimes last for three days and worried his housekeeper, but he would reassure her when he woke up that he had merely been talking with friends on a higher plane.

Swedenborg believed that all men live in two worlds at the same time—the natural world and the world of the spirit. Although our conscious minds are concerned with the material universe, our deeper selves are in close touch with the unseen world and our thoughts and actions are influenced by it. Swedenborg also believed in the Platonic theory of "correspondence," that all material things are reflections of a permanent idea in the non-material world.

Swedenborg did automatic writing and said that in much of it his hand was guided by spirits. He claimed also that many long passages in his books were the words of spirits he heard in his inner ear.

Swedenborg, Goethe, Aristotle, Dostoevski, Mark Twain—these are but a few of the names that crop up in the literature of astral projection. The list also includes many famous kings, queens, and emperors, such as Catherine of Russia and Napoleon. Today, in the 1970s, prominent men and women throughout the world continue to project by day and night, but we won't know about it until time has passed and the stories are revealed in their books and in posthumously published letters and other private papers.

Chapter 20

OOBEs in Childhood and Adolescence

A great gap separates the psychic world of children from that of adults. Up to a certain age children accept their paranormal experiences as natural, everyday events, while adults either dismiss theirs as coincidence or block them out of their minds. Out-of-body experiences are often frightening to adults, at least until they have had one or two. Most children take them in stride, especially the very young ones.

Tacey White, the daughter of a psychic mother, Linda White, began to project at the age of four. Each night she found herself floating to the ceiling in her second body, while her astral eyes calmly regarded her physical body lying in bed. From the age of four to nine she floated around her room at night, but she never told her mother about it. Didn't it happen to everyone, adults, too?

One day, when Tacey was nine, her mother was entertaining a group of friends when the discussion turned to astral travel. Mrs. White had just read Paul Twitchell's *Eckankar*, which describes "soul travel," a form of mental projection to different planes.

Twitchell, said Mrs. White, had warned that there are dangers in projection if the physical body is moved while the second body is away. The etheric body might not be able to return and the apparently dead body might be buried prematurely.*

When Mrs. White's guests had gone, she was surprised to see Tacey looking at her strangely, the child's face deathly pale.

"Is it true, Mommy?"

"Is what true?"

"Can they take your body away and bury it if you haven't got back into it yet?"

Mrs. White looked at her daughter in amazement.

"What on earth——"

Then it came out. Tacey had been projecting since she was four years old, but Linda White never knew about it.

Schoolchildren Out of Their Bodies

At what age do children start to have OOBES? In *Out-of-the Body Experiences* Celia Green states that one woman in her radio survey claimed she had first projected at the age of eighteen months. She recalled that she saw her room from her second body as "a complete and detached picture, as one viewing a scene from a play." Most of the cases I have studied indicate that four is usually the age when OOBEs begin.

One of Crookall's correspondents wrote that when he was seven years old, he woke up one night feeling thirsty. He went to the washstand but saw that the pitcher of water was empty. As he walked back to his bed, he noticed with astonishment that someone was in it—himself. Then he was "suddenly and quickly drawn up in the air and, with my feet at the feet of my body, I was quickly . . . down into it."

A New Jersey child discovered that he could leave his body at will. It happened the first time when he was on his way to school. He pictured himself arriving at the school, heard a popping sound, then found himself in the classroom. Later he told a friend everything that happened in class when his physical body wasn't there.

Children often go through the same process as that of many adults when their astral body leaves. In another Crookall case re-

---

* This is highly unlikely. Any disturbance to the physical body is usually the signal for a quick return of the double.

ported in *More Astral Projections,* a nine-year-old boy suddenly "shot out" of his body about six feet into the air and was conscious of his double in a horizontal position over the bed. He could see his physical body below. When parapsychologist D. Scott Rogo was five years old, he had the sensation one night of being lifted out of bed, floated around the room, then placed on the floor, and finally brought back to his bed.

Imaginative details that may have symbolic significance are a feature of many child OOBEs. In *The Enigma of Out-of-Body Travel* Susy Smith tells how a teacher in Connecticut learned about the OOBEs of his young charges when he asked them to draw pictures illustrating strange experiences they had had. One of the children said that after praying in church, she began to float up to the ceiling. A red line came down from the sky and went through her double to her heart, which then gave off a golden glow that spread through the rest of her astral body.

Another child drew a picture of herself lying in bed "sort of half awake and half asleep," when a blue wave came down and entered her head, then circled through her arms and legs and back to her head again. She felt herself floating up to the ceiling and saw her physical body lying in bed. Her double passed through the ceiling and traveled to different places in town, one of them the house of a friend. Her friend was unaware of her presence.

Color and light are, of course, characteristic of astral projection, particularly in a religious or spiritual context. Even when there seems to be no religious or other motivation in the OOBEs of children, however, their love of fantasy is a predisposing factor. To young children fantasy, sometimes the fantasy of flying, becomes merged with reality. They are rarely surprised, then, when they find themselves out of their physical bodies and floating around delightfully in their astral vehicles.

Since children are as sensitive to social and personal situations as adults, they often have psychological motivations for going out of their bodies. Kathy Crumish, a college student living in New York City, told me of her strange OOBE at the age of eleven. She had been pressured by her parents into joining the Girl Scouts, although she was reluctant to do so. Once at a Scout meeting in church the other girls were playing a game, but they did not invite her to join them. Feeling left out, she suddenly began to rise out of her body and went up very high to the vaulted church ceiling.

Below she could see the tops of the girls' heads as they played their game, as well as her own physical body watching them. She stayed up for about half an hour, then slowly descended and merged with her body, feeling refreshed and no longer "out of it."

As Kathy told me her story, the thought came to me that rising out of her body to this great height enabled her to be "above" the other girls and thus to feel superior and compensate for their neglect of her. One might feel this way in fantasy. For the eleven-year-old girl the ability to project made it a reality.

A Drowning Child Visits the Dead

Extreme stress may bring on an OOBE in a child as well as in an adult. A five-year-old youngster was being taught to swim by his brothers when he was swept away by a waterfall and in danger of drowning. He felt himself going through a tunnel that ended in a pinpoint of light that he knew he must squeeze through. He wriggled through this opening and was "released from all pain and pressure" as he floated down a peaceful stream.

The lad heard soothing music and felt great bliss. He opened his eyes and was happy to see other people—men, women, and children—drifting along with him, all "carried up towards the stars." They finally reached a distant shore and were pulled out of the river by people gathered there. The boy saw many dead relatives that he recognized from family albums and with them his smiling mother, who had died the previous year. As she reached out to him, "a black cross slipped out of her blouse and hung on a thin silver chain." The boy's eyes were dazzled by "the sparkle of seven stars which flashed from the dark background of the cross."

Suddenly he was pulled back by a whirlpool and as the river carried him away, his mother became smaller and smaller until she vanished. The boy woke up vomiting water which the fire brigade was pressing out of his body. He had been lying on the sand for half an hour while they worked to restore his breathing. He was carried home and put to bed.

When his father came into the room, the boy told him that he had seen his mother and mentioned the black cross with the seven flashing stars. At this his father stiffened and left the room. The boy found out later that his mother had died three days before her birthday and that his father had bought her a birthday present—a black onyx cross with seven silver stars in it. While his mother was in the coffin, his father had slipped the cross into her folded hands.

This story, which first appeared in *Fate* magazine and later in *More Astral Projections,* might be dismissed as a dream except for two striking features. One was the child's consciousness of actually seeing his mother and his other dead relatives. Second, he had never known about the gift. He and his brothers had been sent to the home of an aunt when his mother died, and his father had kept the existence of the cross a secret.

OOBEs of an Adolescent Boy

Why did Kevin Lampro leave his body at the age of fifteen? I thought I knew the answer as we talked in the living room of the comfortable Lampro home in the Berkshire Hills of Massachusetts. Kevin, now twenty-one, spoke quickly and nervously, sometimes inaudibly into my tape recorder.

When it first happened, Kevin was between boyhood and maturity. Young people in adolescence are often uncertain who they are, where they are going, and what their relationship is to the world. Just as very young children accept their psychic experiences as commonplace and adults tend to thrust them out of mind, the adolescent is often drawn to the unknown yet frightened of it, especially when it comes in the form of an OOBE.

Kevin had awakened one morning when he was fifteen, unable to move, his body cataleptic. The same thing happened the next morning and several mornings after that. Sometimes it would last for half an hour, and he would hear voices but couldn't make out what they were saying.

Then, one night, as he was falling asleep, he heard someone screaming, "Kevin, I'm going to get you." He was petrified with fear as invisible hands lifted him out of his body and carried him three times around the room. He felt very light as he floated in a circle, the room spinning around him. It lasted only a few seconds, then he was jerked back into his body. He lay there for some time, shivering in terror, then gradually drifted off to sleep.

As Kevin told me this story, his little niece, nine-month-old Sarah, laughed and gurgled in her crib, her happy screams punctuating Kevin's remarks. His nephew, three-year-old Gabriel, played on the living-room floor. A brother and sister-in-law went in and out from time to time. Kevin's mother came in occasionally to listen to the interview. It was a pleasant, easygoing family atmosphere, contrasting with Kevin's rather macabre tale of astral projection.

What happens during a paranormal experience has its roots in the individual—his temperament, his history, what he may be going through in his personal life at the time. The stress of adolescence may determine the form of an OOBE. Kevin admitted that he had always been somewhat nervous and fearful, a worrier, but he insisted that he had not been dreaming, that his I-Consciousness had truly left his physical body.

Although he had always been interested in the psychic, Kevin had never heard of astral projection when he had his first OOBE. After this experience, he began to read about it as he did other aspects of the paranormal. The next time he felt his body stiffen into catalepsy, he was still fearful but less so. This time, however, he went out only partially. He had several partial projections over the next few years. His double would begin to leave his physical body, but fear would drive it back in.

When Kevin was nineteen he had what was probably his most meaningful OOBE. He came home drunk one night about 1 A.M., went upstairs to his room, lay down on the bed, and immediately flew out of his body. By this time he had a pretty good understanding of astral projection and he was not afraid—he just allowed it to happen. He glanced back and saw his physical body lying like a "lump" on the bed, then moved to the stairs and lurched down from step to step, "still drunk in my mind."

Although everyone had gone to bed when he came home, he saw his brothers Jim and Keith on the stairs tinkering with a car radio. In the kitchen his mother and sister, who should have been asleep in their rooms, were eating breakfast. They were not aware of his astral presence. Now a strange thing happened to the kitchen window—it melted into a circle that gave off psychedelic effects such as "swirlies and symbols" and finally coalesced into a dome. Through the dome Kevin saw a clock, the hands pointing to five, and in the distance a white-and-brown painted pony walking down the street.

The old worries returned.

"What am I doing here, man?" Kevin asked himself. "Am I freaked out?"

Fear is the enemy of projection. He began to glide quickly up the stairs and back into bed. He woke up some hours later in his physi-

cal body, saw that it was morning, got dressed, and went downstairs. His mother was in the kitchen cooking. He told her what had
happened, and she listened sympathetically. She believed in psychic experiences.

What was the meaning of this bizarre happening? Time and
space had dissolved into what seemed like a surrealistic dream. But
OOBEs are often like dreams, and sometimes a sleeper wakes up in
his dream and finds that he is out of his body and the dream is real
(see Chapter 26). As in dreams, the time sequence of an astral projection does not always follow that of reality. Kevin saw his mother
and sister in the kitchen as he had seen them many times through
his physical eyes. He learned later that his brothers did fix a car
radio but it was after he had his OOBE. Kevin was sure that the
dome, the pony, and the clock were symbols of events to come. He
never did find out what the dome and the pony meant. But the next
afternoon, exactly at five o'clock, his brother Terry, whom he hadn't
seen for several months, pulled into the driveway.

Kevin's last OOBE occurred four months before our interview.
He was lying in bed one night with a very high fever, so uncomfortable that he began to pray for relief. His body became cataleptic, he broke out in a cold sweat, and his I-Consciousness suddenly
flew out in an arc and went around the room twice. Everything in
his bedroom appeared the same except for a crucifix on the wall that
had not been there before. When he went back into his body, his
fever had broken and he was well.

This was probably a classic example of a self-healing projection
during illness, when the double picks up energy which it transmits
to the ailing physical body. The sudden cold sweat was simultane-
ous with the projection, and it makes one wonder how many times
the breaking of a fever has been due to an OOBE.

Kevin's out-of-body experiences show many of the features we
have seen (and will see more of) in thousands of other cases. His
first was of the type in which other entities, good or evil, real or
fancied, seem to be present and exerting an influence on the projector. (See Chapter 27 for a discussion of "hinderers" and the
"Hades" conditions during projections.) In common with other first-
time projectors, Kevin didn't know what was happening and was
quite frightened. His physical body was cataleptic in most of his
projections.

Kevin's OOBE at nineteen was an example of the kind in which the space-time reality becomes blurred, and he saw or sensed events that either had not yet happened or had taken place in the past. Symbolism—in this case the pony, clock, and dome—is a universal feature of both dreams and psychic experiences, and the symbols often have a deeply personal meaning that must be worked out.

The OOBE during Kevin's illness illustrates how the double may restore the physical body to health, sometimes dramatically so. There was also a religious element in the last OOBE. Kevin prayed and saw a crucifix that was not there in reality. Most psychics have a spiritual orientation, even when they do not attend church. Kevin comes from a Catholic background that still exerts a strong influence on his thinking. He has studied Hinduism and other Eastern religions and believes in reincarnation and the survival of the soul.

Kevin has had many psychic experiences other than astral projection. He has been able to read other minds. He has developed into a good psychometrist—when he holds an object belonging to another person, he can often tell that person details of his private life and sometimes what will happen in the future. Once, while psychometrizing, he told a friend to watch out for "blue spree." A week later his friend bought a motorcycle with that name.

Kevin is clairaudient, that is, many of his psychic impressions come to him through hearing voices, as in his first OOBE. Once when lying in bed at 3 A.M., he heard a high-pitched, rather child-like voice outside trying to call him. He went to the window but no one was in the street. When he told his mother the next morning, she said, "Now why would a child be standing outside in the middle of the night calling for help?"

The next day they learned that Kevin's aunt had had a serious operation the night before. Mrs. Lampro said that when his aunt recovered and phoned later, her voice sounded weak and high-pitched, just as a child's voice would and as Kevin had heard it the night of the operation.

When I first met Kevin, he impressed me as so many other boys and girls of his age do, as being rather self-centered, vague about his goals, and lacking the ability to concentrate. He smoked incessantly and was full of nervous mannerisms. But I soon found out that what appeared to be indifference covered up a truly spiritual nature and an intense yearning to find out the meaning of living and dying. I discovered that Kevin really cares about other people, and I met many of his friends, boys and girls, who gave me the same feeling of caring but of being a bit frightened in a world that is not easy to understand.

Kevin has not yet found himself. He dropped out of high school because he thought that his teachers were not interested in him. Like many of his contemporaries, he plays the guitar and dabbles in writing music. At the moment he is interested in herbalism—using herbs rather than drugs to cure the body in illness. He has a strong interest in psychic healing, and once helped a girl heal a broken leg by laying his hands upon it, a practice that goes back to biblical days.

Kevin is fortunate in having an understanding family that allows him to go his own way until he finds out what he really wishes to do. There is an atmosphere of relaxation in his spacious home, with Kevin's many brothers and a sister, nieces and nephews, coming and going. His father has the very practical occupation of woodsman. His mother is a good-natured woman who is comfortable to be with. It is a devout household but also one in which ESP and other strange phenomena are accepted as part of reality. There are many psychics in Kevin's family, including an aunt who had an out-of-body experience.

What happened to Kevin when he went out of his body has probably been duplicated by thousands of teenagers who overcame their first fear when they understood the nature of their experience. An OOBE in adolescence probably has a special purpose. Perhaps it is saying that the miracles in the Bible can happen to them. Perhaps it is a way of gaining insight into the unknown. It may be telling them that they can heal themselves mentally and physically and that the developing physical body, with all its problems, is supported and sustained by a spiritual body.

Chapter 21

A College
Teacher Sees a Ghost

"Thoughts are like arrows. If you give a cry for help, some-body somewhere will hear it."

The speaker was Diana Marble, a pseudonym for a young woman who teaches English at a New Jersey college. Miss Marble was tell-ing me about her experiences with the out-of-body phenomenon and what it means to her. Like Ed Corsino and others who have helped and healed friends and strangers, she believes that need is the determining factor in OOBEs. It was need that brought the face of a man and the image of a woman to her apartment in one of the most unusual psychic happenings in this book, an OOBE rich in symbolism and drama.

Miss Marble had a startling introduction to the psychic world when she came home late one night in March 1972 with her friend Art. Art, who had had many astral projections, sensed the presence of a ghost. He asked the ghost to materialize, and after sitting in the dark for fifteen minutes, they saw lights shimmering around the grandfather clock in the living room. The lights then took the shape of a very tall woman with an upswept hairdo, wearing a long dress with puffed sleeves that tapered down to her wrists.

Diana and Art both cried out, at the same moment, "My gosh, she's pregnant!"

The ghost's stomach began to grow before their eyes, and as it did so, the woman's hair fell rather wildly over her face. She appeared to be very agitated. Suddenly the ghost reached for an invisible weapon and plunged it into her stomach. Diana, very much upset, began to cry, and Art quickly turned the lights on. The image faded away.

After that, whenever Diana came home late at night, the ghost would be standing in front of the grandfather clock, still pregnant. When Diana turned on the lights, the image disappeared but she knew the ghost was still there. She wondered who the ghost was and when it had lived. The woman's long dresses suggested an earlier period of history, but why should she pick Diana's modern apartment in a New Jersey suburb to do her haunting? And what did the gesture of plunging the weapon into her womb mean?

One night in April, a month later, Diana was sitting in the living room with Art when the ghost appeared again. This time a man's face was superimposed on her womb. The man had very deep-set eyes, a high forehead, and a mustache. During Diana's Easter vacation the face on the womb grew a beard to go with the mustache. The beard stayed for a week and then disappeared.

Up to this time Diana and Art were sympathetic toward the ghosts and tried to make them feel comfortable. Perhaps they had lived through a deeply traumatic experience, a tragic birth or death, and were compelled as ghosts to keep repeating it. But now a third character appeared, this time in the kitchen—a short, stocky man with receding hair. How many more ghosts would invade Diana's apartment and claim her sympathy? Art ordered the shadowy visitors to leave: "Out—out—all of you."

The three ghosts faded away—and did not return.

Several months later Diana's sister Melanie and her husband Bill, who had been living in Arizona, arrived unexpectedly in a camper truck. As the truck pulled up in front of her house, Diana saw the face of a strange man peering through the curtained windows of the camper. It was the face on the womb—the same mustache, deep-set eyes, and high forehead. When Melanie walked in with her husband, the "ghost" followed them, and they introduced him to Diana and Art as a friend from Arizona who was on his way to Washington, D.C.

It was an unusual dinner party that sat around the living-room table—Diana and Art, Melanie and Bill, and the "ghost," whose name was Yves. Art, who had been eying Yves with growing astonishment, finally blurted out, "Do you know a woman who wears her hair up, long dresses, and is pregnant?"

Yves dropped his fork and stammered, "Why, why yes—my former wife. She remarried after our divorce, and she is going to have a baby."

Diana chimed in: "And did you grow a beard over the Easter vacation?"

Yves stared at them and said, "My God!" He went out to the camper and brought back a photo showing his face with a beard. He had grown it early in April and shaved it off the week of Easter.

With all eyes on her, Diana told the story of the pregnant ghost, Yves's face over the womb, and the third ghost who had appeared in the kitchen. Yes, the third ghost answered the description of his former wife's present husband. Yes, the woman had been very agitated and almost suicidal because she was not in love with her husband and preferred to have Yves's baby. The conflict, which was very disturbing to Yves, had reached a peak in March, when the ghosts first appeared.

All the characters in this true-to-life scenario were intelligent and responsible human beings. Yves was a biochemist on his way to a convention. After listening carefully to Diana's story, he readily accepted the possibility that he had projected either his own double or a thought-form of himself and his former wife, with their conflict dramatized in front of the grandfather clock.

But why would Yves appear in his double or project a thought-form to Diana, whom he had never met?

Melanie thought she could provide some clues. She and her husband had met Yves in Paris, where they had been living three years before. Yves's wife came from an aristocratic Parisian family and she wore the long dresses of an earlier period. The previous year Melanie and Bill had come back to America with Yves, now divorced and their close friend, and settled in Arizona. Melanie, noticing that Yves was going through a trying period, told him about

Diana, her calmness and spirituality. Somehow the thought of Diana was soothing to the Frenchman, contrasting with his own inner turmoil.

Yves decided he would like to meet Diana, feeling that her calm presence would have a therapeutic effect on him. Melanie may have told Yves that Diana practiced meditation and that this contributed to her mental peace. Yves began to meditate and found that it quieted his nerves.

In our interview Diana pointed out that the meditator automatically becomes a psychic receiver: "If any human being on earth needs something badly enough and he turns either to prayer or meditation, somewhere that prayer will be heard." Since both Yves and Diana meditated every day, a psychic exchange began that took the symbolism of the pregnant woman and the face over the womb.

Symbolism seems to be the key to this very strange experience in which there was some form of projection. Diana has made an intensive study of dream symbols and finds the same kind of symbolism in literature. Just as ideas appear as symbols in a dream or a story, psychic impressions are often received in symbolic form, and they must be interpreted. As in Kevin Lampro's experience with the window that turned into a dome and a clock, many astral projectors find themselves in another dimension in which the symbols are related to the reason for their projection. Given Diana Marble's kind of mind and value system, it is understandable that the pregnant ghost and the face over the womb would appear to her as "a cry for help."

Characters in a Psychic Drama

There are many more links in the psychic chain that culminated in Diana's ghosts. Although Yves had never seen Diana, he established a psychic link with her through Melanie and Bill. He thought about her much of the time, feeling that in some way she could help him. Diana, in turn, was open to the idea of psychic healing, no matter who would send the appeal for help. Diana also had a link to Yves through her sister. These links were strengthened through meditation, which they often practiced at the same time.

Art now enters the picture as yet another link. Until Diana saw the ghosts, she had been unacquainted with psychic phenomena and the possibility of astral projection. If she had been alone, she might not have seen the ghosts or having seen them, might have been too frightened at first to know how to deal with them. Art was already deeply into the psychic field and had had many OOBEs. He had the necessary knowledge and understanding of the situation to help her absorb what was happening and find meaning in it.

Art provides another strong link. Like Yves, he had been married and divorced. His wife, too, had not wanted her child and he had been afraid that she might harm the baby or even attempt suicide. Diana had a strong affection for Art and shared his concern over this situation, which in turn allowed both of them to see the ghost of the pregnant woman and the face over the womb. Diana summed it up with this thoughtful comment: "Don't we attract only the people and events that have something to do with our innermost selves?"

Although the persons in this psychic drama were tied together by links of family affection and friendship, to Diana the basic motivation was need—the need of one human being that can be answered by another, whether relative, friend, or stranger. Yves's need was to overcome his agitation, to find peace, which only Diana could give him at this time.

"If someone has a deep enough wish," Diana said, "he will automatically go toward it, and in this case I believe that one of Yves's bodies had a desire to be here and it traveled here as a symbol of peacefulness."

The White Robe and the Lotus

I asked Diana if she had ever gone out of her own body in a helping-healing situation. She hesitated before replying.

"I don't know what 'out of the body' means, but I do know that I have experienced another dimension. There was one September night when I felt I was going to die. I was very ill from an infection. I don't know whether I was asleep or awake, but I went to some plane where there was another form of lighting. A lovely blond-haired man in a white robe handed me a lotus. I knew then that I would be well. If it was a dream, it was so real that I thought I would find the water lily beside me in bed."

She did improve and later had a dream in which the symbolism of the lotus was explained.

"It was the hand of God. My hand was, in a way, placed in the hand of God."

The white robe is spiritual dress, a common symbol in dreams and OOBEs. The man in the white robe, she said, made her feel peaceful. He was surrounded by a golden glow. She was so moved by her dream or vision that she got out of her sickbed immediately and painted the dream figure in water colors by the light of a single candle.

"I wanted to keep the experience, to freeze it."

Diana didn't recall being cataleptic or her double's rising in the horizontal position, but she did mention "distinctly passing through a tunnel," where she heard voices with "a hollow, echoey sound." In one of her dreams, she slipped out of her body and looked down on it from above.

There was another helping-healing dream that gave her information about a friend who had a problem, a man she had not heard from in more than a year. In her dream she asked if she owed karma to any person on earth, a debt to that person incurred through her past actions. The next moment she felt herself flying to her friend and saw him in his office.

"What are you doing here?" he asked.

"Did you want me to tell you something?"

He told her that he had not been well. He had had an attack of nerves that had affected his spine, but the doctors did not know how to help him. She said in the dream, "You must change your diet." When she woke up, she tried to call her friend in the middle of the night but was unable to reach him. He must have received her psychic message, however, because he called her by phone the following Sunday.

"How is your spine?" were her first words. "Are you all right?"

"No, it's still bothering me. Hey, how did you know about it?"

She told him about the dream, then outlined a diet for him, which he followed with good results.

Diana said that in this dream the sensation of flying, an out-of-body symbol, was very real, very vivid. It should be noted, however, that since it was late at night, it was hardly likely that Diana's friend was in his office. This is suggestive of other night-time OOBEs in which the space-time dimension is altered. Perhaps Diana's friend also flew out to meet her because of his need, and both created a thought-form of the office he would be in the next day.

Astral Views of the Future

Diana has other dreams in which she goes forward or backward in time. She has seen New Jersey in the years to come, when the coastline will be drastically changed. She believes that "every human being prepares long in advance for every major thing he goes through," and dreams are the most fruitful channel for this preparation.

Sometimes the dream gives her a literal description of the future event, other times it comes in symbols. Diana had a recurring dream about a panel truck, but she took the word "panel" literally. Three months later a day came when she needed help, which would have been available if she had realized that the word referred to a "discussion panel."

Diana has met people in dreams before she meets them in her waking life. She has received help in dreams that in some cases came from the projected thoughts and possibly the projected double of a friend, in others from the source of all wisdom within. The friend arrives in the dream when she is wrestling with a problem and gives her advice, often starting out with "Look, you've got to come at this problem from another angle."

Her dreams tell her where to go when she needs a job. In one dream she was told to visit a college in another state located near a city ten miles from the state boundary line. There, said the dream, she would find a man of American Indian extraction who would be eating peanut butter cups and would be very receptive to her ideas. She went to this city a few days later and found that there were three colleges in the area.

Choosing one of the three, she walked into the office of an administrative official and saw the peanut butter cups on a table. She asked the official if he was part Indian. He was. After they talked awhile, he invited her to lecture to his students. Another link is present in this situation—Diana's grandfather was also part Indian.

Does Diana go out of her body in her dreams? There are clues:

the tunnel effect, the sensation of flying, the vividness of her dreams, the fact that she once saw her physical body from the outside. Many of her dreams give evidence of what is happening or will happen elsewhere or of a thought that may be in someone else's mind. She dreams of or visits during her dreams those with whom she has an emotional affinity—the friend with the bad spine who needed her help, the friend who comes to help her with a problem, the part-Indian college official she met later who was sympathetic to her ideas and offered her a lecture engagement.

Like many other psychics or at least those who have frequent psychic experiences, Diana seems to have inherited her sensitivity. An uncle was a medium, a grandfather an astrologer. Her sister Melanie has traveled astrally. One night while Diana was asleep, she was rudely awakened when something hit her leg. She left her bedroom and resumed her slumbers on the living-room couch.

Later she received a letter from Melanie, who was still in Arizona, apologizing for waking her up. Melanie had involuntarily gone out of her body that night and had flown east over two thousand miles, making an accidental landing on her sister's leg. In her letter she not only gave the correct date of her astral trip but accurately described Diana's apartment, which she had not yet physically seen.

Diana never found out what happened to the ghost woman who was pregnant. It seemed to be exclusively Yves's projection, however, with his ex-wife no more than a thought-form. Diana feels that he was helped by the experience and by the sympathy she and Art extended to the ghosts. Once more in our interview she recalled the American Indian proverb that thoughts are like arrows, and when there is a need, someone will know about it.

Chapter 22

Astral Flights of Young Women

Their names are Linda, Laura, and Flo. They do not know each other. Their worlds are widely separated. They pursue different careers. Yet they have something, many things in common.

Linda White is a young married woman living in New Brunswick, New Jersey, who spends a great deal of time reading, working at a job, and going to meditation classes. Laura Randall (a pseudonym) is an opera singer, actress, and writer now studying in Italy. Flo Thompson is a housewife in Ohio whose main concern is her family —her husband and three children.

They are about the same age. Each woman is lively and outgoing, intensely interested in all that life has to offer. Each is strongly attracted to metaphysics and the spiritual. All three have had out-of-body experiences.

"Just Let It Happen"

I sat with Linda White in the living room of her New Jersey home, my tape recorder on the table. Linda, a slim, attractive woman in her early thirties, recounted her OOBE adventures in a quick, eager voice, her eyes dancing as she talked. She had no secrets to hide, nothing to hold back. She had had many out-of-body experiences, she believed in them and she wanted the world to know about them.

Linda's home was alive with people, children and adults. Many persons wandered in and out of the room—her husband Joe, her children, a visiting couple. The youngest child, four-year-old Michelle, climbed on my lap and said she wanted to go home with me. She was a distraction throughout the interview, but a pleasant one. At times I was tempted to forget why I was there and just play with her.

It was fun to be in Linda's home, getting the "feel" of her surroundings, trying to understand what she was like. Too many books about psychic experiences give only superficial accounts of the experiences with little or no attention to the persons involved in them. I wanted to dig a little deeper, to find out more about the personality of the projector, her goals, the people she loved, the environment in which she lived. I wanted to know, if possible, *why* she had a particular OOBE at a particular time and in a particular place.

I wish I could have been in Asia Minor in the first century A.D. and talked with Aridaeus about his out-of-body experience. It would have been fascinating to watch Chief Ngema Nzago make preparations to cover four days' travel in one night as he lay entranced on the floor of his hut. Imagine hearing about Swedenborg's journey to the heavens from the scientist-mystic himself. Or sitting in Mark Twain's living room as the humorist chuckled over the time his "ghost" turned into a flesh-and-blood visitor.

"Gigi first projected at the age of six when she had scarlet fever. Her father was a spiritualist."

I shook myself. What was Linda talking about? Who was Gigi?

"Gigi was my neighbor when I was living with my family at Longwood Lake in Oak Ridge, New Jersey. She told me that when she was a little girl and ill in bed, her father thought that her body would heal faster if she were away from it, so he taught her how to project her double. She just left her physical body in bed for awhile and felt much better when she got back. Gigi and her sister used to project all night long, and her mother complained bitterly to her father that it was hard to get them up in the morning and off to school."

The story of Gigi was interesting, but when did Linda have *her* first OOBE?

"That's where it happened—at Longwood Lake. As I dropped off to sleep one night, I had a strange feeling that I was going over the lake. Gigi and our other neighbor, Wes, were already there floating over the water. Wes kept saying, 'What am I doing here? I want to go back. What am I doing here?' Gigi just sort of smiled. Her features and her body were distinct, but I could see through her. My own double was as normal as my physical body, but I could see through it, too.

"When I went over to have coffee with Gigi the next morning, I told her about this very funny yet very real dream of flying over the lake. Gigi just smiled and said, 'I see you remember it!'"

I watched little Michelle anxiously as she played with the electric cord plugged into the tape recorder. Gently removing the child's hand, I asked Linda, "What was the angle of your double—were you vertical, horizontal, or what?"

"We were suspended in a looking-down position. Right after it happened, I woke up in bed, and it was very vivid in my mind. Then I fell asleep again, and when I came to in the morning, I recalled it all in the sharpest detail. The strange thing is that it was late winter at the time, yet everything seemed to be reversed. There were leaves on the trees and the water was clear, not iced over. While we were floating in the air, Gigi said that it was summer."

"How did you get out of your body?" I asked.

"I went out through the top of my head. Like I was sucked out—a suction effect. It took about five minutes before I was free, and I was floating over the lake for fifteen minutes."

At this point Michelle spilled a glass of water on the tape recorder. I smiled and winced at the same time while Linda rushed into the kitchen and came back with a paper towel. She wiped the machine carefully. No damage done.

That crisis past, Linda talked about her oldest girl, twelve-year-old Tacey. Although Linda had never been able to project at will, Tacey could go out of her body anywhere at any time. To her it was a natural process and she wondered why adults made such a fuss about it.

Linda and Tacey were in a meditation class, and one night the teacher showed the group how to project. She told them to stretch out on their cots and imagine that their foreheads were blank screens. Linda, concentrating on her forehead, got a light, floaty feeling. Her body began to tingle and grow rigid and she gradually lost consciousness of every part of herself except her head, then felt herself being pulled out through her forehead. The upper half of her double went out three feet and stopped.

Partially projected, she felt a strange presence near. She looked over and saw a man standing there and smiling, a complete stranger. He was bald and wearing "some kind of funny draping." Frightened, Linda slammed back into her body, returning as she had left, through the forehead. Tacey was speaking to her: "Mother mother, I went out and I saw a man there!"

The teacher had seen both Linda and Tacey go out of their bodies.

One of Linda's OOBEs was generated by mental stress. Linda is divorced from her first husband, Tacey's father, and the child is frequently troubled by this. One night Tacey was so upset that Linda also became upset and couldn't fall asleep. Finally she began to doze. The bed started to rock violently, Linda began to spin around, and she felt the covers moving across her body.

Someone or something grabbed her ankles, pulling her to her feet, her legs thrashing about as she rose. But when she opened her eyes, she saw her astral legs moving, not her physical ones. Then she was suddenly gone, taken to a strange place where there were many strange people. She was shown a machine with numbers and told that when a child is born, it has several numbers tattooed on its stomach—a birth number, a draft number, a death number, and many more. Then she was whisked back to her sleeping body.

As the experience of Kevin Lampro, Diana Marble, and so many others have shown, the projector does not always glimpse the real world but sometimes perceives symbolic pictures that have a deep meaning for him. Linda's concern about Tacey seemed to generate this unusual OOBE with its Kafkalike setting. She may have dramatized a feeling that circumstances are sometimes beyond one's control. We are helpless against fate, and the numbers tattooed on our bodies may mark our destinies.

A certain tension had crept into Linda's voice as she told this story, but now she stopped and smiled. She couldn't be somber long.

"I suppose I should tell you about the lasagna."

Michelle, a bit bored, slipped off my lap and went into the kitchen. Another daughter, Jayme, came through the front door and greeted her mother, then joined her father in the kitchen as he was getting beer out of the refrigerator.

"One evening," Linda went on, "we had a dinner date with Joe's aunt in Flushing, Long Island. Actually, I didn't feel like going. I was very tired after working all day, and I took a bath, then lay down on the couch to rest. I began to get that light feeling and I said to myself, 'Oh not now, please. I must get to Flushing. I have no time to leave my body.'

"Well, to my surprise I found myself in my aunt's apartment, getting a preview of the dinner. But what a change since my last visit! When I was there before, the wallpaper had been painted over and looked horrible. Now all the walls had beautiful new black-and-white paper. And instead of the crummy old light, there was a gorgeous new chandelier. Quite a decorating job, I thought —and that's when I smelled the lasagna."

"You could actually smell when you were in your second body?"

"Yes, and it was coming from the kitchen. I went in there and saw Joe's aunt and cousin bending over the stove."

I made a quick note: "Sense of smell operating. This is unusual —mention it in chapter on sense impressions during OOBEs."

Linda continued: "I looked inside the glass door of the oven and saw a tray of lasagna inside, and what a wonderful aroma was coming out! Well, that was the end of my scouting trip. Back I went—in a flash—to my body relaxing on the couch in New Brunswick. I slipped right back in—through my feet this time. My head went in first, then the rest of me."

Now more alert and refreshed, Linda told Joe that she had just been over to his aunt's and that they would have lasagna for dinner. Joe was accustomed to Linda's astral trips, but this he would not believe. His aunt never served lasagna to guests—never —always a roast and potatoes. Linda repeated firmly that she had seen and smelled lasagna. She told him about the new wallpaper and the crystal chandelier, but he was still doubtful.

Linda smiled as she spoke into the mike of the cassette recorder.

"This was one OOBE I could prove. The moment we walked into his aunt's apartment, Joe stopped and gawked at the new wallpaper and chandelier, just as I had seen the room in my double. Yes, his aunt said, she had had a decorator come in and she thought that Joe would be surprised. We had highballs, then sat down for dinner. Joe still looked a little dazed but he hadn't given up. He had a wait-and-see expression on his face.

"The next moment he grinned triumphantly at me as his cousin came out of the kitchen carrying a steaming tray of chicken and string beans. And then his aunt followed with another tray—the lasagna."

This OOBE was unusual in other ways. Linda had left her body while lying on her stomach, her double going out through the lower part of her back. I asked if she knew why.

"Yes, I often have trouble with my back. It is one of my weak spots. I can also go out through any one of the chakras."

The "chakras" are names given by yogis to centers along the spine that when stimulated awaken the hidden powers of mind and soul. During meditation Linda often experienced a release of energy from one or more of these centers.

How did Linda feel about her ability to project? Was she eager to develop it, to reach the point where she could do it at will, as Muldoon and others had done?

"No, I prefer to leave it alone." Like Ed Corsino, Diana Marble, and other projectors, she thought that OOBEs had a humanitarian purpose. "It should only be done at special times, when someone needs your help. Like psychic healing. Otherwise I am happy just to have it happen when it does. I don't care to go out unless I am called."

The tape ran out, and I put the mike and cord back in their cubbyholes in the cassette recorder. Joe and the other couple were talking and drinking beer in the background. Michelle, seeing me get ready to leave, came over and wrapped her arms around my leg, announcing that she was going home with me. She was quite insistent about it until her attention was diverted by a candy bar. I patted her vaguely on the head and said good night to the adults.

For Linda White an out-of-body experience is just another happening in the life of a young mother whose day is filled with interesting events. Sometimes she is amused by her OOBEs, sometimes they are colorful and exciting, and on rare occasions she finds special meaning in their symbolism. But she firmly believes that no one should make an effort to project. If it happens, just let it happen.

"I Struggled for My Life"

Laura Randall is one of those persons of either sex who will climb a mountain just because it is there. She has climbed many mountains in Italy, one of them at Assisi where she visited the shrine of St. Francis. Physically active and loving the out-of-doors, she also meditates and has studied many religions and philosophies, including Hinduism and Buddhism. Her greatest passion is to sing. She has sung with several opera companies in America and Europe and has been continuing her musical education in France and Italy. She is an accomplished actress and, when she has time, does considerable writing.

For Laura, being an artist means more than just performing on the stage or in the concert hall. It means living life to its fullest, being totally involved in every experience and finding significance in it, whether it is studying the texture of a rose in a garden or stopping to play ball with a youngster in the yard of an Italian home. She sees tenderness and pathos, drama and humor, all around her.

Laura is highly psychic, and we have done many successful ESP experiments, with myself as sender of the psychic message and her as receiver. But she feels that psychic experiences, OOBEs or others, should not be ends in themselves but should point the way to deeper truths, truths of the spirit. She has many times had that most spiritual of dreams, seeing a man in white robes.

In front of me is a letter in which Laura describes the most dramatic out-of-body experience of her life:

It happened the second night I was in Vienna. I woke up in the middle of the night and found myself in a mass of energy. I wasn't in my body—I was up by the ceiling and I looked down and saw my body on the bed. I remember thinking that I was exactly at the point between life and death. I remember being aware that when we die there is no such thing as rich or poor because as we come to God we have no material self—all that vanishes. I remember thinking that it is not of our choosing if we live or die, but there is a force that gives life to us or takes it away. I understood the God without—in contrast to the God within.

I recall struggling as never before in my life as I struggled for my life. I was aware how simple it was to resist the temptations of this world, for in this struggle I knew that we have such a power within us that has not the slightest inkling of its strength, for we tap perhaps one millionth of it. I remember crying from the depths of my soul—oh how deep it was—begging God to let me live, for I had not yet fulfilled my place in this world. And in these tears I knew that we are all God's children.

Finally after this great struggle, I went back into my body, but I was paralyzed. I understood what one feels when he has a stroke. I could not move but then, finally, I began to have feeling in my limbs.

Herb, I think I did experience that point between life and death. I surely felt in contact with my Maker.

Yes, we are scarcely aware of the great potential that is in us—mental, artistic, spiritual. For if each of us has a second body that can soar through time and space, we may also have the power to transcend in other ways the limited abilities of the physical body.

For Laura Randall the paranormal experience, the out-of-body flight is a dramatic, an artistic, a spiritual event. It may be the point between life and death, but it is also a unifying force that erases the boundary line between them.

Music as a Point of Contact

Flo Thompson accepts her second body calmly, as she does her physical body. She believes that going out of the body is just another experience, like being in it, but it can also be a deeply personal experience.

Flo was fortunate to grow up in a family where the unusual was taken for granted. Her father talked to ghosts. Her mother once saw Flo's astral body on the stairway. Flo's oldest boy, Brad, was watching television one day when a vase floated off the top of the set and descended to the floor. Even Ginger, the family dog, has a different way of wagging his tail—it goes around in a circle.

This may sound like an eccentric family in New York's Greenwich Village, but they are actually part of what is called "Middle America." Flo lives with her husband and three children in Xenia, Ohio, while her mother and father, recently deceased, lived in Pennsylvania. Paranormal events can happen anywhere at anytime to anyone.

Flo is a very attractive young woman with the kind of youthful enthusiasm I also found in Linda White and Laura Randall. Like the other two, she enjoys being with people but must also spend much time with herself, meditating and reflecting. Like Laura Randall, she loves flowers, the sea, and the mountains and spends solitary hours on the beach, watching the waves and thinking, becoming one with nature. All three women are in touch with life, but they look forward to their mystical moments.

Flo and I first met in the summer of 1972, when I was the guest on a network television show that originated in Dayton, Ohio. She was in the studio audience. When I started to do this book, I wrote to her and we arranged to meet in her parents' home near Harrisburg, Pennsylvania. Her father, who had been in the hospital with a serious illness, was a talented musician and music teacher and played several instruments. He and Flo shared many psychic experiences when she was growing up. Flo's mother was a bit skeptical but willing to admit that strange things did happen to the psychic members of her family.

Flo had her first OOBE when she was three years old. While walking down the stairs in her house, she was conscious of placing her physical foot only on the first and last step, floating above her body the rest of the way. She did this many times when she was alone, but her three-year-old mind reasoned that it might not be socially acceptable behavior. When her mother and father were with her, she stayed in her body and walked all the way down.

I asked Flo if she had had any problems at the age of three that might be connected with leaving her body, but she couldn't remember any. Nor could her mother or father, who were sitting across the room as Flo spoke into the tape recorder. To three- and four-year-old children, floating above one's body while lying in bed or rising above it when walking down the steps seems perfectly natural. Only grownups, who no longer believe in miracles, think it can't happen or look for deep-seated psychological motivations.

Flo had a normal, happy childhood. Inspired by her father's love for music, she learned to play the piano and the clarinet. Music is a very important part of her life today. She uses it as a "point of contact" in going out of her body.

When she was about twenty, strange things began to happen again. One day she was out in the yard, hanging clothes and humming to herself, when flaming words appeared before her, announcing a minor calamity: THE CLOTHESLINE IS GOING TO BREAK. She thought, "Well, isn't that silly." The next moment the clothesline broke, and her garments scattered over the grass.

More incidents were announced by banner headlines. She was reading the newspaper one day when two-year-old Brad, her first-born, toddled in. Block red letters flashed over the newspaper: BRAD IS GOING TO SMASH HIS FINGER IN THE DOOR. The next moment Brad smashed his finger in the door.

Flo didn't like the idea of headlines in red appearing in front of her with their predictions of disaster. She read books on the paranormal and theorized that this was just a trick played on her by her psychic sense to call attention to itself. Once she understood this, the red letters never came back. Now she just gets feelings that things are going to happen. And they happen.

The psychic world has its humor, too. Early one morning about 2 A.M., the washing machine in the basement started up and went through the whole wash-spin-dry cycle. No one was near it. The next night it started again at the same time and went through the cycle again. And again the next night.

How silly can a washing machine be? Flo, assuming that polter-geists or other mischievous entities were at work, left a polite note on the machine, pointing out that the middle of the night was no time to start up a washing machine, especially when no clothes were in it. The nocturnal washings continued, then finally stopped.

When her children began to arrive, Flo had more out-of-body experiences. Stress was a factor in two of the cases. Giving birth to her second child, Robin, was not easy. Unconscious from the an-esthetic, she found herself floating above the delivery table. She knew something was wrong. She could see the doctor and nurse working frantically and heard their words as if in an echo chamber. She went back into her body and heard herself cry out, "Someone please help my baby." When the baby was about six weeks old, Flo had a recurring dream in which she saw everything that had hap-pened and could hear what the doctor was saying.

Once when her husband Jack was out of town, Flo became seri-ously ill with pneumonia. Her neighbor, a nurse, spent the night with her. During the night, after hours of painful coughing, she began to have difficulty breathing. Her breath grew shorter and shorter. Suddenly her double was at the ceiling in a corner of the room, watching her neighbor bending over her physical body.

Flo felt calm now, no discomfort, no pain. She had no sense of identity with that poor creature lying on the bed gasping for air. Whatever was happening to that person did not involve the "I" who was floating in the corner of the room. She watched the nurse talk to her physical body and press a cup of coffee to her lips. Her astral lips felt the warmth of the liquid and the next moment she was back in bed drinking the coffee.

Flo told me that she had floated off the bed through the top of her head. Whenever OOBEs happened to her accidentally, it was an easy separation, with no period of transition. When she consciously tried to get out, it was more difficult—she could feel her second body tugging and pulling. During meditation she had many partial projections of this kind, just as Linda White had a partial projection in her meditation class.

The high point of Flo's psychic experiences came in the spring of 1972, when she traveled astrally from her home in Xenia to her parents' home 375 miles away. She had attempted several times to make this "trip." Sometimes she thought she had been to Harrisburg and back, but was never sure. She didn't tell her parents what she was trying to do because she wanted confirmation from them first. The confirmation didn't come—until one night in March 1972.

Flo had gone to bed about 1 A.M. determined to try again. She was wide awake. First she had to establish her "point of contact" to her mother and father—music. She turned on the radio and listened to an orchestra playing. As she relaxed, she began to concentrate. She pictured herself traveling from Ohio to Pennsylvania, arriving in front of her parents' house, going up the steps to the porch, passing through the door and into the living-room, walking up the stairs.

At one-thirty her mother heard the steps squeaking. She recognized the sound from the days when Flo and her sister were little girls. It had to be one girl or the other. But Flo was in Ohio and her sister was with her own family in Virginia. She looked up the stairway and saw Flo, as solid a figure as in her physical body, wearing her familiar "nightie." Suddenly Flo was gone.

Flo had started to project about one-fifteen. She heard the radio music all the way to Pennsylvania, but when she came back at one thirty-five to her bed in Xenia, a different tune was playing. Somehow she had lost the transition between the tune the orchestra was playing when she started her astral journey and the tune she heard twenty minutes later.

Flo was sure that she had been to Harrisburg. She fell asleep wonderfully relaxed, always the case when she went out of her body. In the morning her mother called and said she had seen Flo on the stairs about one-thirty, wearing her nightdress.

Like Linda White and Laura Randall, Flo Thompson sees no reason to spend time and effort trying to get out of her body. There are other priorities in her life. She wishes above all to love and help her family and to grow spiritually through meditation and prayer. If OOBEs just happen and she can astrally visit her relatives, that is enough for her.

Her family is most important to her, the psychic part incidental. When I was interviewing her in Harrisburg, she called her father "Daddy" and her affection when she said it was unmistakable. She showed me a poem she had written, hanging in its frame on the living-room wall. It was a poem of love for her mother—simple, conventional, and straight from the heart. Laura Randall writes poetry, too, poetry of a very high quality that has been published. It is more literary, yet simple, too, in its message.

I didn't ask Linda White if she wrote poetry. It doesn't matter. Each of the three young women is a poet in living and each moves as freely and meaningfully in the body as outside of it.

Chapter 23

The Dramatic Projections of Dorie and Agnes

"When I go out of my body, I feel good. I enjoy it. It's like having a high without being high."

Dorie Lawrence was sitting next to me in the front seat of my Oldsmobile, speaking into the mike of my cassette recorder. I had driven out to central New Jersey on a hot summer day, but when I turned into the town of Belmar, cool, refreshing breezes greeted me from the lake that borders the town. I had planned to meet Dorie in the antique store where she runs a small bookshop in the rear. I arrived just as the store was closing, and we had to talk in the car. It was not unpleasant. From time to time voices and laughter tinkled as people walked by.

Did she get that "high" feeling the first time she went out?

"No, because I didn't know what was happening, and I was really scared. I had gone to bed, but I wasn't sleeping, just thinking about a lot of things, when I felt my body swell up like a balloon. It wasn't my physical body, of course, it was my astral trying to get out, but I didn't know it at the time. My fingertips felt strange—a very, very fine feeling as if they were drawn out almost to infinity. My teeth and mouth seemed to be very big, but they also had that feeling of fineness—like very thin wires. I felt as though a heavy weight or pressure was pushing down on my body.

"I started to pray, but the more I prayed, the stronger it got. Then all of a sudden I was out of my body, above it, feeling very light."

Dorie, a woman in her forties, is a bit tense and speaks in decisive, clipped tones. Like many other astral projectors, she radiates honesty and integrity. She gave me the precise details of her experience.

The mechanics of it were similar to those of other OOBEs. Her double rose in the horizontal position and remained suspended three feet above her physical body. In later projections she went out slowly through her feet. Occasionally, she projects in an instant and finds herself floating above the bed, looking down on her physical body. She never stays out very long, but she knows without question that she is in another body. Sometimes her physical body stiffens into catalepsy, other times not.

Like so many other projectors, Dorie got over her first fear and now enjoys going out of her body—"a high without being high." Could she describe her second body? Yes, it is exactly like her physical body, a duplicate, with only one difference—sometimes it is taller than her physical body. Unlike Dr. Wiltse, however, and other projectors who compensate for an undersized frame with a larger astral one, Dorie is blessed with a full, attractive figure. The taller double is a symbol of her elation during an OOBE—she feels "high" from going up "high" and has that "ten-foot-tall feeling."

The most dramatic of Dorie's OOBEs occurred during an operation.

"It was on December 15, 1971, at the Wickersham Hospital in New York City. The surgeon was an orthopedist who has an office on Fifth Avenue. Do you want his name?"

Dorie wanted me to know every detail—the date, the place, exactly how she felt at every moment, from the time she was wheeled into the operating room until she woke up in the recovery room.

"Although I was physically unconscious from the anesthetic, I was very much awake in my subconscious. I was standing there in my double, watching the doctors bending over my body. The doctor's assistant asked how long the operation would take. The surgeon reassured him: 'It's a minor operation, just a matter of opening up the back and pulling the ligaments together.'"

The operation began. Dorie watched the doctor as he very carefully and precisely probed her exposed spine. She watched with fascination but without fear. She had perfect confidence in the doctor's ability to restore her to maximum efficiency. But she knew something that the doctors didn't know. Before the operation she had told her husband: "Vic, the doctor will find something else and he'll have to dig a lot deeper than he thinks."

The surgeon stopped for a moment, frowning.

"I'm afraid we're going to have to go deeper. I see something on the lung. Holy smoke, it's a tumor!"

The double of Dorie Lawrence looked on calmly as the knife dug more deeply into her back. There was a big tumor on her lung —and seven small tumors around it. Working with extreme care, the surgeon removed them. In her astral body Dorie felt no pain.

Suddenly she saw her physical body thrashing around on the operating table.

"I was fighting, my body was fighting, trying to take the instrument out of the doctor's hands. I was amazed because I—that is, my double—was not afraid. And yet my arms were flailing and my body was writhing on the table."

In most OOBEs the physical body is passive while the double goes about its business. If the sleeping or relaxing body is disturbed, the double may rejoin it or merely make the same movements and gestures until it is quiet again. This was an offbeat astral happening, however—a completely calm double and a violently struggling physical body, reminiscent of the officer whose double watched his panicstricken physical body rolling on the ground (see Chapter 14). The second body, particularly in its soul body aspect, is often more alert in thought and sharper in perception than the physical, which is more animal-like in its reactions. At this point there were two Dorie Lawrences, one very much superior to the other.

But the double cannot stay emotionally divorced for very long. Suddenly Dorie was back in her struggling body.

"They wheeled me into the recovery room, holding me down while I thrashed around. I don't know why I was so frightened."

Dorie finally fell asleep. When she woke up, she knew the operation had been a success and she would be all right. She remembered being out of her body and decided that when the doctor came in to see her, she would repeat word for word what he had said when she was supposed to be unconscious.

When the doctor visited Dorie the next day, she said, "Doctor, I am going to tell you something. I'm going to repeat everything you said in the operating room. From the vertebrae you had to cut deeper into the lung because you found some tumors growing."

The doctor turned white and left the room without saying a word. His reaction was unusual. In other cases when a patient tells the doctor that she observed everything that happened during an operation, the doctor might show surprise and disbelief, but he wouldn't push it abruptly out of his mind.

Had this happened to Dorie's doctor before—did other patients of his go out of their bodies and watch their own operations? As Dr. Sava wrote (see Chapter 16), no surgeon likes to feel that he is cutting into a patient's body while the patient herself is standing at his elbow, checking every move. If this happens several times to the same doctor, he might begin to question his own sanity.

Dorie paused as a siren screamed in the distance. When the noise had died down, I asked her if she had seen the connecting cord during her hospital projection.

"Yes, it was like a very thin silver wire. It started at the head of my physical body, ran down the length of the body, then up the length of my double."

Could she go out of her body at will? No, she could not project experimentally. It just had to happen. It can happen to her anywhere and at anytime. She doesn't have to be lying in bed. Sometimes, in a flash, she finds herself far away, often several thousand miles distant.

Once she was having dinner with a friend in a New York City restaurant when suddenly she was in England, in the apartment of her friend's mother. She had never been in England and did not know the lady. She told her friend what she saw—what her friend's mother looked like, how she was dressed, the way her hair was set, how the apartment was laid out, the location of the furniture. Her friend verified everything she said. Dorie even went back in time and saw the funeral of her friend's father. She described his appearance and the coffin in which his body lay.

Sometimes, Dorie told me, she might just be dozing when she projected to these far-off places.

"Could it be your imagination?" I wondered.

"No." Her answer came out crisply, decisively. "It is not my imagination. Once I found myself in England, in London. I knew it was London because I saw the clock—Big Ben. It was about two A.M. in New Jersey but there people were walking in the street. It would have been about eight A.M. in London. I was floating over the street. In another projection I visited a temple. I don't know where it was—it wasn't an oriental country—and I saw masses of people filing in."

What does her second body wear? When she goes out late at night, is she dressed for visiting or in her nightclothes?

"No, I wear the same clothing I would wear during the day." She smiled. "I get undressed when I go to bed but my astral body doesn't." The colors of her clothes are not very vivid to her, but she knows she is dressed for an astral trip.

Like other psychics, Dorie meditates, not in a group but by herself. She is an ordained minister of the Church of Ageless Wisdom. She is creative. She has danced professionally and taught dancing. She loves music and plays the piano.

"And when I play piano," she said with emphasis, "I put my feelings into the music. That's the way it should be."

Most projectors, most psychics have strong feelings. And Dorie is unquestionably a psychic. She is also a medium and gives readings to those who wish to communicate with the dead. Spirits contact her with their messages. She won't give the message unless it is very clear and detailed. That is her nature.

"I won't piddle around with initials, like other mediums do. That is ridiculous. I must give complete, clear information—names, dates, places."

Dorie comes from a psychic family. Her grandmother was psychic, also her mother. But the best psychic in her family was Aunt Mary. I looked at the business card Dorie had given me: "Aunt Mary's Bookshop."

She nodded.

"Yes, it's named after her. She was always helping people with her psychic powers. And she told me that it was the path I would eventually follow."

I looked over at the antique shop that also housed Dorie's books on the mystical and the occult. The store had been a railroad station that was cleaned and scrubbed and converted into a handsome building of natural stone with a black-shingled sloping roof. Everything in the shop was bright and fresh-looking—spacious aisles and tables with their objets d'art and Dorie's bookcases in the rear.

Dorie loves her bookshop. A good deal of her business day is spent just listening to people's troubles. ("Except on Saturday, when I have to do my bookkeeping.") She won't sell a book to a customer who is not yet ready for it. Sometimes she impulsively gives a book away if she thinks it will help someone.

Aunt Mary's connection with the shop is an example of those strange coincidences in time when the psychic forces are at work—what psychiatrist Carl Jung would call "synchronicity." Dorie never thought that she would be in the bookshop business. The previous owner of the shop had come to her because she felt psychically that Dorie was the one who should have it. The purchase price was unusually low, and Dorie knew the money would be there when she needed it. All true psychics and mystics feel that way about money.

Aunt Mary, who had predicted that Dorie would follow the psychic path, died on May 31, 1972. Dorie took over the shop the next day.

Dorie was pensive for the first time in our interview as she looked off into the distance.

"Wherever my aunt is, I am sure she is sitting back and saying, 'I told you so. Eventually you're going to do what you have to do.'"

In the end, everyone does what he has to do, psychics or non-psychics. I looked at the card once more. Dorie Lawrence—psychic, medium, astral traveler—had to buy an occult bookshop and call it "Aunt Mary's Bookshop."

It was also coincidence that I should interview Agnes Adamczyk in her Perth Amboy, New Jersey, apartment on the same day I saw Dorie Lawrence. Both women are psychics. Both have five children. Both have had spinal operations and went out of their body during surgery. Mrs. Adamczyk's OOBE was quite unusual, however, in that she experienced her projection two weeks after the operation was performed. But everything she saw was exactly as it had been during the operation, as though it had been filmed at the time and played back later.

"It was the only out-of-body experience in my life, but it was a real good one," Agnes told me. In 1958, when she was thirty-four years old, she was dying from spinal cancer. She weighed only sixty pounds. She was in constant pain and frequently passed out. The doctor told her that he might as well operate, but even then it was one chance in a million.

It was touch-and-go all through the operation. The surgeon removed the cancerous bones from her back and inserted four replacements from a bone bank. After the operation she was paralyzed from the hips down. She lay in bed for two weeks, without sensation in the lower part of her body and without hope. On the fifteenth day following surgery the doctor came into her room and said that he had done his best, but the prognosis was poor. They would try to make her comfortable.

She accepted his verdict calmly. Mrs. Adamczyk had faced death before when she was a girl in Germany during World War II. Bombs from American and British planes kept dropping on Berlin, and once she stayed in an air raid shelter for two weeks. Of the two hundred and fifty persons in the shelter, only five came out alive. Agnes Adamczyk was one of the five.

After the doctor left the room, she began to doze off. The room faded away and she was once more on the operating table. A figure stood near—a man in a white robe with long sleeves and a heavy silver belt around his waist. He had beautiful brown eyes and long reddish brown hair down to his shoulders. He smiled at her—a tender, gentle smile.

"Did you know who he was?" I asked.

Mrs. Adamczyk smiled and said quietly, "Yes, it was Jesus Christ."

In her vision the medical personnel were gathered around her emaciated body, now mercifully unconscious from the anesthetic. The surgeon had not yet arrived, although she had been told that he would be waiting in the operating room when they wheeled her in. Now he came in and picked up his knife, preparing to cut. She was suddenly afraid that he might sever the spinal cord.

The figure of Jesus bent over her body and drew out her astral self, cradling her double in his arms. He stepped backwards but she pleaded, "Please be careful. You'll rip the silver cord between my two bodies." Agnes did not consciously know but she sensed that when the cord is severed, death follows.

Jesus smiled at her reassuringly.

"I'm here," he said. "Don't worry."

She lived through the whole operation again as she watched it from outside her body. She felt excruciating pain, she saw and felt the perspiration running down her back. She watched the surgeon work silently on the muscles at the base of the spine, carefully avoiding the complex of delicate nerves that must not be cut. She heard the comments of the doctor and his assistants. She took special note of the gown and mask the surgeon was wearing.

At last it was over. Smiling, Jesus stepped forward and gently placed her double back in her body. The silver cord had not been ripped, just as the nerves had not been touched. She was wheeled back into the recovery room.

Now, fifteen days later, she woke up from her dream or vision or whatever one might wish to call it, and felt strangely different. It was as though she had to go through the operation again and make it come out right this time. Something was tingling in her hips and legs. Pain, a joyous kind of pain. She knew that her life had turned around for her.

The doctor walked into the room later and was surprised at her bright smile.

"It was beautiful!"

"What was beautiful?" asked the doctor.

"The operation."

The doctor was puzzled.

"But the operation was two weeks ago." He looked sharply at her. "You feel different, don't you?"

"Yes, I have a lot of pain now. Pain all the way down. It's beautiful."

The doctor stared at her in amazement.

"But you were paralyzed for fourteen days. And now you have feeling there. It's—it's beautiful!"

Agnes told the doctor how Jesus had come to her during the operation and taken her double out of the physical body. The doctor was skeptical. But no matter, the important thing was that she was going to recover. Still, it was very strange that she should dream about the operation two weeks later and think that she had just gone through it.

Mrs. Adamczyk told the doctor all that had happened during the surgery, all the words that had passed between him and the nurse. She added other details: before she was given the anesthetic, they had promised her that the surgeon would be there in the operating room when they took her in. But in her second body she saw that he had not yet arrived.

The doctor admitted this was true, but how could she possibly know? She was unconscious.

"No, doctor, I was unconscious in my physical body but not in the one that counts—my double. And when you did come into the operating room, you wore a white gown and a green mask."

Yes, he usually wore a matching outfit during surgery—a white smock with a white mask or a green smock with a green mask. This time, after he had put on his smock, all he could find was a green mask.

What would be the odds against Mrs. Adamczyk's choosing the right combination of gown and mask? Quite high, when we consider that it was the surgeon's custom usually to wear a matching outfit.

The doctor didn't like this kind of talk. A human being has only one body, not two, and he could name every part of it from head to toe. And when a patient is given a general anesthetic, there is no way on earth she can know what is going on.

The doctor left. The pastor came in to comfort Mrs. Adamczyk and found that Jesus had got there ahead of him. He didn't care for that kind of "double" talk either. (Mrs. Adamczyk could have pointed out that St. Paul had said there was a second body.) He insisted that someone must have told her all about the details of the operation, including the white gown and the green mask. Agnes said rather drily that she didn't think the nurse had come into the recovery room to tell her what the doctor had been wearing during the operation.

Did Mrs. Adamczyk have an authentic OOBE? We know that astral projectors have sometimes gone back into the past and witnessed scenes that have already taken place. Agnes not only saw but experienced her own operation two weeks after she had been in surgery and gave clairvoyant evidence that she knew exactly what had happened, although her physical body was unconscious. Another curious distortion of time during an OOBE.

Was Jesus Christ actually present, as Agnes fervently believed he was? Jesus was a symbol of hope and love for her. It matters not whether the actual Jesus was there or it was the spirit of Jesus; the symbols, including the white robe, are unmistakable. There also may have been a psychological factor in her fear that Jesus would rip the silver cord. The cord may on one level have represented the nerves in her back.

Like Dorie Lawrence, Agnes Adamczyk gives psychic readings. She has also had many premonitions and once saved her husband's life when she warned him to drive with extreme care on a trip to Ohio. While he was on the Pennsylvania Turnpike, a drunken driver came down the wrong side of the road and hit his car head on. Just before the collision he remembered his wife's warning and threw himself flat across the seat. He came out of the accident without a scratch.

Mrs. Adamczyk gave me a reading and told me that I, too, faced danger on the road in the next two weeks. On my way home that day my car overheated, someone threw a rock at it, and a passing truck spattered the windshield with loose gravel. When I got home, I parked the car and didn't touch it for two weeks.

Yes, Agnes Adamczyk had just one OOBE in her life, but it was a "real good one." Not only did it save her life but it was perhaps her most profound spiritual experience.

Chapter 24

Conversation with a Dead Philosopher

In the last few chapters we have listened to the out-of-body stories of children, teenagers, young women, and older women. Let us turn now to the men, among them psychics who have trained themselves to go out of their body at will. Two men who have been subjects of experiments at the American Society for Psychical Research (ASPR) have spoken into my tape recorder—Elwood Babbitt and Alex Tanous. Each is a remarkable psychic in his own way, yet each has a totally different personality and way of life and a different psychic style. Both live in New England, Babbitt in Wendell Depot, Massachusetts, and Tanous in Portland, Maine.

It was an executive of the publishing firm of Simon and Schuster, Bea Moore, who first told me about Babbitt and the man who arranges interviews for him, Charles Hapgood, a retired professor of history. Professor Hapgood invited me to visit Babbitt and discuss out-of-body travel with him. Hapgood gave me little briefing by mail except to state that Babbitt stressed the spiritual approach to astral projection.

One afternoon late in September 1973 I drove up in front of Mary Alden's Restaurant in Erving, Massachusetts, where Babbitt and Hapgood were waiting in Elwood's pickup truck. I followed them for four miles down a narrow dirt road flanked by very tall pine trees, the truck bouncing in front of me while my '60 Oldsmobile shimmied on the uneven surface. Finally we came to a large circular clearing in the forest with a house in the middle and were greeted enthusiastically by Babbitt's three children, several large dogs, a few horses, and a dark brown heifer named Chocolate, who mooed at me from her stall.

Many young people, friends of the family, were laughing and talking in the house. Mrs. Babbitt smiled at me from the kitchen, where she was making banana pancakes. It was a warm, unpretentious household, though far from an affluent one.

The two men took me into a small room that serves as Babbitt's office, then both Professor Hapgood and I set up our tape recorders, while Babbitt sat behind his desk. Elwood, a lean man of about forty-five, spoke softly and smiled as we talked about the "fly-in" experiments at the ASPR. In these experiments, which are discussed in more detail in a later chapter, Elwood projected his consciousness from Wendell Depot to the ASPR offices in New York City and tried to identify objects on a table. He had never seen the ASPR office and had no idea what he would find there.

I asked Babbitt if he was aware of traveling in space during the experimental projections.

"No, it was just a matter of turning my awareness on to the experience they wanted and having it projected right in front of me." A clinical psychologist had once said that Elwood could "jump out of his skin" into various dimensions of the spirit. Space and time ceased to exist for him.

How did he prepare for the experiment?

"I projected three times. The first two I went into trance, but the last time I stayed conscious and just willed myself to see the table. Actually, I could be talking to you and doing my other work spiritually at the same time." Elwood paused. "I don't have the education to analyze it or get into an intelligent rap about it. You should talk with Dr. Fisher, who is a scholar and can explain it better than I can."

Through the window I saw a tan mare whose tail was swishing across her rear. To one accustomed to city noises and pressures, the country atmosphere had a soothing, almost hypnotic effect.

Who, I asked, was Dr. Fisher? Hapgood explained that Elwood

was a medium and Dr. Fisher was the spirit control who took over his body when he went into a trance state. Every day people in the area came for spiritual readings, but it was actually Dr. Fisher who gave the readings. Fisher claimed that he had been a teacher and philosopher who lived in the early nineteenth century. While the dead philosopher occupied Babbitt's physical organism and spoke with his vocal cords, Babbitt would travel in his double. He could go anywhere he chose and had often gone back in time and heard such famous figures of history as Socrates and Pontius Pilate.

"I just turn on the spiritual force," Babbitt explained. "It's like turning on a live cosmic vacuum cleaner. My energy is sucked away, and the other entity takes my body over. Dr. Fisher uses my body as a kind of telephone."

Elwood needed a few minutes to go fully into his trance. While he sat with his eyes closed, Professor Hapgood told me about Babbitt's projection to the United States Supreme Court in Washington when the Court was hearing arguments for and against setting off an atomic blast on the island of Amchitka. Hapgood belonged to an environmental group that had asked the Court to forbid the testing. Babbitt willed himself in front of the high bench on Saturday morning, November 6, 1971, as the judges were filing in to hear the arguments.

"Elwood told me that the judges had already made up their minds, even before hearing both sides, and that the vote would be four to three in favor of permitting the nuclear explosion. Since he doesn't read newspapers or listen to the radio, he didn't know that the Court was shorthanded at the time, with two vacancies that President Nixon was trying to fill. Later we got the news that this was exactly how the Court had divided—four to three in favor of the test."

Elwood began to stir and opened his eyes, but there was a new expression on his face. The voice that spoke was deeper and more forceful, the manner more deliberate, the elaborate sentence structure reminiscent of the nineteenth century. The style was didactic, that of a teacher and abstract thinker.

"Let us look at life," said Dr. Frederick Fisher, "as the diversity of gifts to all humanity, each individual a pebble tossed into the ocean of vitality, and from that pebble radiates the vibrational circles which give force and understanding to the individual according to his or her karmic patterns . . .

"You are earth spirit. Spirit is water. Water is energy electrified by all the cosmic changes and eruptions of solar heat that give man the ability to recognize himself as truth, which is the tree of life that you in your religions teach as God. I myself am the energy of spiritual vibration, vitality, and it is with complete remembrance that I simply flow through all dimensions to the creative energy that is constantly filtering from and to the spirit of the individual encased in flesh . . ."

Dr. Fisher went on for quite awhile in this vein, and I wondered how I could introduce what now seemed to be the mundane subject of OOBEs. Finally Professor Hapgood spoke up during a slight pause and explained to Dr. Fisher why I was there. I asked the philosopher questions about the ASPR experiments—how, for example, did Elwood see the objects on the table? Hapgood had told me earlier that Elwood viewed them as colors and shapes—squares, circles, cubes, etc.—rather than as specific, man-made objects.

Dr. Karlis Osis, research director of the ASPR, had reported that because Elwood did not give the exact names of the objects on the table, he considered the experiment a failure. I discovered later, however, that in at least one of the three projections, Babbitt's results had been spectacular. (See Chapter 28.)

"All that is seen by spirit is color," said Dr. Fisher. "Entering the arena of objects, Elwood saw all shapes and sizes in relative spiritual colors, not defining material objects as you know them but rather as their shape and color only gave definition to the experiment that was in progress."

Elwood had picked up more of the mental and spiritual impressions than the physical. He also saw objects that had been on the table on previous days and ones that would appear in future experiments.

"What would specifically be the spiritual impression?" I asked. "If he saw a box, for example, would there be some quality of the box that would go beyond its physical dimensions?"

"Elwood would see it as a color, square like a material box, but like a box that is painted in scintillating etheric colors, namely, the full potential color of pure white that is the color of the spirit."

This would explain why so many projectors talk of seeing bright light and vivid colors, in either an idealized or a familiar setting, especially when the double has more of the soul body component. Psychics I have spoken with like Babbitt who are able to project at will seem to be more completely in their spirit or soul body and further removed from physical conditions. They often see reality somewhat transformed, as though they were viewing it with spiritual rather than physical eyes. Often, too, such projectors go forward or backward in time and create a problem in parapsychology laboratories, where experiments are set up to produce exact, measurable results.

Dr. Fisher explained the difference between traveling in the spirit and in the astral or etheric body.

"Elwood does not operate from the astral where it is possible to leave the body . . . and see the objects on the table and give the terminology needed so that you would understand that he had the item correct. Astral travel, unless understood, is dangerous and can lead many persons into homes of so-called insanity, and thus I frown upon flowing in the astral to prove a point [that is, to prove there is a second body] which to my dimension is unimportant."

I would have put it more simply, but Dr. Fisher's warning was unmistakable.

"For what would you do if you were to enter the astral and you encountered a thief, a murderer, a rapist? Could you keep his vibration from intermingling with yours? This could cause possession or obsession of your finite intellect and cause you to be placed away in one of your mental hospitals. Jesus warned of the so-called demonic forces of the astral."

Demonic forces of the astral . . . I thought of Robert Monroe, who described in *Journey Out of the Body* how he had visited an astral world he called "Locale II," where reality "was composed of deepest desires and most frantic fears . . . peopled with insane or near insane, emotionally driven beings." I thought also of Robert Crookall and his theory of a "Hades" world that sometimes engulfs astral travelers.

Dr. Fisher went on: "If, however, the astral traveler understands the basic spiritual rules governing his mobile travel, it may not be dangerous."

Although Dr. Fisher did not elaborate this point, I have found that many psychics who can project at will, like Elwood Babbitt, Alex Tanous, and Eileen Garrett, bring long experience and spiritual armor to every kind of out-of-body encounter. The inescapable conclusion is that one should not attempt to will an out-of-body experience unless he is spiritually motivated and equipped to handle the forces of the unknown.

But what of the involuntary projectors, those who go out when they are ill or exhausted, dozing or dreaming, in a stressful situation? What of astral travelers who are motivated by affection for friends and relatives, by the desire to help others or to be helped?

Dr. Fisher replied: "Spirit travels extensively to replenish both body and itself. At such times the spirit is protected, for no one leaves without at least a limited protection. Each has an angel or doctor or guide constantly guarding him when he is making that trip through the material world."

Is the astral or etheric body like the physical body in appearance?

"An etheric body is an exact duplicate of your material body. But it is composed of light, rather than flesh and bone. At the moment of transition [death] you will find yourself in a stronger light, etheric light that is much finer than the density of your earth light. You will be more keenly aware of experience. Your astral plane is an exact duplicate of the one you live upon, and you will have lost only the gross body."

A question occurred to me that is examined more fully later in this book.

"Does the duplicate body at birth determine the shape and form of the physical body? Or do they just happen to come together?"

"They enter together, but there always had to be an original before there could be a fakery of anything in your world. The truth, if you wish, lies in the spiritual part . . . to duplicate a body that could react to the five material senses of the [physical] body and the world. Thus, through strong spiritual desire there was formulated through etheric force the duplicate from the original spiritual body."

I was pleased with the word "fakery." I thought of Plato and his doctrine that everything we see is merely the shadow of an enduring idea.

What of the Theosophical belief that each individual has seven bodies, from the dense physical body to the immaterial spiritual body? Three basic bodies were enough for Dr. Fisher, each with a specific function.

"We are constantly working in trinity. You deal with the trinity of life which you know in your religions as the Father, Son, and Holy Ghost. But we speak of the soul, the body, and the spirit."

To Dr. Fisher the out-of-body phenomenon is only a small piece of the universal fabric. Far more important is the goal of life, the reason for our being here.

"The greatest crisis of the day on your planet is fear rather than the true expression of love, which is compassion, or the sincere belief that all lives and breathes in cosmic consciousness and not in the limitations of oxygen on your planet for bodily needs.

"The defeat lies with humanity in not looking within and proclaiming that spirit is omnipotent. It is humanity that seeks through technology, analysis, and rationale that defeats the very purpose of existence . . . Man, not realizing his thought potential, creeps wearily across the face of the globe searching for answers that lie within the wellspring of his own spiritual nature."

Dr. Fisher had a personal word for me.

"You are searching for a profound truth that still escapes you and shows through your various schoolings that you have encountered on your way of life."

Everyone, said Dr. Fisher, should "be himself." I replied that we keep hearing this all the time—the search for identity, the necessity of cutting through the layers of ego that have been imposed by our culture to get down to the true self. But how can one find out who he is, how can he be himself and live his life to the fullest?

"It is not to live life, young man, it is to flow with it in perfect spontaneity of the moment, and this in turn opens the doorway to awareness."

Not to *live* life, but to *flow with it* . . .

"But now the power is getting weak, and I will have to leave you."

There was silence as the body of Elwood Babbitt slept in trance, awaiting the return of the spirit. I asked Professor Hapgood questions about Dr. Fisher. Had he written any books?

"Yes, he said he had published a book in collaboration with two other authors. I haven't been able to find it, however."

This was understandable, since the book is probably out of print. Professor Hapgood would be grateful, as I would, if someone does come across an old work written in the nineteenth century by a Dr. Frederick Fisher, professor of philosophy.

Elwood Babbitt opened his eyes and smiled shyly. The interview was over, and he asked Professor Hapgood and me to join the family for dinner. The "family" included all his guests, one of them a young woman holding her eight-month-old baby, Govina.

As we sat around the large circular table and ate delicious banana pancakes, our conversation was down to earth. We laughed and joked and talked about food and children and animals. Elwood, who has been a medium since he was a child, makes little money, giving most of his time and energy to people who come for spiritual help. But in the friendly, jolly atmosphere of this home in the woods, money did not seem important.

Is Dr. Fisher a genuine spirit from the nineteenth century or just a subconscious personality of Elwood Babbitt's? This kind of question has been asked time and again of mediums, and there is no definitive answer. What is surprising is the wide gap in temperament and training between the pleasant, shy family man who left school at an early age and worked at odd jobs so that he could devote his life to helping others, and the scholarly philosopher of a hundred and fifty years ago who speaks as though addressing a seminar in metaphysics.

This difference has been noted between other mediums and their spirit controls. There were marked differences between Eileen Garrett and her control, Uvani. The simple housewife Pearl Curran was intellectually a child compared with the brilliant spirit Patience Worth who wrote poems, short stories, and novels on Mrs. Curran's Ouija board.

It is quite true that, in the Jungian sense, secondary personalities may be opposites because they fill the need of the individual to be a whole person, to experience his undeveloped sides. But where there is a great difference in education and knowledge, as between Dr. Fisher and Elwood Babbitt, how does the psychic suddenly acquire a background to which he has never been exposed?

Perhaps the most important question to ask about Dr. Fisher is whether his words ring true. What he says about OOBEs and the astral world is paralleled in the experiences of projectors and the observations of parapsychologists who have investigated the out-of-body phenomenon. The remaining chapters of this book will tend to substantiate the ideas of the dead philosopher.

Chapter 25

The Time-Traveler from Maine

Astral travelers come in all shapes and sizes, their personalities ranging over a broad spectrum from introverted types to those who are gregarious and communicative. An example of the latter is Alex Tanous, a young man of forty-seven, who radiates friendliness and enthusiasm. Tall and lean, with deep-set luminous eyes and a warm, expressive voice, he is the favorite subject of many researchers because he is co-operative as well as talented. His out-of-body experiments at the American Society for Psychical Research, which are discussed in a later chapter, promise to add considerably to our knowledge of OOBEs and how they work.

In contrast to Elwood Babbitt, who prefers to stay home and give trance readings, Tanous lectures throughout the country and makes frequent trips from his home in Portland, Maine, to the ASPR laboratory in New York City. While Babbitt gave up formal schooling to devote his time and energy to his readings, Dr. Tanous has earned several advanced degrees—in history, philosophy, and theology—and teaches these subjects along with parapsychology in both high schools and colleges. Like Babbitt and other advanced psychics, he looks for the spiritual meaning in paranormal events and practices meditation. Tanous gives readings, too, sometimes over radio and television, often by mail, frequently to members of his lecture audiences.

In November 1973 I was Tanous' weekend guest at his apartment in Portland. Like artist Ingo Swann and many others who have OOBEs, he is highly creative. I listened to recordings of several popular songs he has written, all quite melodic and original, and studied the unusual paintings hanging on the walls. I was especially impressed with one of a woman's face looking into the light, and a painting called "Christus," symbolizing the hand of God holding the hand of Christ. Without formal training in art or music, Tanous composes and draws intuitively. He believes that spirits work with him as he paints.

As we sat in the cozy living room with our tape recorders, we spent many hours discussing the fine points of Tanous' out-of-body experiences, psychic visions of the future and past, psychic healing, and psychic photography. Tanous is what I would call a "pure" psychic—not a perfect one as he would be the first to admit, but "pure" in the sense that he moves as freely in the paranormal world as he does in his physical body. Whether he is making predictions, as he has so often done on radio and in the newspapers, projecting a mental image onto a blank screen, or astrally following the trail of a missing human being or animal, he does it instantaneously, with little or no preparation. He can project while lying in bed, sitting in a chair, or taking a walk.

Psychics generally come from psychic families, and in Tanous' case, national origin also played an important role. Though he was born in the United States, his family is from Lebanon, a country where the paranormal is an accepted fact. Both parents were psychic, as are many of Tanous' seven brothers and his uncles and aunts. A Catholic upbringing combined with the Lebanese Arab strain has helped Tanous to develop both psychically and spiritually.

When Alex was eighteen months old, his parents decided to test his psychic sense. Noticing his interest in their phonograph, they would play a record, then slip it into a pile of records and run his hand down the side of the pile. Invariably he would pick out the record he had just heard. His father taught him how to develop the sensitivity in his hand so that he could not only feel the vibrations of people and objects but also learn his lessons by touch. Today he often diagnoses an illness by shaking hands with someone. The ability to absorb ideas by running his hand over the text of a book helped him to master many school subjects faster than he could do it by reading and memorizing.

Before his father died, when Alex was eleven, they often communicated through telepathy. Once when his father had gone to town, Alex sent a mental message: "Bring me bubblegum." A short time later Mr. Tanous, his eyes twinkling, walked in and handed him the bubblegum. Alex found himself communicating with other minds, too, especially that of his third-grade teacher. When she wrote fractions on the blackboard, he often gave the answers before she finished the problem. Once when she picked up a piece of chalk and began to write a poem, Alex called out the last line before she got to it.

Alex had his first out-of-body experience when he was six years old and, like Flo Thompson, it was on the stairway in his home. Standing at the top of the stairs, he could see his double, the exact replica of himself, at the bottom, making the same movements. The double was his playmate for a year and a half until he found himself going out of his body in another way. He began to go back in time and witness scenes from the past.

"Mind-Go!"

There have been many cases in this book of astral travelers going forward in time (precognition) or backward (retrocognition). Goethe saw himself as he would be eight years in the future. Agnes Adamczyk relived an operation performed two weeks earlier. Kevin Lampro wasn't sure whether his brothers were fixing their car radio before he saw them on the stairs or later. These were, however, spontaneous projections. Alex Tanous is able to project at will. He says to himself, "Mind-go!" and then may find himself in the present, past, or future at any time or place of his choosing.

Once, at a gathering of psychologists, Tanous went back to the Russian Revolution and described many of the historic scenes of 1917 as though he were watching a film. He saw the revolutionaries, the soldiers, and the Czar in the Winter Palace at Petrograd and witnessed the unfolding of many events with which he was unfamiliar. He described what he saw in broken English, as if he were a Russian translating from his native language. When Tanous visited Russia a few years later, the settings he had seen astrally looked exactly as they did in his projection.

Tanous' ability to make astral trips to the past has been put to such practical uses as locating missing persons and animals and helping the police solve crimes. He does this by psychically going back to the place where the person or object was last seen and picking up the trail, following it as far as it leads him. In one instance he located a teacher in Florida who had been thought drowned when his boat was found on Lake Champlain in New York. In another he said that a hunter who had disappeared in a swampy area in Maine was alive but some distance away. The hunter was located in Iowa.

When a young boy disappeared in Freeport, Maine, in June 1972, the police called in Tanous at the request of the boy's family. Chief Boudreau of the Freeport force believed the boy had been murdered and had four suspects in mind, but he did not reveal this information to Tanous. The chief took Tanous to the place where the boy had last been seen, between a bowling alley in front of the apartment building in which he had lived and a grocery market near the highway.

Tanous was puzzled when the psychic trail led back to the apartment house. Later, when he was driving along the road, a picture of the murderer came into his mind, and he drew a sketch of the man's face. Chief Boudreau compared the sketch with the photo of one suspect, a man who lived in the apartment building. They went to the man's apartment and found the dead body of the boy under a bed, wrapped in blankets.

The Freeport case was written up in the *National Enquirer* of March 4, 1973. In the article Chief Boudreau said that it was Tanous' sketch that made him decide to search the suspect's apartment, even though the police had no other evidence at the time.

In response to a letter I wrote to Chief Boudreau, he replied that "the facts cited in the article and the questions attributed to me are somewhere near accurate. You may quote me and print any or all parts of the article."

Tanous has received many confirming letters from people he has helped in his psychic work. One letter, from Agnes and Wilbur McGoey of Lisbon Falls, Maine, thanked him for finding their lost boxer dog, who disappeared from their backyard on November 23, 1970. While Tanous talked to them on the phone, he went back in time and told them that the dog had been picked up by three young men and taken in a northerly direction, about ten miles or less, to Bowdoin, Maine. The dog, he said, was alive and well and they would get him back. Although Tanous had never met the McGoeys, he described their house and said they lived on a north-south road.

In a letter dated December 10, 1970, the McGoeys wrote:

We now make the following statements with the greatest of pleasure:

1. We found our dog alive and well, December 7, 1970.
2. The street we live on *does* run north and south.
3. Someone had to have taken our dog to another area as she would not wander away under any conditions.
4. We found her about seven miles away in a northeasterly direction.
5. She was located, dead center, in the town of Bowdoin, Maine.
6. Our home fits the description of the house that you kept associating with the dog.

In other instances Tanous projects himself into the future, as he does when he makes predictions of world events. Two young German women visiting in Portland told Alex that they were looking for a house back home. Immediately he went to Germany and saw a house by the water, which he described to them. Later they wrote to thank him—they had found their "house by the water" and it was exactly as he had pictured it.

Since the time-space dimension as we know it does not exist on the astral plane, many of Tanous' projections give information from the past, present, and future as if they were one. A nun and her sister once approached Tanous after a lecture and told him they were worried about their brother in Germany who had just been jailed on a charge of murdering his wife. Tanous suddenly found himself on the scene in Germany, witnessing all that had happened and seeing the outcome.

"Your brother is all right," he assured them. "He will not be convicted. He did not kill his wife. He will be freed."

As Tanous had predicted, their brother was absolved of the crime.

"I Became That Woman"

Tanous sometimes sees conditions in the present, unknown to others, that give a clearer picture of the future. On the morning of October 31, 1969, a young woman named Lenore Difiore called him from Akron, Ohio, and asked him about the condition of her mother, Mrs. Mary Difiore, who was in an Akron hospital. The doctors, suspecting cancer, were about to do exploratory surgery on her right lung. While speaking with Miss Difiore, Tanous projected himself to the hospital and diagnosed her mother's ailment. In a letter to him on April 19, 1970, Miss Difiore recalled his answers to her questions and compared them with what actually happened.

Q: Is it cancer?
A: No.
   (*Correct. It wasn't cancer.*)
Q: What is it, then?
A: A type of fungus.
   (*Correct. It was a type of tubercular fungus.*)
Q: Will she be all right?
A: Yes, she will have much pain but will be fine.
   (*Correct. She had much pain and is fine.*)
Q: How long will she be in the hospital?
A: She will be in intensive care a few days but will spend only about ten days in the hospital, not longer than two weeks.
   (*Correct. She was in the intensive care unit three days and out of the hospital within ten days.*)
Q: Will they take out any of the lung?
A: Yes, but only a small section of the upper right lobe.
   (*Correct. They removed only a small section of the right lobe.*)
Q: How long will she be in the operating room?
A: Not long, less than two hours. One hour and forty-five minutes.
   (*Correct. The doctors were in surgery one hour and forty-five minutes.*)
Q: What was the cause?
A: Possibly from an old infection she was unaware of having.
   (*Possible, but it could not be medically proved. This was also the doctor's opinion.*)

Alex told me what form his astral projection took in this case: "While talking on the phone to her daughter, I went to the hospital and became that woman. My energy was in her and I saw what was wrong with her."

I asked Alex if he felt any of the pain of people whose ailments he was diagnosing or trying to cure. This happens sometimes, he said, but not in the case of the woman in the Akron hospital.

"A Great Sports Figure Will Die"

Two of Dr. Tanous' most dramatic OOBEs took place during radio interviews and can claim as witnesses not only the station personnel but also thousands of listeners. In one, the "Maine-Line" program of WGAN in Portland, a woman called the station to say that a young married woman she knew was worried about her husband, a soldier in Vietnam. Several letters had been written to him but returned to his wife, who learned that his Army unit had been involved in an explosion and there had been many casualties. The bodies of the dead soldiers could not be identified.

Tanous said, over the air, "I have to go there." In a split second he was in Vietnam hovering over the mangled bodies of the soldiers. He knew that the young woman's husband was not among them and that he was still alive but transferred to another Army post. Back at the station, he informed the older woman that her friend would soon hear from her husband.

The woman had placed the call to the station at 9:20 P.M. Three hours later her phone rang. It was the mother of her friend, who said that her daughter had just heard from her husband—he was well and had been transferred to another Army post. Tanous received a confirming letter from the woman who had called station WGAN.

Tanous had another dramatic OOBE while he was being interviewed on the "Sports Huddle, U.S.A." program on Station WEEI in Boston. The time was New Year's Eve 1972 and the interviewer was Eddie Andelman, who asked him to predict what would happen in the world of sports. Andelman later told me by telephone that Tanous had replied: "A great sports figure, most likely a baseball player now active, will die very soon, and the sports world will be in shock."

This prediction was made at 8:22 P.M. eastern standard time. Early the next morning radio news bulletins announced that Roberto

Clemente, the superstar outfielder of the Pittsburgh Pirates, had gone down on a plane off the West Indies while on a mercy mission to Nicaragua. The time of Clemente's death was fixed at 9:22 P.M. San Juan, Puerto Rico, time, or 8:22 P.M. in Boston.

Alex told me that he had felt himself go out of his body and project to a man in a plane, but he didn't know who it was. He saw the plane going down and knew that the tragedy was "happening right now."

It could be argued that in many of the above cases, Tanous did not go out of his body but merely had clairvoyant knowledge of the past, present, and future. He claims, however, that his I-Consciousness does go instantaneously to the place where he directs it, though without the intervening sense of travel spoken of by other projectors. Although he is not conscious of being in a duplicate body, he feels himself as a mass of energy, a ball of light. This corresponds closely to the soul body, with little or none of the physical component present during other types of OOBEs.

Tanous' belief that he is a form of light energy when he leaves his body may be traced to a suggestion made by a priest in a school he attended. It also gave him a clue to his astral trips to the past.

"If a man could throw himself into the light wave of something that happened a long time ago," said the priest, "he could be right there and witness what had happened."

It will be recalled that other projectors experienced themselves as masses of energy when out of their bodies, also that light from the second body frequently illuminates a dark room. Many projectors have found themselves in very bright light and brilliant color, especially when their astral environment was either of a symbolic nature or in a spiritual realm. Dr. Fisher, Babbitt's spirit control, spoke of the second body as being composed of light.

Tanous says also that he usually feels his "mass of energy" hovering over the place to which he has projected, and that he doesn't receive his information directly—that is, through the senses —but that the spirit of which the energy is composed relays the information back to his physical body. When the ASPR experiments are discussed in Chapter 28, it will be seen that Tanous' projections under laboratory controls show many of the same features as when he goes out-of-body on his own.

"John, John, John"

On at least three occasions, however, Tanous was seen in a duplicate body by witnesses, and on two of them his astral voice was heard. A married couple he knew, living in Wellesley, Massachusetts, went to sleep one night disappointed because they had been unable to find a baby-sitter and had to cancel their plans to attend a conference. In the middle of the night they heard someone speaking and woke up. Tanous' face was on the window shade.

"It's going to work out all right," said Tanous from the window shade. "Your niece from California will baby-sit for you and you'll be able to go to the conference."

Then he disappeared. Somewhat shaken by Tanous' unconventional appearance in their bedroom, the couple went back to sleep convinced that he had "goofed" this time. Their niece was three thousand miles away.

The next day they received a call from the young woman, who had, unknown to them, flown in from California. She said that since she was in town, she would be happy to baby-sit for them if they wished to go somewhere.

Tanous was sleeping at the time and doesn't remember the projection. We have plenty of evidence, however, for materializations witnessed by others while the projector sleeps and dreams or at other times when he is unconscious of going out-of-body. Tanous was happy to perform this service for his friends, even if he consciously knew nothing about it.

While Tanous was lecturing at Lakeland Community College in Mentor, Ohio, in November 1973, two persons in the audience saw his astral body hovering over himself as he spoke. One witness said the double was directly overhead, while the other saw it a few feet to the right of his physical body. I asked Alex where each one was sitting, since the position of the double might depend on the angle of vision. He didn't know.

One of the witnesses, a teacher, wrote to him later: "The etheric double passed from your immediate physical environment and moved to the right of your physical body."

The most dramatic of Tanous' materializations occurred on February 16, 1970, when his solid double appeared to John McCarton, a man who lay dying in a Portland hospital. This is one of the most impressive out-of-body cases in my files, with all the criteria for a valid projection—the I-Consciousness, clairvoyant evidence, a witness to the actual appearance of the second body, the double speaking, and documentation of the experience.

McCarton's wife, Grace, who had seen Tanous on a television program, met him accidentally on Saturday, February 14, as she was coming out of her hairdresser's shop. She introduced herself and asked Alex if he would visit John in the hospital and give him a psychic healing. Tanous said that he had to go north on a trip but would try to go to the hospital on Monday before he left.

While driving on Monday morning, Alex had a sudden impulse to stop the car. As he sat there, he projected to McCarton's room, saw the patient lying curled up in bed, and said, "John, John, John." After looking at McCarton for several minutes, he realized that John would die, and left the room.

When Tanous came back to Portland at the end of the month, he learned that John had died on February 24. Grace said that when she went to the hospital on the afternoon of Monday, the sixteenth, John told her about a man who had come into his room that morning, looked at him for about ten minutes, and said, "John, John, John."

In a letter to Dr. Karlis Osis of the American Society for Psychical Research, dated April 27, 1972, Mrs. McCarton added further details:

> When I went to the hospital Monday afternoon, my husband started talking very excitedly about a man who came in to see him that morning. Said the man had just spoken his name, and then stood and stared at him. John was used to having a lot of different doctors come in to see him, but they all asked him questions. This man did not say a word except to call him by name. He described him, and the description fit Dr. Tanous perfectly, except for the glasses, which no one knew he wore. He kept saying he had never seen such a big, thick pair of glasses.

In her letter Mrs. McCarton repeated what Alex had told her about the hospital room:

> He [Tanous] described the room, which bed my husband had been in, and the fact that the next bed was empty. (This was something

I had not known until I went to the hospital that afternoon, as the man who had been there went home that morning.) Then he described John, the way he was lying in bed, rather huddled up, and the puffiness in his face.

Alex told me that, although he does not ordinarily wear glasses, he has a pair for driving with very heavy frames. The lenses appear thick because of the heavy black frames, designed that way to prevent breakage.

Although John had seen him as a solid body, Tanous was not aware that he had materialized. He knew, however, that his I-Consciousness had projected to the hospital room and that he had said, "John, John, John" and realized that Mr. McCarton was going to die.

"Last Night I Thought I Was Dead"

In most of Tanous' projections, whether he is conscious or asleep, he has a desire to help others—friends and strangers, the police, researchers in the laboratory. Perhaps his most deep-seated motivation, one that finally brought him into the ASPR experiments, could be called a spiritual one, stemming from the many tragic deaths in his family. He longed to find out more about the nature of the soul or spirit and what happened to it at death. One of Tanous' brothers had died in an accident, one from a heart attack, and a third, David, was only twenty and married a year when he succumbed to cancer.

Alex was twenty-six and studying for the priesthood when he heard that David was in the hospital. When he saw David, the young man said: "I'm going to die, but I want to tell you something. Last night I thought I was dead. I was lying in bed and floating over and could see myself in bed. It was so beautiful, I didn't want to come back."

David died that night.

A few years later Alex went to work in a hospital for the express purpose of studying terminal patients, to see if there was anything in their experience that could tell him something about the human spirit and the possibility of survival. Many of them saw the spirits of others just before they died.

When Tanous met Dr. Osis later, they discovered a common bond. Osis had done research in the field of deathbed visions,

interviewing doctors and nurses who said that the dying often
see the spirits of dead relatives and friends. One of the remarkable aspects of Osis' research was that the patients who had the
visions were calm and clearheaded at the time.

The Projection of Images

Another and quite astonishing facet of Tanous' psychic powers
is his ability to manipulate light. Once, at a dinner party in Manchester, New Hampshire, he had a feeling that he could project an
image on the wall. Absorbing the light energy of a nearby lamp,
he felt the light coming out of his eyes and forming an image of
the head and shoulders of a man on the opposite wall. As the
lamplight began to dim, the figure on the wall glowed more brightly.

On another occasion, with eight witnesses in the room, a whole
wall lit up with a picture of a boat that appeared to be sailing
across the wall. He kept projecting images for two hours, while
his audience watched in fascination.

Witnesses to the image-making wrote letters to newspapers describing what they had seen. A letter from Frank Meier of Manchester, New Hampshire, to the Manchester *Union Leader* reads
in part:

> As I glanced towards the wall an image suddenly formed on its
> surface with a surprisingly remarkable resemblance to the head and
> shoulders outline of a man . . . I blinked my eyes, shook my head
> and looked again, but the image remained in position . . . When the
> image first appeared on the wall, it seemed to be a glow of light
> rather than a darkening of shadow, not at all as you would imagine
> an object casting a shadow, but rather an absence of shadow similar
> to the effect created on a surface by a flashlight beam.

Hocus-pocus? Magic? Hypnotism? I realize that professional magicians will rise up in their wrath and state that they can duplicate
this feat. My answer is that Alex Tanous is not a magician, that he
works solely from the mental sphere, and that I saw no evidence in
his apartment or anywhere else of props that might be used to put
on a fraudulent demonstration.

But even more to the point is that psychokinesis, or mind-over-
matter phenomena, has been demonstrated many times. Two remarkable Russian women can move objects on a table merely by

concentrating on them. The controversial Israeli psychic Uri Geller has caused objects to bend or break without touching them, in the presence of many reliable witnesses. In psychic photography Ted Serios has projected thought-forms onto unexposed camera film. What Tanous does in the manipulation of light is essentially what Serios does when he impresses mental images on film.

Tanous is now doing experiments in psychic photography with Len Barcus, an optical physicist. In one instance he created a picture on film that looked like venetian blinds, although there was nothing like this image in the room. Several times there were what Barcus calls "paranormal blackies" on the film caused by a "hologram blockage." A hologram is a multidimensional image usually obtained by laser-beam photography, but Barcus theorizes that holograms may also exist in space as "fields of strain points" and that Tanous is able to impose a holographic field on the film and block out the light.

What does a hologram, the manipulation of light, or the projection of images have to do with the second body? We have speculated that the double may be composed of light and/or electrical energy. This energy may be able to affect electrical fields and patterns of light that move through space and be in turn affected by them. The soul body itself may be the purest form of light. The light of the sun may interact with the soul body to refresh and renew both the semiphysical and the physical body.

"I need a lot of light," Alex told me. "I need electricity. I walk in the sun with light in my eyes. When I absorb light I feel just tremendous."

Dr. Tanous drove back to New York with me after our weekend in Portland. As a non-psychic who has had only one verifiable OOBE, I shrank from the sunlight that poured through the windshield. Alex turned his head toward it and drank it into his eyes as though it were a golden nectar. During long stretches of silence, I wondered if he had jumped into a light wave and returned to some scene of the past that has been written up in history books, hovering over it in his "mass of energy, ball of light," and seeing events as they actually unfolded.

Chapter 26

A Classic
Trio of Projectors

Let's go back a bit in time and examine the work of three projectors, all men, who studied their involuntary OOBEs and developed a philosophy of astral travel and a system for achieving it at will. Their techniques are similar in some respects and different in others, but their combined efforts have given much valuable information to present-day investigators of the out-of-body process.

They were alive, fortunately, during one of the most productive periods in the history of psychical research—the first part of the twentieth century. The British Society for Psychical Research was in full swing, with many of the leading scientists of the day making a close study of telepathy, clairvoyance, and mediumistic phenomena. World War I, with its frightful casualty lists in many European countries, stimulated much interest in the possibility of survival, and the Wilmot case (see Chapter 11) and other cases suggestive of OOBEs gave hope that the soul might live on after the dissolution of the physical body.

It was during this time that a young man in America's Midwest, another young man in England, and a Frenchman somewhat older discovered that they had more than one body and that the second body could, in certain circumstances, leave the physical body and go off on its own. The American had hundreds of such experiences, many of them not far from where his physical body slept. The Englishman had fewer OOBEs, but occasionally traveled long distances, sometimes to curiously distorted settings. The Frenchman often found himself beyond what we call the real world and on other planes of existence.

All three gave much thought to this phenomenon, learned to control it, and wrote books about it. Sylvan Muldoon, Oliver Fox, and Yram were, in a sense, the pioneers of astral projection. Although there had been OOBEs since prehistoric times, these three were among the first to give us a reflective and detailed account of their experiences.

A Technique for Astral Projection

Muldoon lived in a small town in Wisconsin at a time when interest in spiritualism was growing throughout the United States. When he was twelve years old, his mother took him and his little brother to a spiritualist convention in Clinton, Iowa. Mrs. Muldoon was by no means a believer, but she wished to find out for herself if there were such things as spirits. Mother and sons were given accommodations in a house where there were many mediums, and Muldoon theorized later that the psychic atmosphere was responsible in large measure for his first OOBE.

Sylvan did not know as yet what an out-of-body experience was. He woke up in the middle of the night with his body paralyzed—he couldn't move. Then he had a floating sensation and began to vibrate in an up-and-down movement. There was a strong pressure at the back of his head.

Next he was floating horizontally above the bed, rising toward the ceiling. How light his body was! Was he levitating? About six feet up he moved ninety degrees from the horizontal to a vertical plane and descended to a standing position on the floor of the bedroom. He was still rigid and could not move by his own direction. Then he began to relax, still with the uncomfortable tension at the back of his head, and took a step forward.

Now the most amazing part of all—he looked back at the bed and saw himself still sleeping there. He had two bodies, one standing on the floor that contained his I-Consciousness, the other lying passively in bed. Two identical bodies, joined by an "elastic-like cable," one end between the eyes of the body in bed, the other attached to the back of the head of the body he now occupied.

Muldoon thought regretfully that he had died in his sleep. He had better inform the others of his demise. He started to walk but swayed as the "cable" tugged at his head. He tried to open a door but passed right through it. He went from room to room, crying out that he was no longer in his body, trying to shake the sleepers only to have his hands go through them. Bewildered, he walked around aimlessly, not knowing what to do.

The tugging at the back of his head grew stronger. He felt himself swaying once more, zigzagging drunkenly as he walked, then suddenly unable to move. The next moment his double was lifted into the air and jerked back to the bed, where it was suspended horizontally six feet above his physical body. It vibrated in an up-and-down motion as at the beginning of his adventure and dropped into his physical body.

Muldoon thus had a classic OOBE his first time out, going through a process of separation that has become a prototype of astral projection. He had hundreds of OOBEs in the years that followed, and the mechanics were usually the same: physical rigidity, a floating sensation, the double vibrating in an up-and-down horizontal position before becoming vertical, the return of the double in the same sequence as when leaving but in reverse order. Muldoon also experienced the tunnel or blackout effect and saw the cord connection between his two bodies.

He discovered that the zigzagging or swaying of the astral body occurred when it still did not have sufficient control to act on its own—when it was within "cord-range activity," that is, within fifteen feet of the physical body. When he got beyond this range, his second body was free to go where it chose.

Although Muldoon was awake during his first projection, he learned that OOBEs are more likely to occur during a dream but that the projector usually has no conscious knowledge that it is happening. Sometimes consciousness may come on after the bodies have separated during sleep, then go off again. The astral body may be walking about at night when it suddenly becomes aware of itself.

The direction in which the second body separates, according to

Muldoon, depends on the position of the physical body. Since OOBEs happen most frequently when one is lying down or in bed, the second body usually rises from a horizontal position before it uprights itself. But if the projector happens to be standing or reclining or lying on his stomach, the duplicate body will leave in the same position and will return the same way. (Linda White, for example, once left face downward when she was lying on her stomach.)

Muldoon claimed also that the second body usually leaves from every point of the physical body, but other projectors have told different stories, mostly that the double moves out through the head, sometimes by way of the feet. Psychics such as Elwood Babbitt and Alex Tanous, however, who will themselves to leave their bodies, say that they separate instantaneously with no awareness of a physical process. Others first induce a trancelike state but have no recollection of going through the classic procedure. The steps outlined by Muldoon seem to apply mostly to involuntary projectors who release a good deal of the physical component with their doubles.

Many involuntary projectors do not recall that their bodies were cataleptic during their OOBEs. Muldoon contends, however, that the second body is usually rigid until it moves out of cord-range activity and the physical body stays rigid with it. Since most OOBEs occur during sleep, the projector may not remember it, becoming conscious only when the astral body is free to move at will. The sleeper frequently wakes up during the returning stage of projection, when the astral body is settling back into the physical and he becomes aware of his cataleptic state. Sometimes he may wake up in this state with his second body about to project or arrested at a point of partial projection.

Muldoon moved at three speeds during his astral travels. He walked at a normal pace around the room or through his house or even while taking a stroll down the street. Next was the intermediate speed, faster than normal, when "one does not appear to be moving, but everything seems to be coming toward him." The third speed was very fast and enabled him to travel great distances in a very short time. He would have periods of unconsciousness during this mode of travel, since it was impossible for him to register in his consciousness all the details of the passing landscape.

Muldoon firmly believed that separation was made easier by what he called "the morbidity factor"—the depletion of the physical body, a subject explored earlier in this book. Sickly himself, he felt strongly that such "morbidity" was the precondition to astral experience. Bodily depletion seemed to be a factor in his involuntary separations, but since he had to spend much time and effort to project at will, it follows that good health may facilitate voluntary projections.

Of strong interest is Muldoon's development of a technique for consciously sending out his double. His method is by no means easy for the would-be projector and probably of little value if he has not first had the experience of an involuntary projection. It requires much mental preparation, then a strong effort of will to hold the consciousness steady.

Muldoon found the key to his technique when he discovered that dream action often parallels the movement of the double when it leaves the physical body during sleep. For example, he dreamed once that he was in "a massive hall" with "a high ceiling, skylights, and colored windows." As he wandered through the hall, the room began to shrink until it was no larger than a twelve-foot-square bedroom and in place of the skylight there was "one small hole in the center of the ceiling."

In the dream Muldoon was worried because the small hole was his only means of exit. The doors and windows had faded away. His dream self rose in the air and tried to squeeze through the hole, but his body was caught in it. Now in a panic, he woke up and found himself in his astral body, its position just as in the dream. He was half above and half below the ceiling.

Muldoon reasoned that by evolving a method of "dream control," he could learn to project his double into a dream and then wake up in the dream. One way was to construct a "rising" dream before dropping off to sleep and try to project his astral body into it. Another was to recall during the day a recurring dream in which projection may have taken place and to rehearse the dream action mentally and physically, thus increasing the likelihood of waking up in his double when the dream came back at night.

In the first method, Muldoon would watch himself going to sleep each night for several nights, even several weeks. He would try to separate his consciousness from the physical act of falling asleep by holding it well into the hypnagogic state that just precedes sleep. Meanwhile, he would construct a dream that would correspond in its actions with the release of the astral self. He might picture himself swimming in the air, taking off in a plane, or going up in an elevator.

The elevator, for example. The would-be projector lies on his back to facilitate separation and holds the picture of an elevator in his mind. He goes mentally inside the elevator and lies down in the same position as in bed. As he falls asleep, he watches the elevator rise. It stops at the floor above or a higher floor, he gets to his feet and walks out into the room above his bedroom. Then he comes back to the elevator, lies on the floor, and down it goes again. He builds this dream night after night until it bridges the falling-asleep period and becomes his actual dream.

Hopefully, he is now astrally projecting in the dream, but he may be unaware of it. How, then, does he become conscious of his astral body while it is "upstairs" in his dream? Muldoon believed that the more often this dream is induced, the more likely the sleeper will wake up in his astral body.

In the second approach, the would-be projector retraces during the day a sequence he has followed in his recurring dream, trying to fix the details of the dream in his mind. For example, in his dream he walked down a familiar road. Awake, he walks along the road until he comes to a certain place—a tree, a doorway, etc.— that he vividly recalls from his dream. He tells himself that the next time he comes to this same place in his dream, he will awaken in his astral body.

The two methods may be combined in the following manner: as he constructs his elevator dream (or a similar dream) while falling asleep, he thinks of an object on the floor above that will be in the path of his astral body during the dream—a door, a window, a table. Then as he drops off to sleep, he gives himself a suggestion to become conscious when his double reaches the object.

Muldoon thus learned to wake up many times in his double while dreaming.

Sometimes the sleeper wakes up in the middle of the night or toward morning, with his body cataleptic. He becomes anxious and loses the chance to project. (This is what happened to the author of this book, as told in the first chapter.) But if he stays calm and thinks of rising in the air, of floating, his astral body may emerge. The state of catalepsy may also signal that the second body is returning from an astral adventure that took place during sleep.

The going-to-sleep and dreaming periods set the stage for projection. Control is difficult, however, because of the delicate balance that must be maintained between allowing oneself to fall asleep and holding on to consciousness as a bridge to the astral experience.

For Muldoon, many kinds of dreams symbolize astral motion, particularly the flying and falling dreams, what he calls "aviation-type" dreams. The falling dream represents a return to the physical body, and it is often precipitated by fear or another negative emotion in the dream. Once when Muldoon was a child he climbed to the roof of a friend's house from the attic and crawled to the edge. Here he became dizzy and frightened and crawled back to the ladder and down to the attic again.

As he was growing up, he had a recurring dream in which he was floating over the roof. He would start to fall when directly over the spot where he had crawled to the edge. He would then wake up with a start in his physical body, a sensation known to many sleepers. Muldoon wrote: "As the phantom [double] lowered, the dream would be of falling. As the body repercussed, consciousness would return. And this explains the phenomenon of falling dreams!"

Many psychiatrists, psychologists, and dream researchers would disagree with Muldoon's explanation of flying and falling dreams. They would look upon the dream action as symbolic of the sleeper's conflicts and memories. Flying dreams might mirror the games of movement in childhood, the need to rise above obstacles, a sex problem. Since every dream can be interpreted on many levels, however, both the psychological and the out-of-body explanation may be correct.

Muldoon never doubted for a moment that he had been awake in his double hundreds of times while asleep in his physical body. The I-Consciousness was always strong in him, whether projection occurred when he was drowsy, dreaming, or wide awake. In *The Projection of the Astral Body,* he wrote: "When one is consciously projected, there is no question about it; one knows it; I know it."

Oliver Fox and the Dream Control Method

Oliver Fox, like Muldoon, spent years experimenting with astral projection in England and developed his own theories. It was not easy, and he had many setbacks. Like Muldoon, he was sickly as a youth and had to expend much effort to achieve his results. Before reaching the point where he could project voluntarily in the waking state, he went through the stages of what he called the "Dream of Knowledge," the "Trance Condition," the "False Awakening," and "Instantaneous Projection," and he learned to concentrate on "an imaginary trapdoor in the mind" as a means of exit for the second body.

Fox believed, as Muldoon did, that we project during sleep and that by controlling our dreams, we may be able to wake up in them. The critical faculty must be in the ascendant, even as we sleep. But how does the critical faculty work when the conscious mind has given up control, as in a dream? When Fox was sixteen years old, in 1902, he had a dream that gave him the clue. In the dream he was standing outside his home when he noticed something peculiar about the paving stones along the curb—they had changed their position. Instead of lying at right angles to the curb, they were now parallel to it.

He knew then that he was dreaming. When he woke up later he thought how wonderful it would be if he could step into his own dream and direct it, even making it last longer and enjoying it all the more. If he could notice an incongruity in the dream, such as the position of the paving stones, something so at odds with reality that it could not escape his critical attention, he would recognize that he was in a dream and could take charge of it.

Fox learned how to project his double into the Dream of Knowledge, then control the dream for short periods of time. If he held the dream too long, however, he got a severe pain in the forehead that he thought came from the area of the pineal gland or hypothetical "third eye," which Yogis believe to be the seat of mystical powers. (In many projections it is observed that the connecting cord starts from the middle of the forehead and ends at the back of the double's head.) He knew that he was losing control also when his I-Consciousness was in both his physical and astral bodies. He could stand beside the bed in his double and at the same time feel himself in bed.

He resolved to fight the pain and stay in his astral body. When he made the attempt a few times, the pain went away and with it the sense of dual consciousness. He was "locked out" in his dream and he wandered freely along what appeared to be a seashore. But when he willed himself to return, nothing happened. Once more he seemed to be losing control. When he finally got back into his body, he was paralyzed as he lay in bed. Finally the paralysis broke, but he was ill for several days.

When he was in what he called the Trance Condition (catalepsy), he discovered that he was not really awake but in a strange state of unreality, hallucinating with "terrifying sensations, shapes, and sounds." This was the False Awakening. Once more he was controlled, rather than doing the controlling. Then it occurred to him that the Trance Condition might precede projection rather than follow it and could be induced consciously to bring on an OOBE when he was awake. This way the Dream of Knowledge could be dispensed with and he could project at will anytime of day or night.

The pain in his head gave him another clue. Just as so many other projectors have conceived of the double leaving through the head or symbolically through a narrow opening such as a tunnel, Fox directed his thoughts as the trance came on to an "imaginary trapdoor" in his mind. To induce the trance he would lie down, relax all the muscles of his body, and concentrate upon the "pineal door." As his body became numb and he was in the Trance Condition, he would see his room bathed in a golden light.

"My incorporeal self rushed to a point in the pineal gland and hurled itself against the imaginary trapdoor, while the golden light increased in brilliance, so that it seemed the whole room burst into flame . . . Once the little door had clicked behind me, I enjoyed a mental clarity far surpassing that of earth-life."

Fox also discovered a way to bypass the "pineal door." After a self-induced trance, he would project his double by "a strong effort of the will." The second body would literally fly out of the room, through the walls and out into space. This was Instantaneous Projection.

Although Muldoon's experiences were mostly in everyday surroundings, Fox sometimes found himself in the physical world, at other times in an environment where reality seemed to be transformed. As in many of Tanous' OOBEs, past, present, and future were often blended. He visited cities such as London that seemed to be larger than usual, with many new buildings that may have been thought-forms from an earlier era or had not yet been built.

He often traveled great distances, in one instance finding himself in a Far Eastern city where there were "street bazaars and shining white oriental buildings . . . a curious fountain: a huge kneeling elephant, sculptured in black stone." Sometimes the scenes were symbolic. In one projection he witnessed "a roadway of golden light stretching from earth to zenith . . . countless coloured forms of men and beasts representing man's upward evolution through different stages of civilization . . . suddenly there came a culminating vision of a gigantic peacock, whose outspread tail filled the heavens."

The temptation would be to regard these scenes as the stuff of dreams rather than the visions of Fox's astral eyes. We know, however, that in a good percentage of out-of-body experiences, both the familiar and the unfamiliar are seen through the lenses of the deeper layers of mind. Linda White could in one instance smell lasagna in the oven, in another watch numbers being tattooed on the bodies of newborn children. Fox, too, could also come down to the earth he knew in his physical body, as he did when he projected to his friend Elsie's bedroom and was seen by her.

Fox's double was quite agile during his out-of-body excursions. He could walk, glide close to the ground or high in the air, levitate, and "skry"—travel through a series of great leaps into the sky. At times, however, he encountered strong "astral currents" that carried him far off course, especially during Instantaneous Projections.

"Like Taking Off a Suit of Clothes"

In contrast to the complicated, sometimes painful methods developed by Muldoon and Fox was the facility with which Yram learned to project his double. Yram was the pseudonym of a Frenchman who wrote *Le Médecin de l'Âme*, later translated into English as *Practical Astral Projection*. Yram believed, as Elwood Babbitt and Alex Tanous do, that one could leave his body "with greater ease than taking off a suit of clothes." He did not suffer from the illnesses that plagued Muldoon and Fox for so many years.

Yram also believed, as many theorists do today, that the double is composed of two basic elements, one semiphysical, the other spiritual.

"The substance which we are using to give form to our double," he wrote, "returns to the physical body, and it is with a far more ethereal body that we soar into space." Each of us has a series of bodies that are available for travel into different dimensions.

Although he often projected in the spiritual or soul body, Yram sometimes found himself on the material plane when too much of the physical component was present. At such times his movements were impeded by objects such as walls and doors (see Chapter 6). At other times his double was arrested on a lower astral plane (the Hades of Robert Crookall and Locale II of Robert Monroe), where he was menaced by hostile entities. He sensed the evil thoughts of those he encountered on this plane and was once chased by men dressed in black.

After much practice Yram learned to project to a higher spiritual plane where he felt a sense of oneness with the environment and those who dwelt there. Although still unified within himself, he was able to radiate his energy outward as though from the "center of a sphere," to "multiply" himself and become both macrocosm and microcosm. This is the true mystical experience, known as "cosmic consciousness."

On the higher plane Yram enjoyed what Crookall calls "Paradise" conditions and what other projectors, sometimes in a heightened emotional state, have spoken of as "heaven." He felt the essence of superior beings who had no form but whose aura radiated a positive energy and an intense love.

Yram projected in several ways. One was by imagining a means of exit that the physical body would ordinarily use, such as a door, a window, or "anything which gives us the idea of passage from one plane to another." Another method was through bodily movement such as a swimming motion that would simulate the flight of the double.

Yram evidently had a loose connection between the bodies, for he speaks of a sudden forceful ejection of the double. In what he, too, called "Instantaneous Projection," his second body would suddenly be torn out and hurled through space, on one occasion "shot out violently like the shell from a gun." In another kind of OOBE, "Projection by Whirlwind," he had the sensation of "being sucked up violently by a sort of huge vortex."

Yram echoes Dr. Fisher when he cautions that the would-be projector must first reach a higher awareness before trying to leave his body. The plane to which he will be attracted will correspond to his mental and spiritual development. If he is not ready for projection, he will find himself on a lower astral plane with a murky atmosphere and unpleasant entities. Meditation is helpful—lying down and relaxing body and mind, removing nervous tension, and thinking benevolent thoughts without any suggestion of evil or hatred.

The high-flown, frequently vague style of Yram's writings has made many students question whether he had OOBEs or merely dreams and flights of fancy. Yram insisted that he knew the difference between dreaming and astrally projecting. In one dream the symbol of a pure white dove appeared and settled on his forehead. At this point his thoughts became crystal-clear and he was conscious both of his sleeping body and his double in the dream.

In addition to waking up in his dream, there are other similarities between Yram's OOBEs and those of Fox, Muldoon, and other projectors. He sometimes experienced the cataleptic state and the tunnel effect, writing that once he had the impression of being "in a sack whose narrow opening was no more than a crack." As with Fox, he was sometimes carried away by astral currents. He was aware of the connecting cord. (Fox, strangely enough, never saw his silver cord although he knew it was there, possibly because it never occurred to him to look back.) He sensed the higher density of his double when closer to his physical body.

Yram shared the almost universal belief that out-of-body experiences, particularly when they are on the higher planes, bring sharper clarity of mind and more vigor to the physical body: "These extra vibrations give one splendid strength and energy. We think and act during the day with unparalleled ease. Without effort, complicated problems are solved."

The
Scientific
Approach

Chapter 27

Scholars of
Astral Travel

In recent years many persons trained in academic disciplines have been making a serious study of OOBEs. The late sociology professor Hornell Hart found evidence for the survival of the soul in the literature of astral projection. Physicist Russell Targ and psychologist Karlis Osis, among others, have taken OOBEs into the laboratory. A young parapsychologist named D. Scott Rogo analyzes and writes about OOBEs as he and others have experienced them.

The outstanding scholar of astral projection is an Englishman in his eighties. Robert Crookall, a graduate biologist and geologist, has added greatly to our knowledge of the phenomenon through an analytical study of more than a thousand cases from the past and present. He has noted similar patterns from case to case, charted the conditions under which they occur, and divided the cases into several categories.

Before we turn to Crookall's work, however, something should be said about D. Scott Rogo, a disciple of Crookall's whose own OOBEs support Dr. Crookall's theories. Rogo, who has received grants for research from the Parapsychology Foundation, has written several books on the subject. One of them, *Nad,* includes cases in which projectors hear music during their OOBEs. In *The Welcoming Silence* Rogo tells about his spontaneous OOBEs and the techniques he has developed for voluntary projection.

In 1965 Rogo made several attempts at projection but was unsuccessful. Then on a hot afternoon in August, something happened to him as he fell asleep that is reminiscent of Muldoon's first OOBE.

"I felt very passive," he writes, "as though I were enveloped in a liquid or density of some sort. I tried to move of my own volition but found myself cataleptic. My mind began to get clearer and I observed that I was floating above my body . . . For an instant I lost consciousness. I . . . found myself standing at the foot of the bed, to the right of it, viewing my physical body."

As Rogo felt himself pushed through "a dense liquid" toward the door, he began to sway, unable to control his double. Again he lost consciousness and woke up in his physical body.

A few weeks later he had another spontaneous OOBE when he lay down one afternoon for a rest. As he drifted off to sleep, his body began to pulsate and he thought it was moving. He turned over on his left side, his face pressing down on his left arm.

After a momentary blackout, he found himself kneeling on the floor in his double, then he stood up. There was a strong pressure on the left side of his face. He had no vision in his left eye but his right eye was normal. He floated toward the door and went through it as though through "dense liquid or jelly." His two dogs began to bark at him. He lost consciousness again and woke up in his physical body, "the left side of my face crushed by its having lain on my arm exerting the same pressure on my face that I felt during the projection."

Learning, as Muldoon and Fox did, that astral projection was likely to occur during the falling-asleep or waking-up period, Rogo developed a projection technique similar to Muldoon's but simpler in execution. He discovered that by controlling the images that went through his mind as he was falling asleep, he could eject his second body. Once, for example, he had the sensation of driving at great speed on a California freeway.

"It flashed upon me," he writes, "that if I could crash my car off to the side of the road, I could project myself. In my image, I threw the steering wheel to the side and crashed my car. Instantaneously, I felt myself floating pleasantly above my body. I was fully awake."

Natural and Enforced Projections

Robert Crookall has written thirteen books based on his research. His theories derive from a study of the classic projectors such as Muldoon, Fox, and Yram; OOBEs throughout history and in different cultures; cases that have come to his personal attention; and the accounts that come through mediums.

Crookall found that, although many first-time projectors do not know what is happening to them and are not aware that it is happening to others, they go through the same process of physical catalepsy, momentary blackout, leaving through the head, rising to a horizontal position, and other steps in the classic separation of the two bodies. In refining his theory, however, Crookall discovered that these and other characteristics depended on the circumstances of the projection—whether it was "natural" or "enforced."

A person who leaves his body naturally—while resting, falling asleep, or when ill and otherwise below par physically—will often go through the gradual process described above. Generally, he will be mentally sharper and his senses more acute than usual. Natural projectors are frequently clairvoyant and able to pass through objects but less likely to touch or move them. When not on the earth plane, natural projectors are attracted to the Paradise realm.

When the double is forcibly ejected from the body—through rapid physical motion, after taking drugs or anesthetics, following an accident or in another stressful situation, when in a hypnotic trance—the quality of the experience is likely to be different. If the projector is on the earth plane, he has a lower level of awareness and is less likely to remember later what happened to him; or he may be in an unearthly, misty atmosphere with unpleasant and frequently threatening entities, the Hades environment.

The Double as a Composite

Crookall discovered that bodily constitution plays a role in the quality of the OOBE and this led to his concept of the double as a composite—made up of a soul body and varying quantities of a semiphysical body or vehicle of vitality. Psychics, mediums, and others who may have a loose connection between the physical body and the vehicle of vitality—those with a "mediumistic" constitution—would tend to experience the Hadeslike conditions of enforced projections. Those with less of the semiphysical component are more apt to find themselves in the Paradise setting when they get beyond the earth plane.

An important factor also stressed by Yram and Dr. Fisher that cuts across other conditions is the degree of advancement of the individual. Those on a high moral and spiritual level, psychics or not, are more likely to enter the Paradise realm. Dr. Crookall joins Dr. Fisher and Yram in warning against attempting to project through will power if one is of unstable temperament or is not spiritually advanced. He would, in fact, discourage any deliberate attempt to project.

If the spiritually advanced psychic has the mediumistic constitution, he may pass temporarily through Hades conditions until he finds his true level. This is also the case with many non-psychics. Thus the double often goes through a two-stage process. In the first stage the vehicle of vitality, which Crookall equates with ectoplasm, surrounds the soul body and creates the kind of misty, foggy, liquidy atmosphere in which Rogo found himself. In the second stage, often after the double has changed from the horizontal to the vertical position, the vehicle of vitality drops off and returns to the physical body, allowing the soul body to travel more freely on the earth plane or to experience realms of great beauty peopled with benevolent entities.

When the second bodies of Rogo and Muldoon were swaying and falling while still near their physical bodies (within cord range), they were controlled by the vehicle of vitality. During this stage the double tends to follow the lead of the physical body rather than demonstrate a will of its own. It is positioned in space as the physical body is in bed or on a chair, and it apes the movements and feels the sensations of the parent body, as Rogo's double did when he felt pressure on his left side. Muldoon also had many experiences of this kind.

During this stage, consciousness may wax and wane, often staying in the physical body or shifting back and forth between the two. In dual consciousness the projector has some awareness in both bodies. Before Fox's soul body broke loose and sailed off to the seashore, he was conscious of both standing by the bed and lying in it. In one of Rogo's projections, his "consciousness and sight stemmed from a point *not* within either body . . . I was viewing both bodies from another side of the room." Once the soul body gets beyond cord range, consciousness stays in it and becomes clearer.

Non-mediumistic persons of advanced spirituality leave their bodies in only one stage—that is, with the soul body in the ascendant. The projector either stays on the earth plane with his awareness and senses immeasurably sharpened or goes to the Paradise realm without first passing through the Hades environment. There are some psychics whose soul body, not the vehicle of vitality, is loosely connected to the physical body, and they project with little or no experience of Hades conditions. Examples are Elwood Babbitt and Alex Tanous.

Crookall also points out that there are "intermediate" cases of projectors who sometimes go through the two-stage, at other times the single-stage projection, or who may experience elements of both stages in the same projection, depending on the balance between the semiphysical and the soul body components present in the second body when it leaves or even while it is out of the body. Crookall writes, in *Out-of-the-Body Experiences: A Fourth Analysis:* "The differences between mediumistic and non-mediumistic persons, between healthy and more or less sick people, are neither sharp nor permanent. For example, non-mediums may be temporarily mediumistic when ill."

Crookall found that there are two silver cords as well as two aspects of the double, although most projectors see only one. One cord starts from the pineal gland area, the other from the solar plexus of the physical body, and both go to the back of the astral head. The solar plexus connection is to the vehicle of vitality, the pineal gland connection is to the soul body. There are a few projectors, one of them medium Gladys Osborne Leonard, who have seen both at the same time.

Dr. Crookall bases his theories in part on what has come through mediums about conditions after death. It appears that dying is also a two-stage process. The "astral shell," which is the equivalent of the vehicle of vitality, sleeps or wanders for three days in the dreamlike Hades region, then disintegrates, leaving the soul body free to enter the brighter realms. During life there is always some of the physical substance present during soul body projections, but it drops away completely after the three-day period following death. The cord, too (or cords), which supplies life-giving energy to the physical body, is severed at death.

Crookall theorizes that ghosts are the astral shells of the dead, with hazy consciousness and without intelligence, that manifest to the living. So, too, during the first stage of a two-stage OOBE and an enforced projection, the vehicle of vitality clouds the consciousness and intellect that reside in the soul body.

Crookall has made several charts in which he likens the vehicle of vitality to the aura surrounding the physical body, with its natural home the Hades environment. The superphysical soul body also interpenetrates the physical body but extends even further beyond the aura and finds its natural habitat on the Paradise plane. After death each body goes to its own realm.

Guides on the Astral Journey

The astral traveler may be accompanied by guides, whom Crookall calls "helpers" or "hinderers," depending on which realm he has contacted. Yram wrote, for example, of the malevolent beings he encountered on the astral plane and the kindly souls who joined him on the spiritual plane. Sometimes the helpers aid in the process of projection and guide the astral traveler on his journey.

The case of William Dudley Pelley, cited by Crookall and other researchers, dramatically illustrates the function of guides as well as other aspects of projection. Pelley, a writer living during the 1920s in Pasadena, California, woke up one night in a state of terror, his body cataleptic. He believed he was dying. Suddenly he was projected into a whirlwind that carried him through "blue space," but just as suddenly two guides appeared, one of them saying, "Take it easy, old man. We're here to help you."

The guides carried him in their arms and placed him on a marble slab, while they watched over him. He discovered, as Dr. Wiltse did, that his body was nude, and they told him to bathe in a nearby pool. When he came out of the pool, he saw that he was clothed, although he was not quite sure what he was wearing. He was quite certain that he had died, but death was a very pleasant experience. He was truly in Paradise, conscious of "a beauty and loveliness of environment that surpasses chronicling on paper." Suddenly he was caught in a whirlwind again and carried in a blue vapor back to his bed and into his physical body, which was in a sitting position.

Pelley, writing later in the *American Magazine* ("Seven Minutes in Eternity," March 1929), insisted that he had been fully awake at the time and that his experience convinced him he would live on after death. His projection illustrates the two-stage process— first passing through the frightening blue vapor of the Hades realm and then emerging into Paradise conditions. In the two-stage process, the projector often returns in reverse order, as Pelley did when he passed briefly through the blue vapor on his way back from the land of the dead.

Psychic Styles in Out-of-Body Experiences

Do the cases in this book illustrate the validity of Dr. Crookall's theories? Most of them do, a few are doubtful. I do not believe that Crookall has given sufficient attention to voluntary projectors and the special nature of their experiences, particularly in a laboratory setting. The results of contemporary laboratory experiments, which are described in the next two chapters, suggest that reality is often transformed during a willful projection when, as Dr. Fisher has indicated, the physical world may be seen through spiritual eyes.

It should be pointed out, however, that most of Crookall's books were published before the current era of laboratory OOBEs. I believe, too, that Crookall would put Tanous, Babbitt, and a few others I have investigated in the category of those whose devotion to religion and what might be called a spiritual approach to life would take them into a supernormal kind of reality.

Certainly the way Tanous and Babbitt go out to both earth and spiritual planes is atypical. It may be argued, as it was by Robert Monroe in a lecture before the American Society for Psychical Research in 1973, that such projectors are not really in their second bodies but are only using their clairvoyant faculties. There is room, however, for all kinds of projections, and the quality could well depend, as Crookall says, on the spiritual development and the physical constitution of the projector. Just as personalities differ in ordinary situations, the projector may have his individual style of astral travel.

He may walk, fly, glide, skry, perhaps cover hundreds of miles in an instant. He may or may not see his physical body or his cord(s). He may move through foggy realms or bright lights. He may experience reality with something added or taken away, as Fox

often did. He may see objects as smaller or larger than they are
or in different spatial relationships to each other (see Chapters 28
and 29). He may, like Kevin Lampro, project his state of mind
into his astral environment. He may project a symbol, as the man
did whose face appeared over the womb of his former wife. The
psychology of the projector, his genetic constitution, his physical
and mental condition at the time of projection, the historical period
and the culture in which he lives, his reason for projecting, his
psychic style—all determine the quality of his out-of-body experience.

In many of our cases there is a mixture of elements, sometimes
the very real with the unreal, as with Oliver Fox and Kevin
Lampro. Caroline Larsen never left her home and she heard her
husband's chamber group playing all the time she was in her
second body. The fact that she could see herself in the mirror would
indicate that a good deal of the physical component was present,
but she saw herself as much younger and wearing a flowing garment. As she came down the steps, a strange but helpful entity
told her to go back.

Muldoon claims that all his experiences were on the earth plane,
but there are reports that he did visit other realms but did not
wish to write about them. Mrs. Leonard, whose first OOBE was in
her own home and in a very mundane situation as she listened to
her husband talking with the gas man and the maid, also had
unearthly experiences on the same night. She heard singing and
playing on an instrument that she knew was not in her home and
saw a grand piano and a young lady who had died. Dr. Wiltse
was very much on the earth plane until the invisible hands of
guides lifted him up, and he saw the symbolic black rocks that
divided life from death.

Joy Snell, the nurse, was helped by guides. The Indian chief
White Thunder also had guides, both Indians, who took him along
a river (Crookall equates water with the Hades realm) and into
heaven where his dead friends were living in wigwams. Agnes
Adamczyk relived her operation and all its details with the most
compassionate of helpers, Jesus, at her side.

The Christian saints who projected at will to help others—
Ignatius of Loyola, Alphonsus Liguori, Anthony of Padua—appeared
in very solid bodies. Was the physical component predominant?
Given the character of the saints and their advanced spirituality,

we must allow, as the Catholic Church did, for miracles, without regard to theories about what happens to lesser souls who project.

We have the two-stage cases, such as the man who pictured himself projecting to his lady friend and her daughter by going up the steps and ringing the bell. There were mind-over-matter phenomena in the beginning when the maid heard the doorbell ring and the daughter heard footsteps. When the projector appeared to his lady friend first as an ovoid figure in a "luminous mist," it could have been his soul body surrounded by the vehicle of vitality, which finally dropped off as his bodily outline and features became distinct. On the other hand, many who have projected in their soul bodies think of themselves only as a luminous mist or a mass of energy.

Crookall puts OOBEs under anesthesia in the category of enforced projections, in which there is likely to be either a dreamlike state on the earth plane or the Hades conditions of fog and mist. But there are instances in which the projectors were mentally alert and quite clear about what was happening in surgery. Dorie Lawrence, Dr. Sava's patient, the woman who saw her daughter buy a get-well card, the man who traveled down the hall as his surgeon went for another instrument—all noticed every detail connected with the operation and often what was going on elsewhere. Other patients who nearly died as they lay ill in bed or on the operating table had the most spiritual of experiences during their projections and gained the conviction that life goes on after the death of the physical body.

I believe, on reflection, that other factors are at work in hospital anesthesia cases in addition to the effect of the anesthetic. The patient about to go under the knife is often in a highly emotional state and has probably been thinking that he might die. His mind and soul may be concerned with thoughts of heaven and hell. Small wonder then that so many of these projectors report meeting the dead, being attracted to higher realms, becoming indifferent to their physical bodies, and being sent back by those they meet in heaven or paradise, or at the halfway point.

It must be said, in spite of what may appear to be contradictions at times, that Crookall has performed a monumental service in fitting all OOBEs into appropriate categories. If one looks closely, he will find a place for every kind of projector and every kind of circumstance and condition in which projection takes place. The physical processes of projection that have been documented by Crookall appear over and over again in the cases in this book.

It is not every OOBE, however, that can be put neatly into a box and labeled. This is the way of the physical sciences, but human beings resist being categorized. Paranormal phenomena, dealing mostly with the mind, are too elusive for absolute classification. Even the physical body, which has been microscopically explored and charted, keeps surprising doctors and physiologists by the way it behaves. Biologists, biophysicists, biochemists spend years trying to unravel the mysteries of the life process. If the nature of the physical body is still not completely known, it will certainly take some time before we have a clear understanding of the second body.

What can be said, however, is that there is a second body, the human double, and that Robert Crookall has done more than anyone else to find out what it is like and how it behaves under various conditions.

Chapter 28

"Trapping the Soul" in the Laboratory

The most exciting laboratory research in the paranormal during the 1970s is in out-of-body phenomena. The only comparable period of such research was in the early twentieth century when Hector Durville and other experimenters were using hypnosis to project the double and detecting its presence with chemical screens and other devices. The experimenters, most of them French, claimed that the double not only caused physiological changes in the hypnotized subject but could consciously observe and feel and even move objects at a distance (see Chapter 7).

After these experiments, which have been more or less discounted by contemporary researchers, interest shifted to other psychic areas when in 1930 Dr. J. B. Rhine began his card tests in clairvoyance at Duke University. So little attention was paid to OOBEs that nothing much happened for thirty years. Robert Monroe, who began having OOBEs in 1958, complained that for a long time he could find no parapsychologists interested in his experiences. The climate changed somewhat in the 1960s when Robert Crookall's first scholarly studies were published, but the only significant laboratory research was the sporadic testing of subjects by psychologist Charles Tart, a university instructor.

Tart worked with two psychics, one of them Robert Monroe, checking their physiological responses as they attempted out-of-body travel. His first subject, a young lady who had had many spontaneous OOBEs, went to sleep in one room of the university laboratory while in the next room Tart watched her brain wave tracings on the EEG (electroencephalograph). On a shelf suspended from the ceiling in her room was a paper with a five-digit number written on it, out of her visual range. For five nights she tried to project to the ceiling and look at the number. On three of the nights she experienced a floating sensation and on the other two was completely out of her body. On the fourth night she went to the ceiling and correctly read the number.

Monroe's attempt to project experimentally points up the difficulty of consciously reproducing psychic events in the laboratory, whether OOBEs or other aspects of the paranormal. Tart tested Monroe at the University of Virginia Medical School. On eight nights between 1965 and 1966 Monroe tried to go astrally into the next room, observe the technician who was controlling the recording equipment, and read a five-digit number on a shelf six feet above the floor. He was unsuccessful in the first seven trials. On the eighth night he had two very brief OOBEs. He said correctly that the technician was out of the room and that a man (identified later as her husband) was with her in the corridor.

Two years later Monroe and Tart tried again, the subject having two very short OOBEs. During one of them he became disoriented and found himself in unfamiliar surroundings. In these experiments and the earlier ones he had difficulty in controlling the movements of his double. Although many of the psychics in the later experiments at the American Society for Psychical Research were able to project long distances from other cities to the ASPR building in New York, they frequently had the same problem when they arrived. A primary goal of experimental subjects who are able to project at will is to gain control over the process and thus meet the requirements of the research.

Four Centers of Out-of-Body Research

It was a dramatic courtroom trial in Arizona in 1967 that in part touched off the present era of laboratory research in OOBEs.

A miner named James Kidd died, leaving a fortune of several hundred thousand dollars and stipulating in his will that the money should go to anyone doing scientific research to prove the existence of the soul. The judge, after hearing the claims of 133 individuals and organizations, ruled in favor of the Barrows Neurological Institute of Phoenix. On an appeal from the judge's decision, however, the Arizona Supreme Court awarded the money to the American Society for Psychical Research, which then granted part of the bequest to the Psychical Research Foundation (PRF) in Durham, North Carolina.

Since one kind of evidence for the existence of the soul is the reality of the human double, the ASPR and the PRF have begun intensive programs in out-of-body research. Similar projects are under way at the Division of Parapsychology of the University of Virginia, and the Stanford Research Institute (SRI) in Menlo Park, California. All four projects are different in design but, taken together, the results may go a long way in proving that there is a double and that it may survive physical death.

As stated in its *Newsletter* of spring 1973, the ASPR looks for the following kind of evidence for the reality of the double: "introspective awareness" of the projector; "observations" by witnesses; and recordings by mechanical devices of physiological changes in the subject and changes in the energy patterns of the target area. Those taking part in the ASPR project include psychologists, statisticians, physicists, and members of the staff.

In planning the experiments, Dr. Karlis Osis, director of research at the ASPR, has tried to separate a clairvoyant vision from a true out-of-body experience. Each of the many experiments that began in the latter part of 1972 was designed to show that the projector was actually present at some point in space in the target area and not merely getting extrasensory impressions in his physical brain.

The Projections of an Artist

Artist Ingo Swann was chosen as the subject of the first ASPR experiment. A shelf divided by a partition with a tray on either side containing target materials was suspended two feet from the ceiling, out of Swann's visual range as he sat in a chair six feet below. Swann was connected by cables to a polygraph in the next room, where researcher Janet Mitchell recorded changes in respiration, blood pressure, brain-wave tracings, and other physiological processes. Swann reported over an intercom what he saw on the trays as he went out of his body and returned.

To rule out clairvoyance, Swann was asked to station his double at various points around the trays and to make a drawing of what he saw from each position. If he was out of his body, his astral eyes would see the target materials as they would appear to his physical eyes, with the partition blocking one tray when he was viewing the other from certain angles. In clairvoyance he could presumably see or "scan" both trays without leaving his body. The materials on the trays were of strong colors and clearly formed objects such as an umbrella, a cross, and a black leather case. Some of the objects were of unusual geometric designs.

Swann was tested on eight occasions, with impressive results. The target materials in one experiment were cut out of construction paper: on one tray a red heart with a black dagger across it; on the other a bull's-eye within three circles, the outer circle in black, the middle in green, and the inner circle in red. Swann sketched almost exactly what was on the trays, although he reversed the colors in the bull's-eye design, with the targets appearing from two different points of view just as they would to his physical eyes.

On another day Swann correctly sketched a cross against a white background, a large red circle and a smaller quarter moon in red against a blue background, and an egg-shaped figure in white, naming the correct colors and drawing the figures as they appeared to him from the position of his double. In a later experiment he referred to some irregular geometric figures that resembled dumplings as "round dumpy things" and accurately sketched them.

In one test the objects were hidden from view in a closed box with a small opening and could only be seen reflected in a mirror. Swann saw the objects reversed as they would be if he were physically looking at the mirror. Two words with an arrow to the left were seen as two words reversed with a dot to the right.

Colors and shapes were clearer than minute details, a general condition of OOBEs. It was difficult for Swann to identify letters and numbers. In one test he was able to describe a white frame around the picture of a tiger's face but could not make out the face. His astral eyes were sensitive to light: materials that absorbed light were easier to see than those that reflected light such as plastics, glossy pictures, and glass.

Advanced psychics who go out in their soul bodies on the earth plane often have much sharper astral than physical eyes, so sharp that objects may appear in brighter light and may break down into their electrical and atomic components. With the physical environment thus transformed into a superphysical or spiritual reality, it was sometimes more difficult for Swann and other subjects to see the target objects exactly as called for by the experiments. According to Janet Mitchell in her article for *Psychic* magazine (April 1973), Swann "perceives . . . the forms of certain light rays and ionization of the air around changing light sources."

Possibly because of this keener inner vision, along with the subjective factor that affects perception in many OOBEs, Swann often saw distorted spatial relationships between objects. At times he was forced to mentally create the dimensions around a target as they would appear to his physical eyes. He did this by visualizing points in space where the shelf would be until his astral eyes could focus upon it.

The tests were evaluated by a psychologist who correctly matched the eight sets of targets with Swann's descriptions of them. Statistically, there was one chance in 40,000 of achieving this result. Of added interest was Janet Mitchell's report that although physiological processes such as blood pressure and body temperature showed no significant changes during Swann's OOBEs, there was a loss of voltage recorded on the EEG. Dr. Tart also reported a loss of voltage in his experiments.

The "Fly-in" Experiments

The next project designed by Dr. Osis was the "fly-in." One hundred psychics throughout the country tried to will their doubles from their homes to Dr. Osis' office on the fourth floor of the ASPR building. Each psychic was instructed to make his astral flight at a prearranged time, stand in his double on an "X" mark in front of the fireplace, look at objects on a coffee table, describe the objects and sketch them, then report by mail or phone what he had seen. Either Vera Feldman or Bonnie Perskari, Dr. Osis' assistants, would be sitting on the sofa on the other side of the table. Dr. Osis himself was frequently in the room, and sometimes another psychic was present who tried to see the doubles of the projectors.

There were usually four objects on the table, two on either side of a high barrier in the middle, arranged so that the double at the fireplace could only see the objects on his side of the barrier. The objects were chosen for size (small objects were harder to see), ease of identification, and in some cases for distinctiveness and individuality, such as a stuffed monkey whose arms could be moved to various positions.

Most of the psychics projected several times, and fifteen of the hundred gave good evidence that they were present in their doubles. Once again, the ability of advanced psychics to see a different kind of reality, added to such factors as mood and psychic style, brought curious results. Although some objects were seen exactly as they were, others were distorted in size and in spatial relationships to objects around them. The targets were often not identified but received as visual impressions in which their shapes and colors came through strongly.

Many of the projectors had circular or globular vision—seeing in all directions at once. The barrier on the coffee table, designed to rule out clairvoyance by blocking the view of the other side, was transparent to many projectors, and because there were paper clips and rulers that held the barrier in place, many reports were of objects that looked like rulers or were in the form of paper clips. The objects on both sides of the barrier were often combined in such a way that they had to be mentally separated into their original parts to be recognized.

Light as usual was an important factor, even the light emanating from the physical bodies of those in the room. On Elwood Babbitt's first projection, the auras of Dr. Osis and another man in the office gave off such a strong violet color that they blotted out the rest of the room. At times lights would mysteriously come on and go off in the room and in a few cases seemed to be activated by the projectors.

Strange Happenings in the Laboratory

The time as well as space dimension was blurred. Alex Tanous and others often saw objects that had been on the table in the past or would be there in the future. A student projector, George Kokoris, saw the stuffed monkey a week before it was actually used, with its arms moved to the exact positions they were in later. Projectors who thought they had cancelled their astral appointments were seen by other psychics who were sitting in the room. Since the extrasensory world is crowded with people and objects, there were many such intrusions along with what appeared to be legitimate projections.

The law of emotional association in OOBEs was dramatically illustrated. A projector from Toronto, Canada, Mrs. Terry Marmoreo, was drawn to a burning building a block away. Another projector flew into an apartment across the street, attracted by more interesting things than were happening in Dr. Osis' office. In one case, a psychic who admitted she was stimulated more by people than by objects, found herself on the first floor of the ASPR building, where several persons were preparing an art exhibit. She accurately described what a young woman was wearing and saw a man carrying a long box to the back yard.

The mode of travel differed from psychic to psychic. Some, like Alex Tanous, merely had to think of the office and they were there in a flash. Elwood Babbitt believed that the office was psychically brought to his awareness. Claudette Kiely, of Granby, Massachusetts, passed factories on one of her trips to New York. Terry Marmoreo was conscious of flying from Toronto and saw ships in New York harbor. When she got to the building, she was momentarily trapped in the hall on the fourth floor. Ann Jensen, of Enid, Oklahoma, passed over Louisville, Kentucky, on the way to New York, but had trouble getting through the door of the ASPR building. Paul Neary, who made it from Atlanta, Georgia, to New York in five minutes, floated over Columbus Circle a few blocks away, then glided up the steps of the building.

Astral Visitors from the North

Alex Tanous' projections from Maine to New York were typical in some ways of his out-of-body style. As in his other OOBEs, he tended to come in from above and had difficulty in stationing himself in front of the fireplace. He hovered over the coffee table and saw objects from a different perspective, with the barrier appearing below him as a wall.

From overhead Tanous often saw elements and partial shapes of the objects rather than seeing them as separate, identifiable entities, a problem other projectors also had who were standing before the fireplace. Yet it was clear to at least one of the experimenters, Vera Feldman, that he was seeing what was on the coffee table. Miss Feldman called Tanous an "excellent subject" and said that although he did not always give exact descriptions of the objects, "it was apparent that he had seen them in such a way that they were hard to describe."

Miss Feldman recalled one experiment in which Tanous drew the barrier as it would appear from above rather than from the fireplace. The experimenter climbed up a ladder and saw that the barrier was as Tanous had sketched it.

In spite of distortions, however, caused by his position in space, Tanous often correctly identified the objects or gave the right shape and color. One "hit" was a basketful of fruit. Another time he saw a candlestick. Once he noticed a cup of tea on the coffee table that had been placed there by one of the girls in the room. Sometimes his visual focus was restricted to the area immediately below him, but at other times he had circular vision and could see the whole room at a glance.

Although Tanous thought of himself only as a ball of light, his double was once seen by psychic Christine Whiting, who was sitting in the room. She saw him "jackknifed" above the floor "next to the target-table . . . unable to straighten his 'body' upright." Although she had never met him, she gave an accurate description of his physical appearance and said that he was astrally dressed in brown corduroy trousers and a long-sleeved white cotton shirt with the sleeves rolled up to his elbows.

When I spoke to Alex later, I asked him to describe what he wore during his fly-in episodes but did not tell him how he had appeared to Miss Whiting. He recalled wearing a cotton shirt with sleeves rolled up and brown slacks which looked like corduroy trousers to most observers.

Alex appeared as a solid figure to Miss Whiting, who also saw other projectors as solid, with clear facial features. When she met Tanous some months later, she recognized him as the man she had seen "jackknifed" over the coffee table.

The Smiling, Brown-tinted Girl

Although Dr. Fisher told me that Elwood Babbitt usually saw physical objects in their spiritual qualities, on Babbitt's last projection he had a sensational "hit." His instructions were to come through the door of Dr. Osis' office and from that angle of vision take note of what was on the table. He correctly saw the brown-tinted plasticine figure of a smiling girl on the righthand side of the table. He also saw a very large plant that was at the right rear of the office and a picture hanging on the wall. A small toy chair had been placed behind the girl's back so that it could not be seen from the doorway. Babbitt sent in a sketch with each object in its correct position, but did not include the toy chair.

The projectors did not feel restricted to what was on the coffee table. When Terry Marmoreo flew in astrally from Toronto, her double was attracted to a crystal paperweight on Dr. Osis' desk. The crystal had a hole on the bottom side. She tried to slip her astral finger into the hole and saw light reflecting from the crystal like "a hall of mirrors." Also on the desk was a booklet, on its cover stars arranged in a circle. She told Dr. Osis over the phone later that she had seen "circular stars" and "snowflakes in May." There was a pattern of snowflakes inside the booklet.

Mrs. Marmoreo, who had never visited the ASPR building in her physical body, told me that the office appeared to her double as filled with light, much brighter than physical light. She said that colors on the astral or spiritual plane are more vibrant and that a person's traits show up more clearly than when observed from the physical body.

One evening when Terry was scheduled to make her astral trip, Dr. Osis and Bonnie Perskari brought three cameras into the office with the hope of photographing her or any other psychic or supernormal visitor who might wander in. About the time Mrs. Marmoreo was scheduled to arrive, Bonnie took a picture of the fireplace with her camera. Fifteen minutes later Terry called from Toronto and said that while she was in the office in her double, she saw a woman in the doorway holding a camera. A light flashed in her double's eyes and the woman's face kept getting in front of the lens.

Parapsychologists and psychics know that very often when a breakthrough is imminent, gremlins or devils or other ill-meaning entities put on their hex. Before Bonnie could have the film developed, the camera was stolen from her apartment.

The Boy on Roller Skates

In a paper prepared for the 1973 convention of the Parapsycholog-ical Association, Dr. Osis told how Christine Whiting saw and accurately described Claudette Kiely, a Massachusetts psychic and teacher who projected to the office on January 11, 1973. Even more startling was the fact that the double of Mrs. Kiely's twelve-year-old boy, Gerard, also appeared to Miss Whiting and was wearing astral roller skates. Mrs. Kiely was not aware that Gerard was with her, and the boy did not know that he had projected. Gerard had fallen asleep while watching a television program featuring waitresses on roller skates.

Miss Whiting described Mrs. Kiely as a blonde and said that she was wearing a "long bright-green skirt (or perhaps it was wide pants) of some shimmery material, acetate or silk perhaps, short-sleeved white blouse (or could have been very soft sweater), her hair done up in a bun at the nape of her neck—and pulled back from the forehead." Mrs. Kiely appeared to be between thirty-five and forty years old.

When she projected on January 11, Mrs. Kiely was wearing "a gold negligee under an indigo blue silk quilted bathrobe." Al-though the colors did not strictly match, Miss Whiting accurately saw the silk material and "shimmery" quality of Mrs. Kiely's negligee and bathrobe, which has a sateen finish. Mrs. Kiely, thirty-seven years old at the time of the projection, wore her blond hair swept up from her forehead but with a plain top and a "twist" at the back of her neck that looked like a bun. Although she was not wearing a blouse, she had a "long bright-green skirt" in her closet.

Miss Whiting gave Gerard's exact age—twelve—and said that he was slender (he was underweight at the time) and that he had "dark brown hair with bangs over his forehead." Mrs. Kiely de-scribes her son as a brunette and sent me a photograph of him that shows "bangs over his forehead."

The boy's astral presence seemed to discourage Dr. Osis, who felt that instead of Mrs. Kiely taking a trip to New York, Miss Whiting may have "scanned" her at home with Gerard in Massachu-setts. Osis said that "no boy was scheduled at the time." It is possi-ble, however, that the lad made an unscheduled astral visit with his mother. The target area, Dr. Osis' office, could hardly be restricted to those who had been booked in advance to drop in.

Since Gerard was asleep, he was in an appropriate state of consciousness for projection. He had an understandable motivation —children like to go with their parents on trips, even if the journey is astral and not physical. As for the roller skates, since the image was in Gerard's mind when he fell asleep, he may have taken the skates along as a pleasant thought-form, perhaps as a symbol of movement.

I wrote to Mrs. Kiely and learned some facts that support the reality of a mother-and-son projection. Mrs. Kiely and her son are emotionally very close and have psychic rapport. Gerard is keenly interested in her projections and prayed for her success the five times she attempted the fly-in. He was praying for her on January 11 when he dozed off with the images of the roller skates and his mother's out-of-body flight in his mind.

Perhaps the most significant fact of all is that Gerard dreamed of "flying in an airplane."

Mrs. Kiely had a subjective experience while she was seen with Gerard that may be as meaningful in its symbolism as the out-of-body impressions of Kevin Lampro, Diana Marble, and other projectors and witnesses described earlier. During the fly-in of January 11, she had abdominal sensations similar to her uterine contractions when Gerard was born. Mrs. Kiely writes:

> The same sensations of the labor room and Gerard's delivery process were duplicated and relived in this astral projection experience . . . I am still thrilled over the notes recorded on the abdominal process —the process of "delivery." I wonder in reality if one "flyer" can deliver another to a place—if Gerard needed my assist and power to travel.

Mrs. Kiely emphatically disagrees with Dr. Osis' assumption that she was in Massachusetts and not New York on January 11. She recalls standing on the "X" mark in front of the fireplace and "lining my feet up on the cross cards of the 'X'—duck style! I also did a yoga squat on the 'X.'"

On another trip Mrs. Kiely seemed to give evidence that she was present in some form. She projected while wearing her indigo blue robe. On the way to New York she saw an industrial smokestack with, in her words, "smoke billowing high into the dark heavens."

She had a feeling of oneness with the smoke and thought, "I am the smoke! I AM that smoke!"

At the same time in New York Bonnie Perskari saw what she described to me as either a ball of white light or a blue haze at the fireplace. Christine Whiting, who was also in the office, saw a large blue light or haze which grew larger and formed into an object. Mrs. Kiely then tried to flick a light switch on the wall near the door, and Miss Whiting saw a flash of light.

Since I have not been given access to the ASPR files, I do not know whether Mrs. Kiely correctly identified the objects on the coffee table during her astral visits. The information in this chapter from the experimenters' point of view was told to me by Dr. Osis and ASPR staff members Janet Mitchell, Vera Feldman, and Bonnie Perskari. Much of this material corroborates what the projectors said about their own impressions of what happened during the fly-ins.

Perhaps Claudette Kiely should have the final word about her astral flight of January 11. She writes: "I *know* I was in the office that night . . . and I will never be convinced otherwise!"

Dr. Osis does have a valid purpose in trying to separate out-of-body experiences from purely clairvoyant ones, and from his point of view what seems to be an extraneous factor may defeat the purpose of the experiment. Psychic phenomena, however, OOBEs or otherwise, rarely come as isolated events, and whatever is added should also add more meaning rather than be set aside as superfluous. The significant role played in other cases by such factors as motivation, symbolism, and emotional association suggests that there is very strong, if not conclusive, evidence that both mother and son projected to the ASPR office on January 11.

One may reject every psychic experience by finding an element in it that can be explained in other terms, even other psychic terms. There is a tendency among parapsychologists to dismiss one kind of psychic happening by calling it another kind. Thus the evidence for mediumship or astral projection is explained by a kind of super-ESP. Ghosts or spirits, second bodies are illusions, psychological constructs based on supernormal knowledge processed in the physical brain.

If this kind of mental gymnastics were carried to an extreme, no OOBE would be safe from it. For example, take the case of

Babbitt's correctly sketching the smiling figurine of a woman on the coffee table as seen from his position in the doorway. Was he really there in his double? Or did he read Dr. Osis' mind and did while in trance what hypnotic subjects often do to please the hypnotist? Knowing clairvoyantly how all the objects were arranged in the room, he then sketched them as they would appear if he had been standing in the doorway, leaving out the hidden chair, and thus fulfilling Dr. Osis' expectations at the time.

It is possible that a psychic plot of this kind was hatched in Babbitt's subliminal mind, but it may be easier to believe, as I do, that Elwood was out of his physical body and viewing the smiling brown figure as his double stood in the doorway.

The Box Experiment

The next ASPR project utilized an "optical image device," or "box," designed by physicist Len Barcus. This time the subject was not home but lying in one room in the ASPR building and attempting to project to another room where the box was located. In the box were a wheel divided into four colors and a carousel with different pictures on it. When the experimenter pressed a button, the wheel and carousel spun around and stopped at random with one of the pictures locked into position with one of the colors.

About halfway up the box was a small "porch" from which the projector could look through a glass at the color-picture combination and tell the experimenter over the intercom what he saw, and whether the combination was in one of four positions—upper right, upper left, lower right, or lower left. For example, a set of five pictures mounted on the carousel would be used in one experiment—a man, a fish, an elephant, etc.—along with four colors: red, black, green, blue. At one time a fish might appear against the color green in the upper right quadrant, another time an elephant against red in the lower left.

With four colors, five pictures, and four positions possible, the projector had one chance in eighty to get the right combination of all three. He might have a complete hit or just a partial hit in which he would get color and position and but not the right picture, or the correct color and picture in the wrong position.

The color-picture combination was actually an optical illusion and could be seen only when the double stood on the porch and looked through the glass. If the subject "scanned" the contents of the box clairvoyantly without leaving his body, they might appear to him as a complete unit, with the carousel and color wheel separated as they actually were inside. When the double was truly on the porch, he would see only the restricted portion—the four quadrants of the color circle with the picture optically superimposed on one of them.

Telepathy, which was a possibility in the fly-in experiment since at least one person always knew which objects were on the table, was also ruled out because the mechanism worked electronically, and the combination came up at random when a button was pressed. The experimenter did not know what the targets were until after each day's run.

Ingo Swann was the first subject to try the optical viewing experiment. After a month of testing to adjust to the conditions of the experiment, a second month's results were judged statistically significant.

Alex Tanous came in from Maine on several occasions—this time physically—to do the box experiment. Alex told me that during the first trials his "ball of light" was jumping all over the box instead of stationing itself on the porch as instructed, sometimes being in the box, sometimes over it, often to the right or left. Once he found himself in a black area between the back of the wheel and the wall behind the box. His objective during this series of tests was to gain control over the double so that he could direct it to the porch.

Alex said that he sometimes created too much light of his own, and this light got in the way of the targets. As he gained more experience in going to the box, he managed to modulate his light. He found that the less conscious he was in his physical body, the better the results when he went out. He did better also when he worked quickly, in clusters, without too much intervening time from one run to the next.

Tanous generally saw positions and colors more accurately than the pictures, which were small in size and, as in the fly-in experiment, might be received as impressions rather than definite objects that could be named. Once he complained that there was too little light in the box, and it was learned later that there had been a mechanical failure. In one of Ingo Swann's projections, he had also complained that he couldn't see the target, and it was found that the light had gone out.

On one trip to the box, instead of being pure energy, Alex's double seemed to have some dimension. He was on the porch but at too low a level, and he stood on his astral toes to see what was inside. A piece of paper was then put on the porch and Tanous felt himself as being taller.

According to Dr. Osis, Tanous did better in the first tests than later when he was making adjustments to control his inter-room flights. The statistics of his first trials have been judged "significant." When I told Dr. Osis what Alex had said about jumping around too much during this period, Osis replied that "it was mighty good jumping."

Recently a new color wheel was designed, a less complicated device than the box, with the subjects viewing the target from above, as Tanous usually does on his out-of-body trips. Alex has given promising results in this test, once getting three hits out of a possible four.

In striving for control over the OOB process, Tanous has found that when he makes his "ball of light" more compact and concentrated, he can see the target more clearly. He calls it "fine tuning," and Dr. Osis now believes that these periods coincide with his successes. Another criterion for his success in seeing the colors and pictures is a feeling of transcending the ego, a sense of unity with the rest of the world.

Since Elwood Babbitt does not travel, at least physically, Bonnie Perskari and staff physicist Jim Merewether took the optical viewing mechanism to his home in Wendell Depot, Massachusetts, and twice tested him there. With Elwood sitting in his bedroom and the apparatus set up in his office, he made an extremely high score the first time but did not do as well later, when he was distracted by the noise from the crowd of people who are usually in his house.

Bonnie said, however, that Dr. Fisher, who had been critical of Dr. Osis and scientific testing of OOBEs, was delighted with the procedure this time.

In an article in the ASPR *Newsletter* (summer 1974), Osis states that the best tests in the "fly-in" experiment were those in which the projector was not fully conscious when leaving his body and went instantaneously to the target area. Those who had difficulty in getting out of their physical bodies and were conscious of traveling through space in another body or "vehicle" did not do as well. Thus Tanous, Swann, and Babbitt, who project with ease and seem to take the least amount of the physical self with them are apparently in a purer form most of the time and more truly out of the physical realm. The design of the experiments must always be taken into account, however, and psychics who did well in one type of test were not always as successful in another kind—and vice versa.

Although Dr. Osis states that the results of the experiments to date seem to be "consistent with the OOB hypothesis," he does not believe that he has reached his goal of "trapping the soul" in the laboratory. As a scientist, he prefers to keep testing and retesting his subjects and devising new ways to isolate the out-of-body experience.

What, in Dr. Osis' judgment, would give proof positive of an OOBE? He might not be prepared to call it conclusive, but he would be quite encouraged if bona fide second bodies or what he calls "apparitions" could be seen and photographed during the experiments. I thought of Christine Whiting's clear view of many doubles in the office and wondered why Dr. Osis did not give more weight to her testimony.

What of the future? The projects will continue with new designs as ingenious as the ones in use the past two or three years. Dr. Osis hopes that non-psychics as well as psychics will volunteer as subjects and witnesses. The electroencephalograph and other machines that detect changes in physiological processes and energy fields in the environment will be used as non-human means of detecting the double.

And best of all, hopefully, a solid, touchable, photographable apparition will appear in the laboratory and prove that the soul can live apart from its physical body.

Chapter 29

More Laboratory Experiments in the 1970s

At the Psychical Research Foundation in Durham, North Carolina, emphasis in the out-of-body experiments is on witnesses as well as subjects—human beings, animals, and mechanical devices. The human witnesses are members of the PRF staff, friends and acquaintances of the projectors, and other persons who have had OOBEs. The animal "detectors" are cats, small rodents (gerbils and hamsters), and a snake. The mechanical devices—thermistors, wire coils, photomultiplier tubes, and a spectrum analyzer—measure changes in the energy patterns of the target area visited by the projector.

The witnesses—human, animal, and machine—are stationed in a detection room where they will hopefully respond to the projector when he arrives in his double from a building some distance away. The animals are placed in enclosures, and their behavior is studied before the tests begin and compared with their actions when the OOBEs are taking place. If there is any significant change, such as from a pattern of moving about the cage and making sounds to a period of calmness and quiet during the OOBEs, it is an indication that the animal may be aware of the double's presence.

The projector, as in the ASPR experiments, must know when he is leaving his physical body and must bring back clairvoyant evidence of what he has seen in the detection room. To induce the physical and mental conditions of spontaneous OOBEs, he first goes through a "cooling down" period in which he relaxes every part of his body and stills his mind. As he leaves his body and returns, he describes what is happening over an intercom to a technician in the next room, where his physiological states are recorded on a polygraph.

Gaining Control Over the OOB Process

The star subject of the PRF experiments is Stuart Harary, better known as "Blue," a student at Duke University and a part-time member of the PRF staff. Harary, who was also a subject in the ASPR project, has had many spontaneous OOBEs, usually when he is relaxed or asleep. He told me that in both his spontaneous and experimental OOBEs, his I-Consciousness takes three forms. In one he is aware of a bodily shape, sometimes an exact duplicate of his physical body. In another he is a ball of light in glowing white, gold, or blue color. In the third form he is a pinpoint in space and has circular vision. At times he is conscious of being simultaneously in all three forms.

Sometimes Blue wears astral clothing over his second body form. The clothing may be a duplicate of what he had on when he projected or of some other garment in his wardrobe. Once he found himself in an astral shirt that did not match the physical shirt he was wearing. It was a shirt, however, that he had been thinking of wearing several days earlier, a thought-form that may have been in his subliminal mind at the time of projection.

Blue's spontaneous OOBEs often occur when he is falling asleep or just waking up. Sometimes he projects while asleep but not dreaming, while at other times he knows he is dreaming and wakes up in his double, reminiscent of Fox's and Muldoon's experiences. Blue can see his physical body, which is frequently cataleptic, lying on the bed his double has just left, but it appears as a dark shadow or silhouette. His shadowy physical body sometimes becomes a window through which he can witness future events.

Harary has had the experience of willing to see a friend, then falling asleep and making the trip without being aware of it until he learned later that the friend had seen his double. Once he was drifting off to sleep at 4:30 A.M. when he thought of visiting a young lady. She called him up the next morning and said that shortly after 4:30 she had seen a ball of light in the corner of her bedroom near the ceiling. When she asked, "Is that you, Blue?" the ball glowed more brightly. Other friends have also seen Blue as a ball of light or a momentary flash.

As Tanous, Swann, Monroe, and other projectors-at-will have found, complete control in the laboratory setting is not easy to achieve. Harary, who is one of the most analytical of the projectors I have met, feels that he is just beginning to gain control over the out-of-body process. Factors that affect the quality of his OOBEs are the thoughts that have been in his mind just before he leaves his body, his physical condition, and the state of his emotions. If body, mind, and feelings are not in balance, what he sees may be distorted or may contain unreal elements.

Hence the importance of the cooling-down period. In preparation for an evening experiment, Blue spends the day trying to be calm and to avoid disturbing situations. Sometimes, in order to slow down his physical and mental activity, he sits and meditates. When he walks into the laboratory and starts the pre-OOB cooling-down period, he is generally in a state of detachment.

The Language of the Soul Body

While the technician watches the polygraph that records what is happening to his physical body, Blue projects his double to the detection room twice during a forty-minute period and stays there for two minutes. He tries to see colored letters that are pinned against the wall and to take note of where the human witnesses are sitting. He also tries to attract the attention of the animals present and influence the thermistors and other mechanical witnesses.

To date the machines have recorded some changes, but the results are inconclusive. Harary was successful at first in describing where the human witnesses were sitting but less accurate in later experiments. This "decline effect" has been noticed in other laboratory experiments in the paranormal. The most interesting and meaningful response among the animals, that of a kitten, is discussed later.

Blue sees the colors of the letters more clearly than their shapes. In some instances, however, he gave the accurate shapes but not always the right name of the letter. One reason for failure of identification is that many letters of the alphabet are similar in shape, another that some of the letters were cut out in a stylized form that made them difficult to recognize. As in the ASPR experiments, identification of the targets depends on their size, dimensions, color, and what emotional significance they may have for the projector. Although geometric shapes come through, each could apply to a wide range of objects rather than the specific laboratory target.

Blue travels easily through all barriers and can get his double into very small physical areas when necessary. This was the experience of Alex Tanous when he found himself as a small entity on the porch of the box and could move around the interior of the box, although its dimensions were far too small for his physical body. It appears from other mind-over-matter cases that Blue in his soul body would have difficulty in affecting the environment of the target area. He points out, however, that his double may cause subtle changes in the spiritual plane of the environment he visits— changes that cannot be detected by the mechanical witnesses.

In common with other experimental subjects, Blue has learned that the world of the double is not always that of the physical body and that his subjective impression may distort the view from his astral position. In analyzing his experiences, Blue says that he probably responds both to his preconceptions of what he will find and to the physical reality that is there, and the picture that emerges depends on the conditions at the time of projection.

What is subjective, however, may well be a direct perception of the spiritual quality of an object and its environment. Harary's sense impressions in the out-of-body state are sometimes far more intense than in his physical body. He sees the target area in "full color," with colors that are often more vivid than usual or perhaps "simply different." His double hears sounds that are of the physical world but sometimes beyond it, sounds that are "incredibly beautiful and harmonious."

In perfecting his laboratory technique, Blue is trying to analyze the information received by the double and to translate it into the kind of perceptual terms his physical brain understands. It is as though the double, particularly the soul body, speaks another language, and a mediator or interpreter is necessary within the same organism.

The Animal and Human Witnesses

The human witnesses did fairly well at first in detecting Harary's presence, one of them seeing a flash of light when he was there. They did less well as the experiments continued. Dr. Robert Morris, research co-ordinator of the project, feels that too much concentration and self-consciousness may get in the way and that it is better for the would-be witness to work at some distracting task and not think too hard about his role as a psychic receiver.

Dr. Morris' theory is supported by what is known in the project as the "periphery effect"—unusual reactions of personnel who were not supposed to be witnesses. Once, for example, Blue made a side trip in his double to the polygraph room next door. The technician felt a shock to his spine and sensed that Blue was there. During another day's experiment, Blue detoured to a room next to the detection room, and a girl there saw him as lines of light.

Among the animals the most significant response was that of a kitten that belonged to Harary. The kitten was in a cage with its floor marked off in squares to measure his activity during the OOB and non-OOB periods. He was normally very active, romping over the squares and meowing at regular intervals. When Blue directed his double to the cage, the kitten stayed quietly in one place and made no sound.

Sometimes Blue did a "pretend" OOBE. Instead of consciously projecting, he just imagined that he was with the kitten. During the "pretend" OOBE, the cat stayed active and showed no unusual response.

There have been many spontaneous OOBEs, some of them mentioned earlier in this book, in which an animal, most often a dog, was a witness. D. Scott Rogo's dog barked at him when he was out of his body. Frederik van Eeden, a Dutch neurologist who practiced projections during sleep, believed that his double was in the garden one night and that his dog stared at him through the window.

A twin project to the PRF's out-of-body experiments is the investigation of haunted houses with animal detectors. At an ASPR lecture on November 7, 1973, Dr. Morris described how a dog, a cat, a rat, and a rattlesnake acted in a house where a young bridegroom had killed his bride and himself in their bed. The rat gave no sign that he observed anything unusual. The other three animals were drawn to a chair in the room. The rattlesnake assumed a threatening posture toward the chair, then seemed to track something from the chair to the window. The dog whined at the chair, while the cat meowed excitedly at it.

Morris believes that the use of animal detectors may give us, along with other kinds of knowledge, more information about the relationship between animals and human beings and tell us how information is processed by different animals. At least for this writer, the possibility that Harary's kitten knew when his double was present supports the theory that emotional bonds are strong motivations for out-of-body encounters, whether the witness is a human being or an animal.

For the future, Morris plans experiments that will show if the animal witness is inclined to move toward a point in space where the projector stations himself. A double projection is also planned in which Harary and another psychic will try to visit the same target area together. In addition, more sophisticated instruments will be used as detectors.

Projection Through Sight and Sound Effects

An experiment at the Division of Parapsychology of the University of Virginia, conducted by John Palmer and Carol Vassar, was designed primarily to bring on the physical and mental conditions that generate spontaneous OOBEs. Rather than screen the would-be projectors, as was done at the ASPR and PRF, Palmer and Vassar called for volunteers, whether or not they had had previous OOBEs. Sixty persons showed up for the tests, most of them in the college age bracket.

Two rooms were used. In one a set of magazine photographs was placed on a table. The other room was darkened while the subjects rested on a reclining chair and were given a progressive relaxation technique similar to the cooling-down procedure at the Psychical Research Foundation. Next they received audiovisual stimulation designed to create a sense of detachment from the physical body. The visual stimulus was a rotating spiral disc, lighted from behind by a strobe light and set about a foot away at eye level. The subject was told to stare at the rotating disc and imagine himself being drawn into it. Meanwhile he listened to a sine wave tone through headphones.

The subject then pictured himself traveling through the wall to the next room and looking at the magazine pictures. After the experiment, he was shown the pictures and asked to match them with his visual impressions. The subjects were also asked whether they had actually left their bodies during the experiment, and 42 per cent answered yes. The impressions of the latter ranged from momentary sensations of separation without imagery to the feeling of being in the other room and even outside the building.

The results of this experiment, which Palmer calls exploratory, were considered negative. Of statistical interest was that of fifty subjects questioned, twenty-nine who had no sensation of leaving their bodies scored at chance (non-psychic) level in their visual impressions of the target, while the twenty-one subjects who thought they had had OOBEs scored below chance. Parapsychologists call the below-chance results "psi-missing"—that is, consciously or unconsciously, the subject may be avoiding the target rather than trying to hit it and may actually be receiving psychic information without being aware of it.

Palmer thought that the "psi-missing" might have resulted from the *active* attempt of the subjects to leave their bodies and look at the target pictures, and that a more *passive* attitude—allowing the image of the target to come into consciousness—might get better results. In a follow-up experiment with forty student subjects, he divided them into two groups, one active as in the first experiment, the other passive. The passive group were not told to try going out of their bodies but were instructed to let the visual impressions come into their minds—a purely clairvoyant procedure.

Instead of using a rotating disc, halves of Ping-pong balls were placed over the subject's eyes, and he was told to stare into a white light. The purpose was, in Palmer's words, to "facilitate the visual component of the OOBE, which in the previous experiment was not as strong as we would have liked." Of the twenty active subjects, this time thirteen reported being out-of-body, while only four of those in the passive condition said they had had OOBEs. The seventeen who "went out" scored significantly above chance, a reversal of the "psi-missing" result in the first test.

As the first experiments in a project that will include many more, they were too brief to be meaningful. Also, since the subjects were volunteers accepted without regard to previous OOBEs, their results, at least in the beginning, could not be expected to match those of experienced psychics such as Babbitt, Tanous, Swann, and Harary. The design of the experiments is a good one, however, and could in time bring on with consistency the states of consciousness that seem to accompany psychic phenomena. By removing tension from the physical body, shutting off outside stimuli, and through sight and sound focusing the attention of the subject not only on but perhaps *into* the experience of leaving his body, the experiment may induce OOBEs even in non-psychics.

Palmer has suggested an ingenious test for OOBEs that might also give strong evidence for survival: a psychic who can go out at will projects to a medium who does not know him, controls her body just as spirits allegedly do, and gives those present information about himself previously unavailable to the medium. If, in addition, he shows personality characteristics that definitely identify him as the projector, an impressive case could be made for an out-of-body experience. While he is presumably in control of the medium's body, machines similar to those in the PRF experiment would be registering changes in the physical environment of the seance room.

Many of the cases described in Chapter 17 of this book come close to meeting the requirements of this test. In the automatic writing and direct voice cases, particularly that of Gordon Davis, the personality of the projector and the information he gave were quite startling. All that was lacking was his awareness of being present. Other projectors, such as Vincent Turvey, however, claimed that they consciously took over a medium's body and spoke through her.

I would like to carry Palmer's proposal a step further. Since the double of a medium has to go somewhere when her physical body is occupied, she might try to visit and take over the tenantless body left behind by the projector. Although he would have the advantage of knowing where he was going, the medium would have to use her psychic ingenuity to find his physical body. This kind of exchange might bring many complications, but it would be worth trying.

Outdoor Areas as Targets

At the prestigious Stanford Research Institute (SRI) in Menlo Park, California, they call it "remote viewing." Physicist Russell Targ, who is conducting the tests with fellow physicist Harold Puthoff, regards the out-of-body concept as too threatening to the subject. It is true that going out of the body may be an unnerving experience for non-psychics, especially first-time projectors, but psychics who are used to it are quite comfortable with the idea. Of the five subjects in the SRI experiments, however, only two were considered psychic in the beginning, one of them Ingo Swann, but the three non-psychics all gave positive results.

Unlike the ASPR and PRF experiments, the SRI project uses outdoor areas as targets rather than what Targ calls "artificial" objects such as the optical viewing instrument, or box, at the ASPR, and the colored letters and animal cages at the PRF. Targ does not believe that numbers or letters are easily seen by the double, and his view has been borne out by other experiments. He prefers that the psychic be stimulated by interesting places to visit, such as other countries and natural settings.

According to Targ, the design of an experiment should fit the needs of the subject rather than those of the experimenter. In one of the tests, he asked Ingo Swann to choose his own target. Swann suggested that he be given the latitude and longitude of a target area and he would attempt to land there in his double. Since distance is no obstacle in psychic situations, Targ gave him a point halfway around the world. While sitting in a chair, puffing a cigar and drinking coffee, Swann projected to the Indian Ocean, to an island so tiny it is not on most maps.

Swann drew a sketch of the island, where there is a French meteorological station. A comparison with a map of the actual island showed that the sketch and the map were almost identical, even to a large white mountain in the western portion.

A second projector was Pat Price, former mayor and police commissioner of Burbank, California, who volunteered for the experiments. Price had had so many psychic experiences during his police career that he was an ideal subject. Given the same geographical co-ordinates, Price went immediately to the same French island and also drew an accurate sketch, even more detailed than Swann's.

He not only saw the island but heard the inhabitants speaking French.

In the fall of 1973 a series of carefully designed "remote viewing" tests were begun at SRI with Pat Price as the principal subject. In each test, one or more members of the SRI staff drove to a location in the San Francisco area selected by a random method and stayed there for half an hour. Back at the laboratory Price sat with the experimenter, generally Dr. Targ, and attempted to project to where the car had gone, although neither he nor Dr. Targ had any advance information about the selected area.

Five SRI scientists, not connected with the project, evaluated the results, correctly matching six of nine locations with Price's descriptions of them. Price does not believe that his view of the target areas was "remote" but that in each case, after a one-minute period of relaxation, he went out of his body instantaneously to the designated area. He believes also that his I-Consciousness occupied a position in space and that he was there in his double for the half-hour period.

Price's descriptions of the target areas, both verbally and in drawings, were often so accurate that Targ could identify the area without being told where it was. Sometimes precognition would be operative, as the subject guessed what the target would be even before it was selected.

One of the areas was a swimming-pool complex in a park two miles south of the SRI building. There were two large pools and a concrete block bathing house. Water could be heard bubbling in the circulation system that fed the pools. Price, whose double observed the complex for half an hour, concluded that it was a "water purification system" about two miles from the laboratory. He sketched the two pools but about 10 per cent smaller than their actual size when drawn to the scale of the map. He saw the bathhouse as a one-story concrete building and sketched it accurately in relation to the swimming pools.

Interestingly, Price also drew two water storage tanks, although there were none in the complex. This appeared to be a subjective image based on his identification of the area as a water purification plant.

What conclusions may be drawn from the results to date of the experiments at the American Society for Psychical Research, the

Psychical Research Foundation, the University of Virginia, and the Stanford Research Institute? How do the experiences of the psychic subjects differ from spontaneous OOBEs as we have examined them and as the psychics themselves have experienced them? What more can we learn from the experiments about the nature of out-of-body phenomena? What do machines such as the electroencephalograph tell us about what is happening to the physical body when the double is away?

Many of the difficulties of other controlled experiments in ESP laboratories are present in the OOB tests. When one goes out of his body naturally, without conscious effort or laboratory controls, his need or the need of others may take him directly to his "target," usually another human being with whom he has a close relationship. Even then, however, his mode of departure and the nature of his OOBE are conditioned by his state of mind and body.

Laboratory subjects are also motivated by the desire to do a successful experiment, but they must project mostly to objects instead of living, breathing individuals. Thus many of the ASPR projectors found themselves going off in search of persons and activities rather than confining their doubles to the designated areas where there were only lifeless objects and machines. Although members of the staff were in Dr. Osis' office during the fly-ins, the focus of attention was on the objects. The PRF experiments did attempt, however, to use human and animal witnesses who had some kind of rapport with the projectors. Blue Harary's bond of affection with his kitten was a factor that led to promising results.

The size of the targets was also an obstacle. There was difficulty in both the PRF and ASPR experiments in clearly seeing numbers and letters. The double was more sensitive to light and color, which may be spiritual attributes. In the SRI tests, the use of natural outdoor settings in bright daylight seemed to have greater appeal for Pat Price and other subjects, as well as being more interesting and more closely associated with life and people.

The attempt to gain absolute control over the OOB process presented a problem but also a challenge to such psychics as Tanous and Harary, who were strongly motivated to master the technique of projection in the laboratory. This kind of dedication promises eventually to yield the results that Targ, Osis, Morris, and Palmer are seeking. To reach this goal, however, it will be necessary to cope with distortions in perception that arise in part from subjective feelings and from the conscious effort required by the design of the experiments. Thus a period of mental and physical preparation, a cooling-down phase, is important.

Harary found that the need for control requires that the experimental projector be in good health. Although Blue has many spontaneous OOBEs when he is ill or very tired, as is the case with other projectors, extreme fatigue is a deterrent in the laboratory because he cannot direct where his double will go. When he goes out of his body in these fatigue states, his double simply "drifts away" instead of heading for the detection room. In spontaneous OOBEs, he may travel great distances but during the experiments it is necessary to keep his I-Consciousness close to his physical body and not let it take off on its own.

The discrepancy between what the experimental projector reports and what is actually there—what Dr. Osis calls the "fantasy" element, may be explained in many instances by the fact that a different, even keener perception is operating, the soul body or spiritual perception postulated by Dr. Fisher. The ball of light of both Harary and Tanous, the ionized particles that Swann sees with his astral eyes, the sensitivity of Babbitt and others to auras and bright light—these are experienced during psychic probes that do not always yield the kind of sensory images registered by physical eyes.

Finally, there is the matter of psychic style. Tanous and Swann fly instantaneously to near and far locations. Price needs only sixty seconds of relaxation before he flashes to the target area. Babbitt either goes into a deep trance that frees his soul body as his physical organism is taken over by Dr. Fisher, or he remains conscious during his OOBEs. Terry Marmoreo is aware of traveling to her destination. Tanous and Harary are balls of light, Harary often a dot in space. Several of the psychics, notably Tanous and in some respects Swann and Harary, do not think of themselves as viewing the targets directly but as receiving information that is relayed to their physical organisms for processing and interpretation.

Mechanical witnesses are still in a somewhat rudimentary stage in terms of their ability to detect what may be physically undetectable, but as more sophisticated equipment is designed and more money is available for such equipment, there may be more definite evidence of energy patterns being affected by the mind-over-matter power of the double. (See the next chapter for examples of such psychokinetic effects.) The fact that these devices are mechanical may at present keep the projector from interacting with them as freely as he might with human beings and animals.

Polygraph tracings of what is happening to the physical organism have not yielded much evidence of changes during OOBEs except in one rather significant function: Ingo Swann, Blue Harary, and Robert Monroe all lost voltage while they experienced themselves in their doubles. This loss of electricity may well be linked to the electrical fields of life that are discussed in the next chapter.

Chapter 30

Of Psychiatrists, Professors, and Perception

In 1969 Sally Marsh, a twenty-three-year-old college student living in New York City, had an OOBE that just lasted a few seconds, but it changed the course of her life. What started out as a beautiful experience turned into a nightmare because of her psychiatrist.

Sally, a bright and impulsive girl with a tendency toward introspection, had been in psychotherapy for three years. From the beginning the doctor had insisted that she suppress her irrational impulses and imaginative fancies and live according to a system of logic. Every move, every decision must be thought out carefully, every strange notion that flitted through her mind must be examined, explained, and discarded. For two and a half years Sally followed this strict mental regime, feeling neither better nor worse but having complete faith in her doctor.

Then something happened to her. She put on a recording one day and as she listened to the music, logic went out the window. In her own words, she "transcended the process." She was transformed, joyful, in love with living. She found pleasure in each moment, in people and nature. She enjoyed taking long walks in the sunlight, looking into the face of the sun and absorbing its warmth. She began to feel happy for the first time in her life.

One day she came in for her therapy and told the doctor how happy she was. The doctor frowned.

"Why are you happy?" he asked.

"Because I am."

"But you don't become happy out of a clear blue sky. There has to be a reason for everything. You have to find the reason."

"Why? I feel happy—that's all."

Sally's relationship with her psychiatrist began to disintegrate, but she found a new integration in herself. The more desperately the doctor tried to make her a rational being, the more she delighted in irrationality and spontaneity, and the more meaningful her life became to her.

She began to feel that a wonderful event was about to happen. Perhaps there was too much ecstasy in her life, too much to support life itself. She wondered if she was going to die. But she was not afraid of death. She even looked forward to it.

One afternoon while working on her part-time job, the feeling became so strong that she thought she would explode. She was on the verge of tears. One of her employers, a woman doctor, noticed that Sally was upset and suggested that she rest for awhile in an unoccupied office. She lay down on the floor and thought about death. But she felt peaceful, prepared.

Suddenly she was out of her body, floating near the ceiling. She was not afraid. She thought, "This is not death." It lasted only a few seconds, but when she returned to her body, she had a sense of sublimity, of being in harmony with the rest of the world. Her employer, who was on her way to a nearby hospital, suggested that Sally go along with her and get a physical checkup. Sally agreed.

At the hospital she told the resident physician that she had gone out of her body and that it was a strange and wonderful experience. Without a word, the doctor went into the next room and called Sally's psychiatrist. Five minutes later two policemen walked in and told her that they were taking her to the psychiatric ward at Bellevue Hospital.

The policemen were apologetic. She didn't look psychotic to them, but they had to follow orders. The doctor at Bellevue found her calm and rational and sent her home. Sally's employer was shocked when she heard later what had happened. She had recommended going to the hospital only for a physical checkup. There was nothing mentally or emotionally wrong with Sally.

But the appearance of the policemen, their official designation of her as "psycho," the trip to Bellevue so disturbed Sally that she has held her feelings in check ever since. She believes now that to have an OOBE is equivalent to being psychotic. I have tried to convince her that this is not so, but I have not succeeded as yet. Traumatic experiences of this kind are not eradicated overnight.

Sally's out-of-body experience was the climax of her discovery that the world could be a place of beauty and joy. Her projection was both actual and symbolic. The need to separate from her psychiatrist and find her own way culminated in the separation from her physical body. The self that rose above her body was the new Sally that was born of her suffering and that promised a richer and fuller life for her. Instead, her psychiatrist sent her rudely back into the old self with its fears and inhibitions, its distrust of life and people.

Is Astral Projection Abnormal?

The point of this true story is that it highlights the opinion of many psychiatrists, psychologists, and doctors that any behavior deviating from what is considered normal must be an aberration. Let me add quickly that most psychiatrists would not have reacted as Sally's did when he heard of her OOBE. They would have said nothing or would have tactfully suggested that her experience, though real to her, did not actually take place but symbolized an inner conflict. I believe that it was symbolic but I also believe that it happened in reality.

Clearly, it was her psychiatrist's problem and not Sally's. But why should an out-of-body experience be regarded as a psychotic episode? It is a common medical belief that to see one's own double or to experience one's consciousness as being out of the physical body is symptomatic of a temporary or permanent brain dysfunction, or, at best, of a neurotic need. Dr. Jean Lhermitte states, in the *British Medical Journal*, that "the appearance of the double should make one seriously suspect the incidence of a disease." According to D. H. Rawcliffe, "the vast majority of the hallucinations in which it seems to the subject that he has left his own body are found among psychotics."

It will be recalled that the writer Maupassant, during a period of physical degeneration, thought that his double came into the room when he was writing and dictated to him. On the basis of the Maupassant and other such cases, doctors and medical writers conclude that all experiences of the double are hallucinatory. Most of the cases cited, however, are of the patient's consciousness remaining in his physical body, not an awareness of being in the double.

If one concedes that psychological and physical abnormalities such as brain damage sometimes bring on the illusion of the double, it does not follow that all OOBEs are hallucinations. Wouldn't it be more to the point to say that because so many normal persons have OOBEs, those in abnormal states may also be having them? It is becoming increasingly evident that psychic experiences, OOBEs or others, are everyday occurrences and that they can happen to anyone, the healthy-minded as well as the mentally disturbed.

The Indestructible Double

The subject of brain damage and psychosis brings us to a crucial question: If there is a double, is it the primary body or is the physical body dominant? Or are both directed by a third body essence, as Dr. Fisher suggested? When a person suffers from senility or other forms of brain deterioration, is his whole psyche permanently affected or is there an intelligence still in control, if dormant? Were Maupassant and others in his condition hopelessly deteriorated in body and mind, or did their doubles, if they had doubles, still retain their psychic health? Is mind generated by the physical body or is it an indestructible force?

The British Society for Psychical Research has recorded a case in which an old woman's double acted intelligently and rationally although her physical brain had degenerated. The case was reported by Dr. F. C. S. Schiller in the SPR *Journal* of 1923–24. The daughter of Mrs. F. B. Robertson wrote to her aunt that her mother "had gone entirely insane" and was now in a sanitorium. Her condition had been diagnosed as "senile dementia due to arteriosclerosis."

While in this condition, Mrs. Robertson ostensibly projected to the seance room of Leonora Piper. She spoke about members of her family and friends, particularly about a man whom she had resented.

"I do forgive Mr. Westerham. I see his weaknesses now. I did not understand so well before . . . Tell G [her sister] I am well and happy . . . Speak to me, G. I have reached you many times, sometimes consciously to yourself, and sometimes unconsciously. I understand so much better now . . . [I] shall be released from my perishing body and go on and on with my own."

Dr. Schiller comments: "The bodily machine may become disordered in ways which irresistibly suggest that the 'soul' is destroyed or deranged . . . All the time it may be leading a life of its own . . . or on another plane, though it cannot express this life through a body which is no longer in its possession in any effective sense."

It is possible, of course, as in the Gordon Davis case, that the living astral traveler who manifests in the seance room is not conscious of doing so, but some part of the personality seems to be expressing itself in an intelligent and meaningful way. Mrs. Robertson's condition was subject to short periods of trance, similar to the altered states such as sleeping and hypnosis, in which the projector may not be aware of his astral trip.

In *Discarnate Influence in Human Life*, Ernesto Bozzano cites cases of soldiers in wartime whose brains were "torn up by shrapnel, with abundant loss of brain matter," yet they got well and showed no sign of mental deterioration. In other cases autopsies have shown extensive brain damage in an individual who gave no sign of it in his behavior while alive. Bozzano tells of an officer who complained of nothing more than an annoying headache. He died suddenly and "an autopsy of his brain revealed the fact that an abcess of slow development had reduced the entire brain to a pulp of pus."

It would seem from these examples that the seat of intelligence must lie somewhere else than in the physical brain, and no amount of damage to the brain is going to affect the true brain that operates from the double or from whatever essence it is that controls the double. A striking example of this kind was given in Chapter 15. It is a tenet of medical science that when the brain is denied oxygen for more than six minutes, the patient either dies or suffers irreversible brain damage. Yet Dr. George Ritchie, medically dead and without oxygen for nine minutes, recovered with his mind intact.

There are many instances of the double being free of the defects in its physical counterpart. Paul Lachlan Peck's double was intact although a blood clot was forming in his physical head. Flo Thompson watched her pneumonia-ridden body from a healthy second self. Bert Slater, who had a cut on his physical arm, saw it healed in his astral arm. Mrs. Webb, near death in the hospital after her brain operation, was able to send an intelligible message through the hand of medium Geraldine Cummins. Ed Morrell, in great pain while tightly bound in his strait jacket, had no pain as he soared aloft in his double. Vincent Turvey, as weak as a child in his physical body, found that his double could lift a bed with two people in it.

Senses such as sight, hearing, taste, smell, that are defective or inoperative in the physical body, are often restored to normal, even supernormal acuteness in the duplicate body. Celia Green gives several examples. One of her correspondents wrote that although it was impossible for her to read physically without glasses, she read two pages of a book with her astral eyes. Another correspondent projected two hundred miles and found herself in a theater. She writes: "A significant point is that I am rather deaf and could never, in the body, have heard stage dialogue without my hearing aid; nor could I have seen so perfectly without my glasses. Despite the absence of both these artificial aids, I found no difficulty whatever in seeing and hearing perfectly."

Another projector wrote that he had lost his sense of taste and smell after suffering a fractured skull. His double could smell quite normally. Out-of-body reports usually stress the visual sense, less often the sense of hearing, and sometimes the sense of touch. Smelling while in the double is rather rare, although the highlight of Linda White's projection to her aunt's apartment in Flushing, New York, was her smelling the lasagna that was cooking in the oven.

OOBEs of the Blind and Near Blind

It is intriguing to think that the blind may have some form of perception closely related to the visual when out of their bodies.

If the double is free of physical defects, a blind projector who was once sighted could see with astral eyes. Dreams should give us a few clues. In his paper "Dreams of the Blind" (*Psychoanalytic Quarterly*, Vol. 27, No. 2, 1958), Dr. H. Robert Blank writes that "a remarkable feature concerning the dreams of the blind is the frequency with which the 'flying' dream occurs. The sensation of floating through the air is quite common. One blind man I know experiences this sensation in seventy per cent of his dreams. For this I have no explanation to offer, but in this case, too, *all objects are perfectly visible.*" (Italics mine.)

Although most dream researchers believe that the blind know in their dreams that they are without sight, psychologist Elinor Deutsch, who is blind, questions this assumption. In "The Dream Imagery of the Blind" (*Psychoanalytic Review*, July 1928), she gives examples of many blind persons, particularly children, who claim that they see in their dreams. The youngsters she interviewed saw such objects as an automobile, a buffalo, a lion, a house, and buildings. Many of them saw colors. Although Deutsch believes that they use the word "see" to describe what they experience through other senses, their dreams are suggestive of another kind of perception in which a visual sense might operate.

The dreams of a blind student discussed by Raymond H. Wheeler in "Visual Phenomena in the Dreams of a Blind Subject" (*Psychological Review*, July 1920), show many features of an OOBE. The student kept seeing "a foggy light," "a heavy fog or thick dust," "a faint brownish haze," and "black, inky water," all suggestive of the semiphysical vehicle of vitality in Hades conditions. He also saw "a circle of rather brilliant light," "a bright and silver form," and other attributes of a Paradise setting. His physical body was cataleptic.

Flying dreams, the foggy light, brilliant colors, physical catalepsy —all are evidential of OOBEs during the dreams of the blind. If there are few actual reports by the blind themselves of projecting in their sleep, it may be because when a dreamer wakes up, his tendency is to think of himself as he is in his waking condition and to reconstruct his dream in "rational" terms. Thus, blind persons might tend to block out any memories of out-of-body experiences and of seeing in their dreams.

There has been too little investigation of the paranormal experiences of the blind, particularly of their OOBEs. An outstanding case, however, is that of Loraina Brackett, reported by Slater Brown in *The Heyday of Spiritualism*. Loraina, who lived in Providence, Rhode Island, in the early 1800s, suffered a head injury when she was sixteen, followed by deterioration of eyesight and blindness at the age of nineteen. When hypnotized, however, she was able to walk around the house and perform as though she were sighted. She could read messages in sealed envelopes and could see pictures by holding them to the back of her head.

Loraina also projected to places some distance from Providence and described them in accurate detail. Once when she was hypnotized, a Colonel William Stone suggested that she go with him astrally to his home in New York City. Although she had never been in New York, she saw the Battery as though she were physically there, gave accurate details about the Astor House, and described both the interior and exterior of Colonel Stone's house, including the pictures hanging on the walls and the appearance of his servants.

What of the congenitally blind? If the double does not share the defects of the physical body, it should have some form of perception akin to sight, even if the physical eyes are sightless at birth. I have tried, without success so far, to locate a congenitally blind person who has had an out-of-body experience. I did, however, interview a young man blind from birth who attends Columbia University in New York City. He did not remember having an OOBE, but he described a recurring dream, or rather a nightmare, that is suggestive of astral projection. He awakens with his body cataleptic and feels himself spinning around. This generally happens when he is lying on his back, the favorite position of projectors.

Does sight depend upon the physical eye and the optic nerve? Take the case of Mme. Bire, who was totally blind until she spontaneously recovered her sight while bathing in the waters at Lourdes, France. A doctor who examined her later protested that she could not possibly see because her optic nerve had atrophied. Yet she saw the doctor, his office, and everything else she looked at. A month later the doctor examined her again and found that the optic nerve was functioning once more.

If Mme. Bire had an atrophied optic nerve, what was she seeing with? What invisible, immeasurable force first gave her sight, then repaired the nerve so that her physical organs could play their

customary role and match what had been happening without their
assistance?

Hypnotherapist Milton Erickson regressed an extremely near-
sighted young man to the age of eight, when he had had perfect
eyesight. In this state he was able to read books he could not
read as an adult and thread fine needles without glasses. If the
young man's physical eyes were defective, what was he seeing
with when he was hypnotized? Did the perfect eyes of the double
take over while he was in trance, just as the perfect brain of the
double may function outside a brain-damaged physical body?

The Nature of Perception

What is perception? Many projectors see a different kind of
reality, particularly when the soul body is operating. The evidence
from cases of astral projection, from dreams, hypnotic trances, etc.,
suggests that seeing, hearing, tasting, smelling are but different
channels for what is a fundamental perception, an attribute of
Mind. At birth there are different sense organs subject to accidents
and to the frailties of the physical body, but also a true perception
untouched by physical events and probably resident in a second
body or soul.

There is more and more evidence that one sense may take
over the function of another—a phenomenon called synesthesia. Recent experiments in dermo-optics—seeing through the skin—give
many examples. In Russia blind children are being trained first to
sense colors through rays of light beamed on their hands, then to
read printed matter. In this country a teacher named Evelyn
Monahan is showing blind children in the South how to read
through the skin.

At the Human Dimensions Institute in Buffalo, psychic Carol
Liaros is teaching blind persons to see colors not by touch but by
passing their hands above pieces of colored paper and detecting the
"energy aura" around them. After learning to distinguish between
colors, some of the subjects are able to make out shapes of objects
and even faces on photographs. One young woman woke up in the
middle of the night with her bedroom bathed in a chartreuse light
through which she saw the outlines of her bed and dresser. She had
sight for half an hour, then remembered that she was blind, and the
scene faded away.

In France Dr. Yvonne Duplessis of the Centre d'Information de la Couleur in Paris is training a person who is going blind to perceive through her forehead, cheekbones, and fingers. Dr. Cesare Lombroso wrote in *After Death—What?* of a patient who, when suffering temporary attacks of blindness, could see with her ears. With her eyes bandaged, she could read lines held against her ear. When Lombroso placed a magnifying glass between her ear and the sunlight, she cried out that she was being blinded.

What is the basic form of perception that is operating in all these cases? The Russians have speculated that what they call the "bioplasmic body" is responsible. Every cell may be a sense receptor. We may go further and say that the double through its own light and electricity can perceive the outer world with all the senses of the physical body and, in addition, experience other dimensions with senses that go beyond the physical.

The Electrodynamic Fields of Life

The subject of perception brings us back again to the question of the primary substance or essence of the double. Is it present at birth as a replica of the physical body or embryo? Is its development parallel with the development of the physical body? Is it regulated by the physical body's behavior or does it transmit life energy to the physical organism through the connecting cord?

The theories of Dr. Harold Burr, late professor of anatomy at the Yale University School of Medicine, suggest that there is a prenatal electrical force that controls the development and behavior of the physical body. There are life-fields (L-fields) or fields of electrodynamic energy that surround organisms and direct their growth. Using a specially built vacuum-tube voltmeter, Dr. Burr was able to predict the structure of a fully developed adult animal or plant by studying the voltage gradients in a seed or an egg. The L-fields of a frog's egg, for example, showed that the nervous system "always grew along the axis with the highest voltage gradient."

In human beings as well the L-fields are the matrix or mold, the organizing principle that determines how the body will grow and maintains its structure throughout life. Dr. Burr points out that the materials of our bodies and brains are renewed constantly. "All the protein in the body, for example, is 'turned over' every six months." If we meet someone we have not seen for several months, we recognize him even though all the molecules of his face are new.

The L-fields preserve the character of the body, no matter how often the body renews itself. An analogy is the action of a magnetic field. If iron filings are scattered on a card held over a magnet, they move into the pattern of the magnet's force field. If the filings are thrown away and new ones scattered on the card, the new filings arrange themselves in the same pattern. The magnetic field is the organizing principle.

Cells that may be removed from one section of a growing organism and grafted onto another section will develop into whatever organ was destined along this line of growth. An example is given by Gardner Murphy in *Three Papers on the Survival Problem:* "The same kind of cells, removed at the same time from the same growing individual, would become, in one environment, skin cells; in a second, muscle cells; and in a third, nerve cells. Growth is an expression of a field."

It is the L-fields, the organizing principle, that determine what the tissue becomes more than the inherent properties of the tissue itself.

The L-fields are, however, subject to another controlling force—the mind. What Edward Russell in *Design for Destiny* calls the T-fields (fields of thought) have priority over the L-fields and can alter them. Psychiatrist Leonard Ravitz found, for example, that when a subject was hypnotized, his change of mood or mental set affected the L-fields around his body. During Dr. Ravitz' experiments there was a loss of voltage when the subject was in a state of "hypnotic catalepsy," comparable to a loss recorded on the EEG when Dr. Tart was testing his subjects and when researcher Janet Mitchell monitored Ingo Swann's physiological processes during his OOBEs. Correlating these processes with the out-of-body state is in its rudimentary stage, however, and no definite patterns have been established.

An important aspect of the L-fields that may have implications for the concept of the duplicate body is that electrodes from the voltmeter do not have to be in contact with the organism. As the electrodes are taken further away from the body, the field is still active. Experiments in the past, notably those of De Rochas and Durville, indicated that there may be a force present at some distance from a hypnotized subject that responds to a physical stimulus, such as the prick of a pin, and that may even move objects.

Researchers in Russia, using sophisticated machines, have detected electrostatic and magnetic fields about four yards away from the human body. The Russians call these "biological fields" and believe they may cause objects around them to move. Nelya Mikhailova, one of Russia's celebrated mind-over-matter psychics, was found to have unusually strong fields that could be measured twelve feet away.

Another Russian with mind-over-matter ability, Boris Ermolaev, who has been successfully tested under laboratory conditions, can squeeze an object with his hands, then separate his hands and leave the object suspended in space. The larger the object, the longer it hangs in the air unsupported. A Russian scientist has called this force "biogravity," theorizing that Ermolaev creates his own gravitational field.

It is not possible to state unequivocally that L-fields and biogravity can be equated with the second body. Dr. Burr points out, for example, that the chemical processes in the body are not under the complete domination of the L-fields but that there is a give-and-take of energy between them, possibly that protoplasm supplies the energy and the L-fields give it direction. Burr did find, however, that the L-field is present in the unfertilized egg of a salamander and that it keeps the same structure after fertilization. This fact would indicate that the future growth of an organism is already determined before conception and can be charted by a voltmeter.

What the L-fields do is to support the idea of an organizing principle that may well be the human double present at conception or even before, that may be measured electrically as a variety of fields surrounding and interacting with body organs and combining into the larger field that embraces the whole body. The L-fields or the double or the mind, whatever one may wish to call this organizing and directing principle, keeps the physical body intact during its lifetime, provides it with spiritual energy that keeps it functioning, and leaves it at death. This principle can be detected photographically as well as electrically through the Kirlian process and may sometimes be seen as the aura by the naked eye. Sometimes it takes the form of a substance called ectoplasm, the semiphysical material that levels off into purer energy as the soul body takes over, and in its purest form may become light as suggested by

Dr. Fisher and experienced by such psychics as Alex Tanous and Blue Harary.

Just as the L-fields may vary from moment to moment or day to day, depending in part on the physical condition of the organism and particularly on the influence of mind and emotions, so the double varies in appearance and substance according to the constitution of the projector, the circumstances of the projection, and the projector's soul development as well as his state of mind. When, as Dr. Burr points out, the pattern of the L-fields shows that there is or will be a weakness in the physical body, it is probably the more physical part of the double that reflects the condition of the body. When the soul body takes over, it is a purer essence not subject to the ills of the physical body and probably cannot be detected by instruments.

Essentially, the double is a thought form, just as the physical body and all physical objects may be, and is shaped and directed by the mind. It may appear younger, taller, in extended or contracted form, with clothing and other objects—however the mind of the projector wishes to present it. In its purer form the double interacts with time as well as space, going into the past or future. Thus, just as the L-fields are constant yet fluid and everchanging, the double too is a constant principle that assumes many guises.

It was theorized in an earlier chapter that various aspects of the double—ectoplasm, ovoid form or etheric envelope, electrical energy, and pure light—may be seen as auras around the physical body, each body extending further out from the physical. The auras have also been identified as an "energy body," "emotional body," and "mental body." These bodies or fields change and interact as physical, mental, and emotional conditions change. The "mental body," furthest away, may be the equivalent of the soul body that creates the L-fields and is itself created by mind or spirit. The "energy body" and "emotional body" may be related to ectoplasm, the vehicle of vitality, the aura, the surround. The L-fields may be an attribute of all three bodies. Admittedly, these are only rough approximations and are as yet theoretical. The L-fields and other discoveries do not solve the problem of the double. They do, however, give support for its existence and help build a solid base for future research.

All bodies, however, are created and shaped by thought, the prime creator and organizer.

When Sally Marsh went briefly out of her body, she was on the way to learning the fundamental nature of her being. She recalls the experience as "a beautiful state of consciousness." If her psychiatrist had not interfered, it could have been the beginning of a spiritual unfoldment.

I have given the young woman a pseudonym because of the trauma that followed. No, she was not psychotic at the time but as normal as thousands of other projectors who have had OOBEs. And she can take heart in the fact that Burr, Lombroso, Bozzano, Carrington, Osis, Morris, and other researchers who are investigating the nature of man have come close to proving the reality of the human double in their laboratories.

The
Ultimate Question

Chapter 31

A Rehearsal for Dying

The story of astral projection comes down finally to the ultimate question: Do OOBEs prove that human personality survives bodily death? Parapsychologists from the American Society for Psychical Research and the Psychical Research Foundation hope that their experiments can give a definitive answer. If it can be shown that human beings do have a second body and that their I-Consciousness can travel outside the physical body in an astral vehicle, it may furnish the most convincing argument for survival since the British Society for Psychical Research was founded nearly a hundred years ago.

There are many motivations for an OOBE and many physical and psychological conditions that generate it, but its main purpose may be to practice the act of dying and in so doing, remove the fear of death. If her psychiatrist had not steered her off course, Sally Marsh might have discovered through projection that the symbolic loss of her old self was a giant step forward in her life and that some day she would gain a new self in physical death. There are many other cases in this book of first-time projectors who were convinced through their OOBEs that life is just a prelude to a new life-in-death. The Egyptian mystery rites, described in an earlier chapter, gave the initiate the experience of dying to incorporate into his life experience.

Evidence of Survival Through Death Apparitions

There are many ways in which the physical act of dying gives evidence of a second body and survival. In crisis apparitions, the double of a dying man appears to a friend or relative at some distance from the scene of death, often when the witness does not even know of the illness or fatal accident. In its first years the British Society for Psychical Research investigated many cases of this kind. Three such crisis apparitions were described earlier in connection with the clothes worn by doubles—the British soldier whose astral apparel had a thin red thread weaving through the pattern, the grandmother of Charles Tweedale who appeared to him at the moment of death in her goffered cap, and the sailor who projected to his sister as he drowned.

In *Footfalls on the Boundary of Another World,* Robert Dale Owen tells about a young English girl who is asked to watch an infant in a country house while the child's father takes his seriously ill wife to a doctor in London. The baby dies suddenly, but this fact is kept from the dying mother. Two days later the young lady goes into a room where the body of the infant lies in a coffin and sees the mother's double sitting on the sofa and looking at her dead child. The double does not speak but points to the infant, then up to heaven, and fades away. The time is between 4 and 4:30 P.M.

The next day the girl receives a letter from the woman's husband, stating that his wife died the previous day, but just before her death she cried out, "Why did you not tell me that my baby was in heaven?" When her husband did not answer, she said, "It is useless to deny it, Samuel; *for I have just been home, and have seen her in her little coffin.*" Then she, too, died—at 4:30 P.M.

Another story of a dying mother projecting to her children first appeared in Richard Baxter's *Certainty of the World of Spirits* and again in the present author's *In Defense of Ghosts.* Mary

Goffe, a young Englishwoman of the seventeenth century, lay near death in her father's home in West Malling, nine miles from her own home in Rochester, where a nurse was taking care of her two small children. At 1 A.M. Mary's breathing became labored and she closed her eyes as though sleeping. At the same moment the nurse in Rochester heard the rustle of a gown and woke up. She saw Mary's double come into the room and look down at her youngest child, who was asleep. The nurse said, "In the name of the Father, Son, and Holy Ghost, what art thou?"

Mary vanished, but in West Malling, a woman sitting at her bedside saw that she started to breathe normally again. When Mary woke up the next morning, she told the woman, "I was with my children last night when I was asleep." Moments later she died.

There were many witnesses to the Mary Goffe projection, in addition to the nurse who saw her double. A neighbor to whom the nurse told the story the next morning went to West Malling and learned from Mary's father that she had gone astrally to Rochester. A Reverend Thomas Tilson investigated the case and interviewed Mary's mother and father, the nurse, two neighbors, the minister, and the woman who had spent the night with Mary.

An early study by physicist William Barrett as well as the recent one by Karlis Osis shows that many of the dying have visions of the dead. Some of the terminal patients do not know that the friend or relative whose astral body they see has just died. In the early 1900s two young schoolgirls who were friends became ill during an epidemic. Jennie died, but Daisy was not told. Just before Daisy succumbed, her eyes lit up and she turned to her father and said, "Why did you not tell me that Jennie had gone? Here is Jennie, come to take me with her."

In Baird's A Casebook for Survival, a marine medical officer tells of a vision that came not only to a young girl as she died at sea but also to the medical officer, the captain of the ship, and several members of the crew. A ten-year-old orphan was on her way back to Japan and in the care of the ship's captain. She became ill, grew rapidly worse, and appeared to be dying. Both the child and the medical officer who was in the room saw a light directly over the bed that radiated waves of blue, white, and gold. The doctor described it as a luminous globe "like a distant light diffused and glowing in a heavy fog." As it came down gently and lit up her face and hair, the girl cried out, "Oh Mama, Mama, I see . . . the way . . . and it is . . . all bright . . . and shining!"

The light rose quickly, dissolved, and disappeared, and at that moment the child died. Seconds later the captain came in with the first and second mate and said they had just seen "a ball of blue fire . . . that appeared right over our heads in the smoking room."

A Vapor Rising from the Head

What may be even more significant for the reality of the double is that many witnesses see a second body emerge from the head of someone who has just died. Very often it starts as smoke, mist, or vapor rising above the head and then crystallizes into a lifelike duplicate of the physical body.

Joy Snell, the nurse who was visited at night by the double of her friend Margaret before the latter became fatally ill, was at Margaret's beside when she died. Miss Snell wrote: "Immediately after her heart had ceased to beat, I distinctly saw something in appearance like smoke . . . ascend from her body . . . This form, shadowy at first, gradually changed and . . . resolved itself into a form like that of my friend who had just died . . . The face was that of my friend but glorified, with no trace on it of the spasm of pain which had seized her just before she died."

Miss Snell said that in her twenty years of nursing, she saw this same phenomenon at death many times.

"The spirit form, in appearance an etherealized duplicate of the human form, takes shape above the body in which life has become extinct and then vanishes from sight."

The same process has been observed at death throughout history. In Chapter 3 of this book it was stated that in Tahiti a vapor could often be seen rising from the head of the corpse, gradually increasing in size, and then taking the form of the physical body. Robert Crookall has given many instances in which the departing double was first seen as a mist, a vapor, a cloud, or a blue light—a gaseous substance that in most cases condensed into a human form.

One of Crookall's accounts is of a seven-year-old boy who was sitting at the bedside of his dying grandmother. Suddenly she sat up and coughed, then lay down again in the stillness of death. A puff of white smoke rose from her body, floated across the room, then drifted through the open window. Eileen Garrett said that as a child she saw "a grey smoke-like substance rising in spiral form" from dying ducks. Later, when her own child died, the smoky substance "curled and wove rhythmically away."

Many observers have seen the aura of the body change as death drew near. In "A Vision of Death" (*Light* Magazine, July 9, 1887), a letter signed "M.A. Oxon." stated that as the writer sat at his dying friend's bedside, the colors of the aura grew "more and more defined as the spirit prepared for departure." Edgar Cayce, who diagnosed illnesses of persons often hundreds of miles away, once saw a neighbor without an aura and feared for her life. She died the next day.

Dr. Walter Kilner, who was able to detect auras with chemical screens, said that the aura faded rapidly at death. This has also been demonstrated by the Kirlian photographic process, which shows the gradual fading out of the aura surrounding all organisms —human, animal, and plant—when death is near.

Most of those who see the second body at death also watch the connecting cord break off. The Tahitian clairvoyants saw a "vapory cord" attached to the head, which disappeared when the physical body grew cold. Dr. Hout, who witnessed the astral projection of three patients while they were unconscious during surgery, was at his aunt's deathbed when there emerged "a silver-like substance . . . streaming from the head of the physical body to the head of the spirit double." He called the cord "a connecting link between the physical and spirit bodies, even as the umbilical cord unites the child to its mother."

The cord usually is severed when the double emerges at death, but occasionally the bodies remain connected for a long period. "M.A. Oxon." wrote that, although the doctor had pronounced his friend dead, "the magnetic cord was yet unbroken and remained so for yet eight and thirty hours." When the cord finally broke, the dead man's face relaxed and lost its look of suffering.

Sometimes there are two or more witnesses who see the double leave at death. In her *Journal*, Louisa May Alcott writes about "a curious thing" that happened when her sister Betty died; "I will tell it here, for Dr. G said it was a fact. A few moments after the last breath came . . . I saw a light mist rise from her body, and float up and vanish in the air. Mother's eyes followed mine, and when I said, 'What did you see?' she described the same light mist. Dr. G said it was life departing visibly."

Two rather detailed descriptions of the double leaving at death come to us from the nineteenth-century psychic healer Andrew Jackson Davis and from an unnamed psychic whose version is given in Chevreuil's *Proofs of the Spirit World*. In his *Harmonial Philosophy* Davis wrote:

> The clairvoyant sees right over the head what may be called a magnetic halo . . . golden in appearance and throbbing as though conscious . . . The emanation is elongated and fashioned in the outline of human form. It is connected with the brain . . . by a very fine life-thread. On the body of the emanation there appears something white and shining, like a human head; next comes a faint outline of the face divine; the fair neck and beautiful shoulders manifest, and then in rapid succession all parts of the new body down to the feet—a bright shining image, somewhat smaller than the physical, but a perfect prototype in all its details . . . The fine life-thread continues attached to the old brain. The next thing is the withdrawal of this electric principle. When the thread snaps the spiritual body is free.

The other psychic wrote:

> *The brain took on a particular brilliancy* . . . I saw another head being formed, which took shape more and more distinctly . . . In the same manner as the fluidic head became detached from the brain, I saw being formed successively the neck, the shoulders, the torso, and finally the entire fluidic body . . . The deformities and defects of the physical body had almost entirely disappeared from the fluidic body . . . the mind or discarnated intelligence raised itself up at a right angle above the head of the deserted body, but before the final separation of the tie, which had united the material and intellectual parts for so long, I saw a vital current of electricity forming itself on the head of the dying one and becoming the basis of a new fluidic body . . . It was impossible for me to know what was passing in this revivified intelligence, but I remarked its calm and its astonishment at the profound sorrow of those who were weeping near her body.

Sometimes a living double will encounter the double of someone who has just died, as the novelist William Gerhardi did when he met his friend Bonzo on the astral plane. During one of Caroline Larsen's OOBEs, she visited the home of a dying acquaintance and saw his double leave at death. The newly dead man, who had been an alcoholic, immediately began searching for a bottle of whiskey, found it, and tried to lift it to his mouth. His astral hand went right through the bottle, much to his disgust. Then he looked up and saw Mrs. Larsen's double, became confused, and staggered out of the house.

Where his double went is not known. Perhaps, a bit too late, he swore off drinking after seeing Mrs. Larsen's "ghost," not realizing that he was one himself.

Photographing the Double at Death

There have been other ways to infer the presence of a surviving body at death. An ingenious doctor, Duncan MacDougall, built scales around the beds of terminal patients and weighed them both before and after death. He found that there was a difference in weight of about one to two ounces. Two Dutch physicists, Drs. J. L. W. P. Matla and G. J. Zaalberg van Zelst, devised a cylinder in which a spirit presumably displaced a portion of the air. They calculated the weight of the spirit as 2.25 ounces.

Claims have been made for the last hundred years or so that the astral body can be photographed at death. Dr. Baraduc, a Frenchman of the last century, took pictures of his son's body every fifteen minutes for three hours after his death. They showed a misty ball of light that hovered over the body and finally faded away. Dr. R. A. Watters, a physicist, photographed cloudy forms over the bodies of animals that had been killed, but his experiments were never successfully replicated.

Since it is possible to create bizarre effects on film either accidentally or by design, such photographs have been discounted as proof that the second body was present. This does not mean, of course, that psychic photography is not possible. Very sophisticated kinds of equipment and processes, such as infrared photography, the Kirlian process that catches the aura around organisms, Dr. Burr's vacuum tube voltmeter that registers the L-fields, the laser beam technique in holography that gives a multidimensional picture of an object or person—all may be put into service some day to record the presence of the double as it leaves at death.

In *Psychic Discoveries Behind the Iron Curtain,* Ostrander and Schroeder cite the experiments of the Russian scientist Genady

Sergeyev, who detected electromagnetic force fields several yards away from a corpse. The man had been declared clinically dead after his heart stopped beating and his brain activity ceased.

Until it can be established to the satisfaction of science that reliable instruments have unquestionably recorded the presence of the second body, not just once but repeatedly, and have identified it with the physical body of a person who has just died, we might listen to the words of Sylvan Muldoon:

For my part, had a book on immortality never been written, had a lecture on "survival" never been uttered, had I never witnessed a seance or visited a medium; in fact, had no one else in the world ever suspected "life after death," I should still believe implicitly that I am immortal—for I have experienced the projection of the astral body.

Chapter 32

The Future
of Astral Projection

In 1890 the British Society for Psychical Research asked thousands of persons this question: "Have you ever, when believing yourself to be completely awake, had a vivid impression of seeing or being touched by a living or inanimate object, or of hearing a voice; which impression, so far as you can discover, was not due to any external physical cause?" Of 17,000 replies, 10 per cent were affirmative. Fully one third of this group said that they had seen the doubles of living persons.

The percentage of those who have had out-of-body experiences themselves is even more impressive. The late Hornell Hart submitted this question to 155 students in his sociology classes at Duke University: "Have you ever actually seen your physical body from a viewpoint completely outside that body, like standing beside the bed and looking at yourself lying in the bed, or like floating in the air near your body?" Thirty per cent said yes.

Psychologist Francis Banks found that 45 per cent of a group of churchgoers had experienced projection. Dr. Jule Eisenbud, the psychiatrist who wrote *The World of Ted Serios,* has estimated the number of projectors at 25 per cent of the population. When astral traveler Robert Monroe asked a lecture audience in New York City how many had had OOBEs, about one third raised their hands. At my own lectures from 25 to 30 per cent of the audience tell me about their OOBEs.

These figures would be even higher if many projectors were not so reluctant to talk about their experiences. Some are afraid of ridicule. Others who are faithful churchgoers may think it is sinful to reveal that they are astral projectors, despite the knowledge that many priests and ministers were bilocators. It is easier to believe that only saints can work miracles, particularly if they lived a long time ago.

Although many of the projectors I have spoken with were quite willing to have their names and stories in this book, others gave me only a few details or refused to talk at all. Some spoke freely about their OOBEs but did not want their real names used for various reasons. In no case did I feel that anyone who spoke into my tape recorder was seeking personal publicity. It was rather the reverse.

Yet, with the concept of the double gaining acceptance in the 1970s along with other kinds of paranormal phenomena, more and more astral projectors are coming out of the woodwork and declaring themselves. The experiments of physicists Russell Targ and Harold Puthoff at the SRI, the carefully controlled tests at the ASPR and PRF, the serious study of OOBEs at the University of Virginia, the knowledge that many prominent persons in history saw and traveled in their doubles or knew of others who had left their bodies—all of this has removed the "taboo" label and brought the investigation of OOBEs into public view.

Astral projection in the laboratory is one of the outstanding facts of this decade. It is true that parapsychologists are cautious about reaching definitive conclusions, yet the striking successes reported in this book cannot be denied. Since OOB researchers know that science is reluctant to accept the validity of their results, they are probably a little slower to declare themselves than scientists would be in other areas of research.

The second body is an elusive phenomenon. One cannot grasp and hold it as he might a test tube in a chemistry lab. The double comes and goes, appears and disappears, shows its presence sometimes but not always, and success in the experiments is not constant.

Dr. Osis is still trying to "trap the soul" in his laboratory. Yet Alex Tanous and other projectors not only gave evidence that they correctly saw the objects on the coffee table during the fly-in experiments, but were frequently seen by other psychics in the room.

Perhaps Osis and the other researchers will only be convinced when someone like Tanous materializes in a second body and can talk and shake hands with those in the detection room. Meanwhile, to clinch the case, a highly sensitive camera will take pictures of him as he fades in, shakes hands, and fades out again. But how will we know that it is not his physical body we are seeing rather than his double? A detective would have to trail him before and after he is tested to be certain that the flesh-and-blood Tanous was elsewhere at the time and not in the laboratory posing as his double.

How will the skeptics explain away his appearance and disappearance? First, it will be said that cameras do lie at times and that film can be doctored. Second, the magicians will step forward and announce that they can work this same trick through methods known only to members of their profession. And even if Dr. Osis and other researchers published their findings in responsible journals, asserting that they had witnessed the materialization of the double and recorded it photographically and electronically, they would be accused of either naïveté or fraud. They would be downgraded in the press, their experimental controls called slipshod. Other researchers would try to replicate the experiments and fail to do so, since the second body is not always producible on demand.

Thoughtful persons are beginning to understand, however, that the reality we know in our daily lives is no more certain than the reality of the double, perhaps less so. The physical world is a façade behind which are atomic structures in constant motion and change. In subatomic physics, particles are behaving psychically rather than according to known physical laws. In one experiment, when an electron was fired at a screen it went through two holes at the same time, acting as though it were not one but two electrons. Does the electron have a double? Sometimes it resembles a particle, other times a wave. It goes forward and backward in time. In short, the subatomic world bears a suspicious resemblance to the world of the paranormal, and the second body would be and probably is at home in it.

The future of astral projection is assured, simply because the double is there and cannot be wished away by doubters. As time goes on, more and more persons will understand that they are alive in two bodies and will become better acquainted with the one they can't see. More parapsychology laboratories in universities and research centers will conduct well-controlled tests with psychic subjects, using other psychics, animals, and machines as witnesses. With rapid advances in electronics, photography, and holography, it may be possible some day to get a clear picture of the double leaving at death. The time of death itself, which is still uncertain, may be pinpointed as the moment when the silver cord breaks off.

What science will find is what has been known by thousands of projectors and by all wise men and women throughout history, whether they were scholars, workers in the field, or hunters in a primitive tribe. Two thousand years ago the Greek philosopher Posidonius, who taught both Caesar and Cicero, said: "The Souls of men, when released from the body in sleep or in ecstasy . . . behold things that they cannot see when bound to the body—they remember the past, see the present, and can contemplate the future. The body of the sleeper is as one dead, but the Soul lives on in the fullness of its power."

Postscript

No sooner was this book completed than more exciting news came in from OOB laboratories as well as more stories from people who travel in their doubles. Experimental subjects are beginning to influence detection devices during their projections. In tests designed by Dr. Gertrude Schmeidler of City College of New York, Ingo Swann has raised and lowered the temperature of thermistors while out of his body.

The American Society for Psychical Research has built an instrument called a "diving pool," an enclosure in which a feather is suspended on a string. The subject sits in another room and attempts to "dive" astrally into the enclosure and move the feather. Any such movement is measured electronically on graph paper. Alex Tanous and other subjects have given what appear to be positive results, but Dr. Osis reports that the widest fluctuation of the recording pen came when Pat Price, the subject of the SRI's remote viewing experiment, catapulted his second body into the pool from forty feet away. Dr. Osis believes, however, that it is too early to state unequivocally that the double is moving the feather.

Tanous, certainly one of the most active of all experimental projectors, has also been working with other organizations. In an OOB experiment at the Energy Research Group in New York City, his double touched an object on the floor which he described as "square" and "soft like leather." It was a rubber mat. At one point he saw "bright lights shining, bright lines running across," and described his feeling as "a unity again, a whole unity . . . the fine tuning . . . and this is when the object became very clear to me."

In Toronto, Tanous was the subject of another experiment conducted by Dr. George Owen, a biologist and parapsychologist who heads the New Horizons Research Foundation. Sitting in Dr. Owen's home, Alex concentrated on two house keys he had never seen before. Then he went out for lunch with Dr. Owen and came back an hour later. One key had bent five degrees, the other ten. The house had been unoccupied while they were gone.

Although this was not strictly an out-of-body experiment, the psychokinetic energy Tanous exerted on the keys is probably closely related to mind-over-matter phenomena during OOBEs.

More about Blue Harary, the star subject of the out-of-body project at the Psychical Research Foundation: In a later experiment one of the technicians, watching the target area through closed circuit television, saw Blue's double in the room.

From my dream diary of July 8–9, 1974:

> I finally did it again. I went out of my body last night while I was asleep, but what a strange experience it was—not like the first time. I floated around the room in a cloudy, misty haze. I could not see the walls or other details of the room and could not fix myself at a point relative to the rest of the room. I tried to see my body on the bed and finally saw myself lying there but not clearly. I must have been in my vehicle of vitality.

In March 1974 a devastating tornado struck the town of Xenia, Ohio, where Flo Thompson lives, bringing a large death toll and extensive property damage. Since the telephone lines were down and communication cut off, I asked Alex Tanous if he could "go there" and see if Flo and her family were all right. He was in Xenia and back instantaneously and told me that they had all escaped injury and that their house had little if any damage.

A few days later I received a letter from Flo verifying what Alex had said.

Writer Ralph Woods reports another offbeat OOBE involving a well-known long-distance swimmer. The man, who prefers to be anonymous, told Woods that whenever his physical body is exhausted during a marathon competition, he relaxes it by floating overhead in his double while continuing to swim. When he re-enters his body, he feels refreshed and can go on for quite awhile without fatigue. The man added that athletes in other sports also go out-of-body during competition, but they don't talk about it.

In August 1974 I met Carol Ann Liaros at the convention of the Parapsychological Association and learned more details of her experiments at the Human Dimensions Institute in Buffalo, where she teaches blind persons to read colors with their hands (see Chapter 30). Many of the subjects are now getting spontaneous visual impressions. One man began to see out of the side of his head. A woman who is totally blind said she saw a shadow walk in front of her.

In one experiment the blind subjects attempt "mind travel"—sending their consciousness to the homes of volunteer workers on the project. They use a step-by-step process, as one might do who is practicing out-of-body travel—picturing themselves leaving the room, flying to their destination, hovering over the house, then coming down and going through the front door. One blind subject smelled the aroma of food and could see a red color. The volunteer was in the kitchen and was wearing a red suit.

Another subject saw toys on the sidewalk in front of the volunteer's home, walked around them (either imaginatively or in her double), then walked up three steps and into the house, where she described in detail the contents of a room. All that she saw was actually there—the toys, the three steps, the objects in the room, even a painting that was hanging on the wall. A woman who had lost her sight at the age of two months projected her consciousness to the living room of a volunteer and correctly described the placement of the furniture by mentally walking around the room with her cane as she would have done in her physical body.

The September 1974 issue of Miss Liaros' newsletter, *E.S.P. and "You,"* quotes one of the blind subjects: "Awareness of my own energy field is developing and I feel as though I can really see myself: I see my hands working, I see my body. I see images and shadows and seem to be able to almost see what is in a room. It seems that I really see it, although I don't, and I am totally blind." In the November issue, another totally blind subject comments: "Imagine my surprise one day when I was sitting in my store and saw the outline of the cellar door on one side and the outline of my father sitting on the other side. It was shocking. I thought possibly I was getting my sight back. I covered my eyes with my hand and it was still there."

October 29, 1974. During a visit to Sir Alister Hardy's Religious Experience Research Unit at Manchester College in Oxford, England, I learned of an eighty-nine-year-old woman who had projected fifty years before. Her letter, beautifully written, described how she had been in her second body for a day and a half, while she watched her physical body go about its chores.

Dr. Karlis Osis invites the readers of this book who can project at will to take part in the experiments at the American Society for Psychical Research, 5 West 73rd Street, New York, N.Y. 10023.

Bibliography

Alcott, Louisa May, *Journal*, 1858.
American Society for Psychical Research, *Newsletter*, No. 12, Winter 1972; No. 14, Summer 1972; No. 15, Autumn 1972; No. 16, Winter 1973; No. 17, Spring 1973; No. 18, Summer 1973; No. 19, Autumn 1973; No. 20, Winter 1974; No. 22, Summer 1974.
Aradi, Zsolt, *The Book of Miracles*, New York: Farrar, Straus and Cudahy, 1956.
ASPR Symposium, "Parapsychology: Today's Implications, Tomorrow's Applications," May 18, 1974, New York City.

Baird, A. T., *A Casebook for Survival*, London: Psychic Press, 1948.
Bardens, Dennis, *Mysterious Worlds*, New York: Cowles Book Co., 1970.
Battersby, H. F. Prevost, *Man Outside Himself*, London: Rider and Co., 1940.
Baxter, Richard, *Certainty of the World of Spirits*, London: Joseph Smith, 1834.
Bayless, Raymond, *The Other Side of Death*, New Hyde Park, New York: University Books, 1971.
Bergen (New Jersey) *Record*, July 22, 1973.
Blank, H. Robert, "Dreams of the Blind," *Psychoanalytic Quarterly*, Vol. 27, No. 2, 1958, pp. 158–74.

Bolen, James Grayson, "Interview: Charles T. Tart, Ph.D.," *Psychic,* Feb. 1973.

Bozzano, Ernesto, *Discarnate Influence in Human Life,* London: John N. Watkins, 1938.

Brown, Slater, *The Heyday of Spiritualism,* New York: Hawthorn Books, 1970.

Bruce, H. Addington, *The Riddle of Personality,* New York: Moffat, Yard and Co., 1908.

Burr, Harold, *Blueprint for Immortality,* London: Neville Spearman, 1972.

Burt, Cyril, "Jung's Account of His Paranormal Experiences," *Journal,* SPR, Vol. 42, No. 718, Dec. 1963, pp. 163–80.

Carrington, Hereward, *The Invisible World,* New York: Beechhurst Press, 1946.

———, *Modern Psychical Phenomena,* New York: American Universities Publishing Co., 1920.

Catholic Encyclopedia, Vol. I, New York: Universal Knowledge Foundation, 1907.

Chevreuil, L., *Proofs of the Spirit World,* New York: E. P. Dutton & Co., 1920.

Cornillier, Pierre-Émile, *The Survival of the Soul,* London: Kegan Paul, Trench, Trubner & Co., 1921.

Cranston, Ruth, *The Miracle of Lourdes,* New York: McGraw-Hill Book Co., 1955.

Crookall, Robert, *Casebook of Astral Projection,* New Hyde Park, N.Y.: University Books, 1972.

———, *During Sleep,* London: Theosophical Publishing House, 1964.

———, *The Interpretation of Cosmic & Mystical Experiences,* London: James Clarke & Co., 1969.

———, *Intimations of Immortality,* London: James Clarke & Co., 1965.

———, *The Jung-Jaffe View of Out-of-the-Body Experiences,* World Fellowship Press, 1970.

———, *The Mechanisms of Astral Projection,* Moradabad, India: Darshana International, 1968.

———, *More Astral Projections,* London: Aquarian Press, 1964.

———, *The Next World—and the Next,* London: Theosophical Publishing House, 1966.

———, *Out-of-the-Body Experiences: A Fourth Analysis,* New Hyde Park, N.Y.: University Books, 1970.

———, *The Study and Practice of Astral Projection,* London: Aquarian Press, 1961.

———, *The Supreme Adventure,* London: James Clarke & Co., 1961.

———, *The Techniques of Astral Projection,* London: Aquarian Press, 1964.

Cummins, Geraldine, *Mind in Life and Death,* London: Aquarian Press, 1956.

D'Assier, Adolphe, *Posthumous Humanity*, London: George Redway, 1887.

David-Neel, Alexandra, *Magic and Mystery in Tibet*, New York: Claude Kendall, 1932.

Davis, Andrew Jackson, *The Harmonial Philosophy*, London: Rider and Son, 1917.

De Liso, Oscar, *Padre Pio*, New York: McGraw-Hill Book Co., 1960.

Deutsch, Elinor, "The Dream Imagery of the Blind," *Psychoanalytic Review*, Vol. 15, July 1928, pp. 288–93.

de Vesme, César, *A History of Experimental Spiritualism*, Vol. I–Vol. II, London: Rider and Co., 1931.

Ducasse, C. J., *The Belief in a Life After Death*, Springfield, Ill.: Charles C. Thomas, 1961.

du Maurier, George, *Peter Ibbetson*, New York: Harper and Bros., 1891.

Ebon, Martin, *They Knew the Unknown*, New York: World Publishing Co., 1971.

Edgerton, James A., *Invading the Invisible*, New York: New Age Press, 1931.

Eliade, Mircea, *Shamanism, Archaic Techniques of Ecstasy*, New York: Pantheon Books, 1963.

Elliott, G. Maurice, *The Bible as Psychic History*. London: Rider and Co., 1959.

Evan-Wentz, W. Y., *The Tibetan Book of the Dead*. New York: Causeway Books, 1973.

Fodor, Nandor, *Between Two Worlds*, Englewood Cliffs, N.J.: Parker Publishing Co., 1964.

——, *Encyclopedia of Psychic Science*, New Hyde Park, N.Y.: University Books, 1966.

Fox, Oliver, *Astral Projection*, London: Rider and Co., 1939.

——, "The Pineal Doorway—A Record of Research," *Occult Review*, April 1920, Vol. 31, No. 4.

Garrett, Eileen, *Adventures in the Supernormal*, New York: Creative Age Press, 1949.

——, ed., *Beyond the Five Senses*, Philadelphia: J. B. Lippincott Co., 1957.

Geddes, Sir Auckland, "A Voice from the Grandstand," *Edinburgh Medical Journal*, Vol. XLIV, 1937, pp. 365–84.

Gerhardi, William, *Resurrection*, London: Cassell and Co., 1934.

Green, Celia, *Out-of-the-Body Experiences*, Oxford, Eng.: Institute of Psychophysical Research, 1968.

Greenhouse, Herbert B., *The Book of Psychic Knowledge*, New York: Taplinger Publishing Co., 1973.

——, *In Defense of Ghosts*, New York: Simon and Schuster, 1970.

Gurney, Edmund, F. W. H. Myers, and Frank Podmore, *Phantasms of the Living*, London: Trubner and Co., 1886.

Hankey, Muriel, *J. Hewat McKenzie*, New York: Helix Press, 1963.

Harner, Michael J., "Common Themes in South American Indian Yagé Experiences," in Harner, ed., *Hallucinogens and Shamanism*, New York: Oxford University Press, 1973.

Hartwell, John, Joseph Janis, and Blue Harary, "A Study of the Physiological Variables Associated with OBE's," paper prepared for the 1974 convention of the Parapsychological Association, Jamaica, New York.

Hastings, James, *Encyclopedia of Religion and Ethics*, Vol. XI, pp. 441–46, New York: Charles Scribner's Sons, 1962.

Hill, J. Arthur, *Man Is a Spirit*, London: Cassell and Co., 1918.

Hives, Frank, *Glimpses into Infinity*, London: The Bodley Head, 1931.

Hocking, William E., *The Meaning of Immortality in Human Experience*, New York: Harper and Bros., 1957.

Holms, A. Campbell, *The Facts of Psychic Science and Philosophy*, London: Kegan Paul, Trench, Trubner and Co., 1925.

Hunt, Douglas, *Exploring the Occult*, New York: Ballantine Books, 1964.

Hutton, J. Bernard, *Helping Hands*, New York: David McKay, 1967.

Jaffe, Aniela, *Apparitions and Precognition:* New Hyde Park, N.Y.: University Books, 1963.

Jastrow, Joseph, *The Subconscious*, Boston: Houghton Mifflin Co., 1905.

Johnson, Raynor, *The Imprisoned Splendour*, New York: Harper and Bros., 1953.

Jung, C. G., *Memories, Dreams, Reflections*, New York: Random House, 1961.

——, *Seven Sermons to the Dead*, trans. H. G. Baynes, London: Stuart and Watkins, 1967.

Karagulla, Shafica, *Breakthrough to Creativity*, Santa Monica, Cal.: De Vorss and Co., 1967.

Knight, David C., *The ESP Reader*, New York: Grossett and Dunlap, 1969.

Koestler, Arthur, *The Roots of Coincidence*, New York: Random House, 1972.

Larsen, Caroline, *My Travels in the Spirit World*, Rutland, Vt.: Charles E. Tuttle Co., 1927.

Leadbeater, Charles W., *Dreams: What They Are and How They Are Caused*, London: Theosophical Society, 1903.

Leonard, Gladys Osborne, *My Life in Two Worlds*, London: Cassell and Co., 1931.

Letters from the Saints (anonymous), New York: Hawthorn Books, 1964.

Liaros, Carol Ann, *E.S.P and "You,"* newsletter, No. 6, Aug. 1974; No. 7, Sept. 1974; No. 9, Nov. 1974.

Light Magazine, 1923, p. 729; July 9, 1887, pp. 310–11.

Lombroso, Cesare, *After Death—What?* Boston: Small, Maynard & Co., 1909.

Marryat, Florence, *There Is No Death*, London: Griffith Farran Browne & Co., 1890.

Mitchell, Janet, "Out of the Body Vision," *Psychic*, Apr. 1973.

Monahan, Evelyn, with Terry Bakken, *Put Your Psychic Power to Work*, Chicago: Nelson-Hall Co., 1973.

Monroe, Robert, *Journeys Out of the Body*, Garden City, N.Y.: Doubleday & Co., 1971.

Morrell, Ed., *The Twenty-fifth Man*, Montclair, N.J.: New Era Publishing Co., 1924.

Morris, Robert, paper prepared for the 1973 convention of the Parapsychological Association, Durham, North Carolina.

——, "Survival Research at the Psychical Research Foundation," *Newsletter*, ASPR, No. 18, Summer 1973.

Muldoon, Sylvan, *The Case for Astral Projection*, Chicago: Aries Press, 1936.

——, and Hereward Carrington, *The Phenomena of Astral Projection*, London: Rider and Co., 1951.

——, *The Projection of the Astral Body*, London: Rider and Co., 1929.

Murphy, Gardner, "Three Papers on the Survival Problem," *Journal*, ASPR, Jan., July, Oct. 1970.

Myers, F. W. H., *Human Personality and Its Survival of Bodily Death*, London: Longmans, Green, 1903.

National Enquirer, March 4, 1973.

New York *Times*, Nov. 7, 1971; Feb. 25, 1974.

Osis, Karlis, paper prepared for the 1973 convention of the Parapsychological Association, Durham, North Carolina.

Ostrander, Sheila, and Lynn Schroeder, *Psychic Discoveries Behind the Iron Curtain*, Englewood Cliffs, N.J.: Prentice-Hall, 1970.

Owen, G. Vale, *Facts and the Future Life*, London: Hutchinson and Co., 1922.

Owen, Robert Dale, *Footfalls on the Boundary of Another World*, Philadelphia: J. B. Lippincott Co., 1860.

Palmer, John, and Ronald Lieberman, "ESP and Out-of-the-Body Experiences: The Effect of Psychological Set," paper prepared for the 1974 convention of the Parapsychological Association, Jamaica, New York.

——, and Carol Vassar, "ESP and Out-of-the-Body Experiences: An Exploratory Study," *Journal*, ASPR, Vol. 68, No. 3, July 1974, pp. 257–80.

Parapsychology Foundation, *Newsletter*, Vol. 16, No. 4, July–Aug. 1969, pp. 10, 20.

Parapsychology Foundation *Review*, Sept.–Oct. 1972, p. 19.

Pelley, William Dudley, "Seven Minutes in Eternity," *American Magazine*, March 1929.

Plutarch, *On the Delay of Divine Justice*, trans. Andrew P. Peabody, Boston: Little, Brown and Co., 1885.

Puharich, Andrija, *The Sacred Mushroom*, Garden City, N.Y.: Doubleday & Co., 1959.
Prediction magazine, June 1936, pp. 207–8, Dec. 1955, p. 60.
Prince, Walter F., *Noted Witnesses to Psychic Occurrences*, New York: Olympia Press, 1972.
Psychic News, August 12, 1961.
Psychic Research, May 1929, p. 267.

Ravitz, Leonard J., "How Electricity Measures Hypnosis," *Tomorrow* magazine, Vol. 6, No. 4, Autumn 1958, pp. 49–56.
Rawcliffe, D. H., *Illusions and Delusions of the Supernatural and the Occult*, New York: Dover Publications, 1959.
Ritchie, George, "Return from Tomorrow," *Guideposts*, June 1963.
Rogo, D. Scott, "Astral Projection in Tibetan Buddhist Literature," *International Journal of Parapsychology*, Vol. 10, No. 3, Autumn 1968, pp. 277–84.
———, *The Welcoming Silence*, New Hyde Park, N.Y.: University Books, 1973.
Roos, Anna Maria, *The Possibility of Miracles*, London: Rider and Co., 1930.
Rose, Ronald, *Living Magic*, Chicago: Rand McNally & Co., 1956.
Russell, Edward, *Design for Destiny*, London: Neville Spearman, 1971.

St. Louis Medical and Surgical Journal, Nov. 1889.
Sava, George, *A Surgeon Remembers*, London: Faber and Faber, 1953.
Sculthorp, Frederick C., *Excursions to the Spirit World*, London: Greater World Association, 1961.
Sherrington, Sir Charles, *Man on His Nature*, London: Cambridge University Press, 1940.
Shirley, Ralph, *The Mystery of the Human Double*, London: Rider and Co., 1938.
Smith, Susy, *The Enigma of Out-of-Body Travel*, New York: Garrett-Helix, 1965.
———, *Out-of-Body Experiences for the Millions*, Los Angeles, Cal.: Sherbourne Press, 1968.
Snell, Joy, *The Ministry of Angels*, London: G. Bell and Sons, 1918.
Socialist Industries, U.S.S.R., Sept. 4, 1973.
Society for Psychical Research (British) *Journal*, Vol. 3, April 1888, pp. 254–56; Vol. 8, 1897–98, p. 250; Vol. 12, Nov. 1906, pp. 322–28; Vol. 21, 1923–24, p. 87; Vol. 34, Mar.–Apr. 1948, pp. 206–8, 210; Vol. 41, No. 707, Mar. 1961, p. 52; No. 710, Dec. 1961, p. 214; Vol. 42, Sept. 1963, p. 126.
Society for Psychical Research (British) *Proceedings*, Vol. 1, 1882–83, pp. 135–36, 141–42; Vol. 3, 1885, pp. 6–7; Vol. 7, 1891–92, pp. 41–46; Vol. 8, 1892, pp. 180–94; Vol. 9, 1893–94, pp. 53–54, 57–59; Vol. 13, 1897–98, pp. 397–400; Vol. 35, 1925–26, pp. 560–89.
Spraggett, Allen, *The Unexplained*, New York: New American Library, 1967.

Stead, W. T., *Borderland*, New Hyde Park, N.Y.: University Books, 1970.
——, *Real Ghost Stories*, London: Carlyle Press, 1897.

Targ, Russell, and Harold Puthoff, "Information Transmission Under Conditions of Sensory Shielding," *Nature*, Vol. 251, No. 5476, Oct. 18, 1974, pp. 602–7.

Tart, Charles T., "A Psychophysiological Study of Out-of-the-Body Experiences in a Selected Subject," *Journal*, ASPR, Vol. 62, No. 1, Jan. 1968.

Theta, Winter/Spring 1974, p. 19.

Thurston, Herbert, *Surprising Mystics*, London: Burns and Oates, 1955.

Turvey, Vincent N., *The Beginnings of Seership*, New Hyde Park, N.Y.: University Books, 1969.

Tylor, Edward, *Primitive Culture*, London: J. Murray, 1871.

Tyrell, G. N. M., *Apparitions*, London: Society for Psychical Research, 1953.

Van Eeden, Frederik, "A Study of Dreams," *Proceedings*, SPR, Vol. 26, 1913, pp. 431–61.

Wavell, Stewart, Audrey Butt, and Nina Epton, *Trances*, New York: E. P. Dutton & Co., 1967.

Wereide, Thorstein, "Norway's Human Doubles," *Tomorrow* magazine, Vol. 3, No. 2, Winter 1955, pp. 23–29.

Wheeler, Raymond H., "Visual Phenomena in the Dreams of a Blind Subject," *Psychological Review*, July 1920, pp. 315–22.

Whiteman, J. H. M., *The Mystical Life*, London: Faber and Faber, 1961.

Wills, Arthur J., *Life, Now and Forever*, London: Rider and Co., 1942.

Yram (pseud.), *Practical Astral Projection*, London: Rider and Co., 1935.

Index

1